Sociophobics

About the Book and Editor

Sociophobics, a new branch of anthropology and sociology, provides the student of human emotions an alternative to psychological interpretations of fear, a universal human experience. Fearing can be efficiently analyzed as a communication technique. Through symbolic means, shared fear meanings are transmitted among humans, tending to confirm and maintain culturally established norms and values. Sociophobics extends the anthropological conception of cultural systems to include fearing as a characteristic feature of learned behavior, thus opening the way to cross-cultural comparisons of an important emotional experience. This study of a specific human affective state rests on a general theory of emotions rooted in the social-cultural nature of humankind. Sociophobics raises the possibility of reevaluating comparisons of human and infra-human emotions and encourages an expanded conception of the character of the individual.

David L. Scruton is professor of anthropology at Ball State University.

Sociophobics
The Anthropology
of Fear

edited by David L. Scruton

Westview Press / Boulder and London

This Westview softcover edition was manufactured on our own premises using equipment and methods that allow us to keep even specialized books in stock. It is printed on acid-free paper and bound in softcovers that carry the highest rating of the National Association of State Textbook Administrators, in consultation with the Association of American Publishers and the Book Manufacturers' Institute.

Published in 1986 in the United States of America by Westview Press, Inc.; Frederick A. Praeger, Publisher; 5500 Central Avenue, Boulder, Colorado 80301

Library of Congress Cataloging-in-Publication Data
Main entry under title:
Sociophobics: the anthropology of fear.
   1. Fear. 2. Fear—Social aspects. 3. Fear—
Cross-cultural studies. I. Scruton, David, 1928–
BF575.F2S65 1986   152.4   85-11621
ISBN 0-8133-7088-4 (soft)

This book has been produced without formal editing by the publisher
Composition for this book was provided by the editor
Printed and bound in the United States of America

The paper used in this publication meets the minimum requirements of the American National Standard for Permanence of Paper for Printed Library Materials
Z39.48-1984.

10   9   8   7   6   5   4   3   2   1

Contents

Preface

The preface and introduction for a book whose subject is not yet part of the existing order of things may be more difficult to write than those for a volume whose topic already has an established constituency. In the first instance these not only present a particular book but also the field of inquiry. Further difficulties may be created by a title that, like the subject it is intended to identify, is unfamiliar. Perhaps this begins to sound like a complaint, but it is not meant to be; it is simply a statement of fact. In any event, I must accept the responsibility for my plight, for any difficulties I may encounter are self-imposed.

Sociophobics is a neologism. I hope it will prove to be a useful one, but that is something the learned community must decide. It appeared that a new term was needed in order to identify a new subject of study, and as nothing suitable lay at hand one had to be created. After all, the scriptures enjoin us not to put new wine in old skins. So, when it began to be clear that the study of fear by anthropologists and sociologists was, for all practical purposes, a new thing, it seemed only reasonable to cast about for a word by which to call it. As the purpose of the study was to treat human fear as a cultural phenomenon the "socio-" readily proposed itself. Somewhat unthinkingly, I applied for the remainder to a colleague in the history department who happens to be a native speaker of Greek, and was a little chagrined when he promptly replied, "Phobos." The current popularity of phobias ought to have brought it to mind.

Having discerned and christened a new or at any rate largely unexplored object of potential anthropological and sociological interest, the next step was to explore it. To this end several colleagues were invited to the campus of Ball State University to scout its possibilities. This first sociophobics conference was accordingly held in Muncie on October 19 and 20, 1981. The meetings were generously supported by James Koch, provost of Ball State. In addition to the convener, active parts were taken by S. Gene Andrews, Enya P. Flores-Meiser, Whitney Gordon, and Jack Whitehead, all from Ball State. Colby R. Hatfield, Jr., the

University of Colorado at Denver; William H. Key, the University of Denver; David Parkin, the University of London; DeWight R. Middleton, SUNY-Oswego; and Larry Perkins, Oklahoma State University, completed the group. Gordon, Key, and Perkins are sociologists, Andrews is professor of English, and the others are anthropologists.

The format of the conference provided for an informal presentation of exploratory papers on various aspects of fear and general discussion of issues that emerged in the course of the sessions. The group's consensus was that useful work waits to be done in the area of fear as a cultural experience and the meetings adjourned with a feeling of enthusiasm. It was held, with Tennyson, that work of noble note might be done.

The first public presentation of sociophobics came in my paper at the annual meeting of the American Anthropological Association in December, 1982 as part of the session on Psychiatry, Therapy, and Culture. Encouraged by its reception Flores-Meiser and I organized a sociophobics symposium for the XIth International Congress of Anthropological and Ethnological Sciences held at Vancouver in August, 1983. Several of us from the 1981 conference continued to pursue this interest: Flores-Meiser, Hatfield, Middleton, Parkin, and myself. We were joined by Molly G. Schuchat and Marcella G. Walder of Behavior Service Consultants and Duane Quiatt of the University of Colorado at Denver. The symposium was well received and the participants were emboldened to think the evident interest in this nontraditional inquiry into a human emotion justified a collection of essays, of which this is the result.

Thanks are due to several people whose work has helped to make this book a reality. The preparation of the manuscript—actually, the preparation of the floppy disks that seem to have usurped the place of manuscripts—was accomplished by Billie Snyder, whose intimate familiarity with the arcane and, to me, utterly incomprehensible world of the computer and word processor was an endless source of amazement. And to Enya P. Flores-Meiser for reading the resulting product in its final version. Also performing yeoman service in ordering and typing the various sections were Bonnie Bowlin and Brenda Whittaker. George Pilcher, associate provost of Ball State University, kindly provided financial support for preparation of the manuscript. To these people all of us are grateful. And how could this paragraph close other than with thanks to the endlessly patient and helpful people at Westview Press—Krista Hayenga, Victoria Yogman, Kathy Streckfus, and Dean Birkenkamp?

David L. Scruton

1
Introduction

David L. Scruton

A common theme unites the seven essays gathered here. That theme is simply stated: an experience which is among the most common, if least desired, of our lives—being afraid—can usefully be approached, examined, and interpreted by the guidance of a principle which is rather different from the one under whose aegis fear studies have usually been conducted. Each of the authors has considered some corner of human fearing, some part of the "landscape of fear," as Tuan puts it, hoping that the application of this principle will help to illuminate what has hitherto been obscure. That landscape is a very broad one; we do not know what its boundaries may prove to be. If we have been fortunate enough to be able to cast some light on it, here and there, showing the existence of a plain, a promontory, a mountain, still, most of the countryside is in darkness. Nevertheless, however tentative and uncertain the results, a beginning has been made.

The common theme referred to above, which gives sociophobics its claim to the attention of social scientists, is that a socialcultural model of fear can provide an effective instrument for ordering and analyzing data. If our interpretation of fear behavior is to be persuasive there must be designed a theory, not simply of fear but of human emotions in general, which centers on that principle. It must be demonstrated that a sociocultural model of emotional behavior can be devised with an orientation consistent with and informed by a commitment to the axiom that individual human behavior, no matter how personal and internal it may appear, can be effectively related to the fact that we are a social animal and are found to live only in a cultural milieu.

The first chapter addresses itself to this task, as well as to an application of the resulting theory to fearing. Even a brief survey of theories of emotion leads to the conclusion that a unified model of the sort proposed is not presently available. Elements of one are about, as are remarks to the effect that emotions are processually part of our cultural apparatus.

They are variously described as cultural artifacts, or social constructions. But a single comment, however much on target it may be, does not constitute a theory. The one which is offered here, an important element of which was anticipated some years ago in a dissertation on the cultural organization of emotions in Samoa, emphasizes the role of emotions as instruments and techniques of human communication. They are cast in the light of social events, not entities or states of being, as they have often been described. An effort is made to link the communication which they accomplish to critical survival needs of our species—needs which can only be satisfied in organized communities through the medium of cultural rules and modes of behavior. Thus, the emotions are encompassed in the conception of human nature which is generally favored by anthropologists and sociologists. It may be that success in bringing the emotions into the stream of our collective lives will help to overcome serious conceptual difficulties that have stood in the way of a truly unified view of that nature.

Fearing, as a cultural mode, is shown to serve important social functions which may lead to the confirmation of and adherence to compelling values and norms. So, it becomes an emotion-action complex which has fundamentally positive consequences—presumably a response to complex requirements laid on us by our biosocial nature. Finally, some consideration is given to the relation between the individual's seemingly private emotional life and the social organization of these cultural experiences.

Chapter 2 is methodological in purpose. In his essay, Key reviews the methodologies of earlier fear studies, his goal being to assess the potential usefulness of these research strategies and techniques for work in sociophobics. His evaluations of a number of these are framed in the context of theoretical perspectives presented elsewhere in the book. This review of fear research shows there to have been a movement from interviews to more formal and structured instruments, as the bulk of empirical research in the past has focused on the identification of various stimuli which are thought mainly to elicit fear reactions in subjects. Importantly for our objectives, he notes that fear research has been carried on chiefly by psychologists and little attention has been paid to the sorts of questions which interest social scientists.

He concludes that the use of objective tests and measurements is inappropriate for the very immature state of social science fear research. He is also troubled by a number of unresolved questions and issues about existing research. He proposes, instead, "soft" techniques as more useful devices at this early stage, anticipating that in the future, as work proceeds there will be developed more sophisticated methods and analytical techniques.

Methodological concerns are also important in the third chapter, by Flores-Meiser. She shifts the emphasis, however, from an examination of what has been done with mainly American subjects to the need for ethnography, and the cross-cultural perspective of anthropology. With Key she agrees on the paucity of data and studies which might excite the interests of those scholars whose realm of discourse is the cultural field of human action. In reflecting on this, she independently pursues a line of thought proposed by Parkin, in a later chapter: since the ethnographer tends to "see" and report the normal—the culture pattern— the absence of fear data in most reports may signal the fact that fear is not highlighted in many nonwestern societies as it is in those of the Judeo-Christian tradition. Additionally, this absence may remind us of the established tradition in the social sciences of ceding the inquiry into emotions to psychology.

In reporting on her own work among the Tagalogs she points up the task, and the necessity that ethnographers presently face, of reexamining and recasting their data. In a sense, (one suspects) this may be as much a reexamination of themselves as of their field experiences. It demands that the anthropologist, who may either not have noticed fear activity among his people (perhaps, as Parkin intimates, it was not clearly evident) or who, having noted it, assumed that it was not his domain but belonged, if to anyone, to the psychologist, return at least in his mind, to his subjects and ask them, in their absence, about their fears. Or, he must reexamine the structural relations of aspects of that society to infer the presence of this culturally induced anxiety. How did the Kwakiutl host feel on the eve of an especially important potlatch, for example? Her essay in this retrospective interpretation of Tagalog culture focuses on fear and shame, and she ends by suspecting that fear among children is gradually melded into another set of institutionalized feelings, called hiya—shame, shyness,—becoming a primary feature of adult response tendencies.

Chapter 4 is an extended test of the proposition that field experience, although retrospectively examined, can provide the basis of sociophobic conclusions, as Hatfield leads us through certain aspects of life among the Maasai and the Sukuma. He looks back from lengthy field experience and considers the means by which fear is patterned in two cultural groups, adjacent but distinct. He selects three broad areas, or foci, of fear experience, first exploring fears that arise in both communities from the discordant clash of expectations and real practices with respect to the roles of women in marriage. The second focus shows us how cultures can redefine objective situations of danger and threat, which might be expected to encourage fear responses. This is the conditioning of Maasai warriors to make them "fearless." For comparison he turns to two

Sukuma organizations which attract young men, although the life circumstances in the two societies are not the same.

Finally, he analyzes ways in which culture may impose fearful characteristics on certain situations and create statuses associated with fear. He dichotomizes these into fears of enemies within, and enemies without. Examples are provided by beliefs in witchcraft and the power of the curse, specific examples of fear categories. Enemies from without are represented by agents of development, specifically those associated with the Tanzanian government, and agencies of education. In this meticulous analysis—a revisitation of the field, so to speak—we learn what the ethnographer can do with what he has already done.

The element of ethnography is present in Middleton's excursion into the urban setting as a source of patterned fear. As in the previous chapter he considers the relations between affective experience and social ecology, as it were, but in this instance his subjects are those who dwell in those curious conglomerations of ethnicities and cultural subtypes. Considering the world trend toward the development of vast conurbations, his concern for fear sources and modalities may be especially relevant not only to future sociophobic research, but to urban studies in general. He identifies, in this pioneering essay, some of the sources of danger and fear in the urban context and the cognitive and behavioral measures that urban dwellers have devised to cope with them. He is especially concerned with migrants to the city, as they inescapably experience a variety of dislocations—physical, cultural, and, not least, emotional. How much must these new urbanites learn, and by what processes, about risks and dangers in their new environment?

Taking the position that cultures produce, communicate, and manage fear he is convinced that contexts which feature a rich diversity of contrasting and often competing lifestyles should furnish us with exceptional opportunities to examine the processes by which groups both generate and cope with fear and danger. Observing fear and avoidance in urban public places, and how people communicate in these respects, ought to make possible insights into the role of "traffic relationships" in managing fear and risk.

In their chapter Schuchat and Walder offer a provocative suggestion that two categories of people, who have at first glance little in common, in fact share a number of significant features. These are the ethnographer, the field anthropologist, and the victim of those intense, abnormal fear experiences called phobias. The authors, commencing from the sociophobic premise that fearing is a cultural experience, propose to clarify the nature of phobias by a comparison and analysis of those common features.

They point out that both the ethnographer and the phobic individual participate in a universe of symbols, which are themselves cultural instruments. Each has in common with the other certain unsettling experiences that take them out of the symbolic universe with which they are, or "should" be familiar. As he departs from his familiar symbolic world into an alien one the ethnogrpher generally experiences culture shock. Although the phobic does not physically leave his usual world, with its familiar symbol cues, like the ethnographer he is in a similar state of disorientation, confusion, and uncertainty. He is ignorant of the significant meanings, the behavioral cues which are essential to an unthreatened existence.

Unlike the ethnographer the phobic is an unwilling foreigner in a strange land. His awareness that he ought to respond to cultural cues as others do is his besetting problem. Whereas the ethnographer, knowing he can map the unknown world and by learning its symbolic geography both be at home in it and report it to others, can cast himself eagerly into the discovery of its system of cues and meanings, the phobic knows he should have that knowledge, but does not, and is terrified by his failure.

By showing that the phobic's fearing can be approached by analyzing the culture shock/fearing of the ethnographer the authors place each of the two in the same perceptual field: a cultural universe. Even these strange and uncontrolled fears are cultural experiences.

In the final chapter Parkin draws, as others have done, on his ethnographic experience in order to review his own interpretation of fear. However, he goes beyond the cultural boundaries of the Giriama, the Luo, and the Judeo-Christian-Islamic worlds, as these provide him with the pivotal comparisons. He offers us a model of human fear which both serves as one of no doubt several possible taxonomies and finally takes sociophobic theory beyond the limits of the descriptive to an analytical level where fearing is grist not alone for the mill of the anthropologist or the psychologist, or even the philosopher. In this reflection this ancient instrument of human survival experience and that uncertain phenomenon we call creativity are juxtaposed.

In this model he draws a careful distinction and creates a typology of fear, i.e. the Raw and the Respectful. The first is the realm of the uncontrolled, the unpredictable, the unforeseen. Respectful fear, on the other hand, has been tamed, domesticated, therefore institutionalized. It is fear that has been brought into the community and fashioned according to human purposes. In the process, and at least in the Western context, it has, as Parkin puts it, been transformed into a commodity and is treated like a thing, subject to rules of production, distribution, even of consumption.

He further notes that it is raw fear that may give us a glimpse of the nature of creativity. There are no institutional rules about how to deal with it—no sovereign or god to placate—so mankind must experiment, innovate, devise methods of dealing with it. In a word, create. And, by creating, transform the feral into the domesticated. In respectful fear—tamed, ordered, institutionalized—we see this emotion adapted to human purposes and interests. There we find utilitarian fearing: fear and the state, religion, the family. This is fear and the social order.

At some point in the book the reader may find himself raising an objection. Surely, the emotions, if they are anything at all, must be considered as part of the individual . . . of you and of me, not a part of that individual's group. Is it not you as you, and I as I who have emotions, who feel them, who actually and actively experience the choking rage, the paralyzing fear, the ecstasy of victory, the despair of defeat? Yet the central feature of these essays, the linchpin of sociophobics' persuasiveness, seems to negate that almost self-evident truth.

In reply we argue that emotions are cultural creations, not individual ones. They are, it is true, rooted in the inescapable fact that the particular and specific human is the least common denominator of all human events. But this does not provide us with analytically efficient instruments by means of which our emotions can be understood. In order to grasp their character, to understand not what the emotions are, for this mires us in a bog of epistemological search for essences and natures, but what the emotions do, we are compelled to turn away from the individual locus of emotion-experience to the community. It is within this community, that elemental unit of human survival identified by its complex web of social relations and its equally complex geography of cultural understandings, that we are at last able to comprehend the most significant fact of our emotions: they are experienced by individuals but their meaning can be found only in our collective existence.

It is a fragment of that collective meaning that these essays on sociophobics lay before the reader.

2
The Anthropology
of an Emotion

David L. Scruton

Introduction

Put fear out of your heart.
William Allen White

. . . a world founded upon four essential
freedoms. The fourth is freedom from fear.
Franklin Roosevelt

To conquer fear is the beginning of
wisdom.
Duke of Wellington

The three quotations, chosen from *Bartlett's*, from which many more
of like import might have been drawn, and the essays that make up
this book are about fear in humans. White, Roosevelt, and the Iron
Duke leave us with the clear understanding that fear is something we
would be better off without. Moreover, they tell us unequivocally that
it is possible to free ourselves from it. This is not simply a dream, but
a goal that we may hope to achieve.

However, if the past is any sort of useful guide to the future, we
wonder if that is a realistic ambition. It does not seem so. If any human
emotion is as old as our species it must, surely, be fear, and the end
of its hold on us is not in sight. Every human being who is possessed
of normal faculties has often found himself in intimate contact with
that pale-visaged specter. Would any of us want to count the hours
spent clasped in the clammy embrace of one of its unpleasant manifestations? The legions of our fears may seem to fall into a number of
broad categories, although this taxonomy is far from exact and is intended
only to be a guide to our memories.

Physical Fears. Many of our anxieties center on fear for our physical selves: the sudden, heart stopping sensation as a semitrailer narrowly misses cutting short one's earthly journey; the fright that clutches the heart when a piton pulls free from its crevice during our negotiation of an overhang on the north face of the Eiger; the remorseless terror that floods us as we watch the grave face of our physician, examining a laboratory report or an X-ray. Such sudden threats to the integrity of our physical fabric prompt fear, panic, terror. These feelings, all representing varying degrees of anxiety, belong to the same unwelcome tribe.

Social Fears. By no means all of our fears for ourselves are physical. Indeed, most are social. The unprepared student fears the prospect of failing a final exam and imagines the consequences of that failure. A salesman whose recent performance has been only marginal waits in the outer office of a customer for a crucial interview whose outcome may determine his future. A young boy, asking a girl for his first date, holds the phone in his sweaty hand and cannot decide whether he most fears rejection or acceptance. The outcomes of such events as these do not involve injury or life's end but it is not clear that they are felt less keenly because of that.

Fears for Others. Much of our fearing is not for self at all, but for others, and these fears can easily reach or surpass the intensity of those for ourselves. Any parent who has lain awake in silent misery as the night wore slowly on, wondering where a son or daughter might be, will remember the bitterness of the fear that knifed through his vitals at the sound of a distant siren, conjuring dreadful images that could only be swept away by the sound of a door softly closing.

We cannot possibly catalog all our fears nor would it serve any useful purpose if we could. Each of us has had too many and these have been too various. We are bothered by the small ones and haunted by the great, dark fears that seem always to be nearby, waiting to lay their icy hands on our hearts and lives. By some examples we remind ourselves what fear is, what it feels like, and what some of the situations are that cause us to be afraid.

It is beyond imagining that anything having so pervasive and persistent an impact on our lives, that so powerfully influences our thoughts and our actions, should have escaped systematic study, resulting in informed responses to it. And, indeed, an array of professional men and women is available to help us combat our anxieties even if, or perhaps especially if, they seem to be irrational, groundless, and unrelated to the real world. Psychiatrists, counseling psychologists, psychoanalysts, priests, and the writers of innumerable self-help books are all at the ready, each armed with special attitudes and therapeutic techniques, each prepared to help us face, deal with, and should we be very fortunate, overcome our fears. Failing this we may hope they can help us endure what cannot be eliminated, thus enabling us to exist in a world in which it seems that to live is to be afraid.

In view of this it perhaps seems gratuitous to introduce still another approach to the study of this phenomenon. Nevertheless, that is what this collection of essays does. We offer a fresh perspective on human fear and the act of fearing and believe it is sufficiently distinct from current approaches, sufficiently radical in its theoretical orientation, and possessed of sufficient potential for improving our understanding of this unwelcome companion in life's journey that it merits consideration.

If its potential can be realized it will prove of interest to anthropologists, sociologists, psychologists, scholars in the humanities, and perhaps the general public. This realization will take time, for the field of inquiry is vast, undoubtedly complex, and deeply entangled with what we already feel, believe, and think we know. Furthermore, some of its principles and conclusions may appear to be inconsistent with current psychological opinion.

We have chosen to call this endeavor *sociophobics*, by which we mean the study of human fears as these occur and are experienced in the context of the socialcultural systems humans have created, lived in, been shaped by, and reacted to for numberless millenia. We propose that human fears are most efficiently understood as social phenomena. Fearing is an event that takes place in a social setting; it is performed by social animals whose lives and experiences are dominated by culture, that complex set of patterns of learned behavior that sets us apart from the rest of the beasts.

It is impossible to understand fully what human fearing is, how fears happen in the individual, how they are expressed both to self and to others, how they are received and reacted to by others in the community, and what their function in our lives is unless we treat fearing as a feature of cultural experience, which people participate in because they are members of specific societies at particular times. Fearing is thus a dimension of human social life.

This is a departure from what is customary. For the most part, fear and other emotions have been assigned to the psychological sciences. The prevailing attitude seems well expressed by Scherer (1982:555): "Along with most other theorists of emotion, I assume that emotion is best treated as a psychological construct." In dealing with their subject psychologists have often been inclined to emphasize organic features with which emotions often seem to be associated. Fear is commonly thought of as an innate human trait, the result of the species' phylogenetic development, something which is triggered by various stimuli and experienced in biochemical terms. Psychological studies of the "fear state" in humans and laboratory animals are prominent features of the literature.

Sociophobics contends that this concentration on fear at the organic level has had the effect of inhibiting the development of an analytical interest at the socialcultural level. As social scientists we accept without objection the view that fearing, indeed all emotional experience, is a consequence of human phylogeny. It is incontestable that the capacity to feel and the ability to communicate, both of which lie at the root of emotions, had significant selective advantages in the lives of ancient populations of hominids.

Of course, all human behavior has its foundations in our evolutionary past. The role of the social sciences is to build upon that foundation and concentrate on the invariable human habit of organizing behavioral potentials which are the results of evolutionary development in non-organic ways. Although our phylogenetic history sets limits on certain aspects of human behavior the range of possibilities remains so great that biology is, in effect, nondirective. If we wish to understand human actions, which are always the actions of men and women in groups, sharing common understandings and habits, we must examine them in terms which are appropriate to those groups, not ones appropriate to a different level of perception and analysis.

It is in consideration of this that we propose sociophobics' guiding principle: fear is a social act which occurs within a cultural matrix. "To fear" and "to be afraid" are social events which have social consequences. A second proposition, derived from the first, is that it is necessary to analyze fear using the methods of the social sciences rather than those employed by the psychological sciences.

Having said this, we must accept that the social sciences have not given much attention to this phenomenon. Fearing as a characteristic yet variable mode of human behavior has been largely ignored by them. Indeed, the social sciences have shown a lack of concern for the entire gamut of human emotionality and have been largely content to accept the hegemony of psychology. Izard (1977:v) notes that "emotion is a truly interdisciplinary subject. Workers in the fields of physiology, neurology, ethology, physiological psychology, personality and social psychology, clinical psychology and psychiatry, medicine, nursing, social work, and the clergy are all directly concerned with emotion." It appears from this that virtually the only people who are not involved in the study of emotions are social scientists. Such a conclusion is not entirely accurate but as a generalization it has considerable force.

One or two have moved to meet the implied challenge. Kemper (1978:1) observes that "there are many theories of emotion, but none is sociological. This is astonishing, because in most cases the actions of others toward us, or our actions toward them, have instigated our joy, sadness, anger, or despair." But he soon accounts for this lacuna in sociological theory. "One reason sociologists pay little systematic attention to emotions is that psychologists have legitimately preempted the field."

He carries his point too far. Preemption suggests the prior seizure of something, by someone, to the subsequent exclusion of others. No field of science would think of doing that. If social scientists have not been interested in emotions it can only be because they have not thought there was much there for them to do, given their particular orientations, and that what was to be done was being properly taken care of by another discipline.

Like every teacher of anthropology I have accumulated a large number of introductory textbooks over the years, most of them published in the last decade. Perusal of their indexes showed that in sixty such texts designed for general anthropology or introductory courses in cultural anthropology there was some reference under emotion in only ten cases. A mere four mentioned fear, none directed the reader to joy, and only one to grief. Anger was an easy victor with twenty-one appearances. Most of those talked about aggression. I did not expect much from this survey but on an elementary level it confirmed my opinion and those of my colleagues that anthropology has not been deeply interested in human emotions.

As a result, the scientific division of labor gives the appearance of being straightforward and unambiguous. Fear is an emotion; emotions are features of the individual and his personality; the particular human and his psyche are properly dealt with by the psychological sciences. The role of the social sciences is to devote themselves to those collective phenomena that are summarized as societies and cultures.

But, although this is traditional, it is not a state of natural reality. Truth may be a seamless garment but the history of our efforts to apprehend its character shows remarkably diverse and compartmentalized perceptions of its unity. This is a truism, admittedly, but it should not be overlooked simply because we are familiar with it. One is an anthropologist, another a psychologist, yet another is a physiologist, or a sociologist, and still another is a student of education. It is no accident that a psychologist sees the world through psychological eyes; he could hardly do otherwise. The same is true of each of us who studies humanity. Reality owes as much to the attitudes of those who examine it as to its own character.

The historical tradition conceding the emotions, among them fear, to the psychologist tells us only what has been. It does not prevent our wondering what fresh, novel, and useful insights might be achieved if specialists of a different sort inquired into them. In response to this wondering we offer sociophobics.

A Cultural Theory of Emotion

It is agreed that fear is an important member of a large, poorly defined class of experiences called the emotions. Efforts by psychologists to classify these conditions have produced little agreement on a roster of mankind's affective events, but there persists a widely shared conviction that it is theoretically possible to construct such a taxonomy.

Although our concern is with a particular one of these, in order to set the study of fear in a cultural perspective we require a comprehensive theory of emotions. A satisfactory response to this need has not yet been fully achieved. We shall, therefore, address this issue first, later returning to fear to apply general principles to a specific example.

Despite the fact that social scientists have not developed much in the way of systematic analyses of the emotions it is not altogether accurate to say, as Coulter (1979:125) does,

> Mistakenly thought of as beyond the scope of social convention and constraint, affective states have been allowed to fall exclusively within the province of psychology. In its turn, psychology has generated a variety of ways of handling the phenomena of affect, but few of them have remained consistent with, or controlled by, the conceptual structure of the socio-cultural dimensions integral to the very constitution of the phenomena under study.

Theodore Kemper and Susan Shott, both sociologists, have proposed approaches to emotion that are intended to fill the gap described by Coulter. Much of value can also be found in Coulter, himself, Shibles (1974), and Solomon (1976). Of these, Kemper's (1978:1) is the most comprehensive and ambitious. He looks at emotions from the point of view of their relationship to social interaction.

> . . . in most cases the actions of others toward us, or our actions toward them, have instigated our joy, sadness, anger, or despair. . . . Social situations influence the expression of emotions, not only in terms of intensity (e.g. the norms that distinguish permissiveness for emotional expression between men and women), but also directly by instigating the qualitatively different emotions themselves.

To Kemper, the emotions are products of social events; one might almost say they are by-products. The interaction event occurs and produces sadness, joy, anger, despair, or fear. Shott (1979:1317-18), for her part, inquires why sociologists ought to pay attention to emotions, since others have marked them out as their province.

> Perhaps the most obvious response is that emotions pervade human affairs, including social ones, and *not* simply as epiphenomena. Indeed . . . certain types of emotions are so central to social control that society as we know it could not exist without them. Hence, for a complete understanding of social behavior, sociologists must study the role of emotion in social life. . . . Even more important, the explanation of much emotional experience requires a sociological perspective.

It should not be presumed that every psychologist is indifferent to the possible relations between affect and society. James Averill (1976:87) observes that ". . . *emotions are social constructions.* That is, emotions are responses which have been institutionalized by society as a means of resolving conflicts which exist within the social system."

These observations, insightful as they may be, are enervated by a tendency to pay inadequate attention to the critical element of any socialcultural interpretation of the emotions: culture. It is largely because of this shortcoming that a workable socialcultural theory of the emotions is not presently available to us. None stipulates clearly that the social relationships within whose framework emotions occur, that is, the actions of people toward one another in socially defined situations, are not only causes of other social events but are the products of cultural understandings. What people do and are to one another are not simply social facts, they are cultural ones, and the varying circumstances in which people interact are mainly cultural in origin. Indeed, it is unclear how social facts involving humans could be imagined, except in a cultural context.

Hildred Geertz (1959:225;237) takes a more satisfying position when she says, "In the course of growth of a given person, [the] potential range of emotional experience becomes narrowed, and out of it certain qualitative aspects are socially selected, elaborated, and emphasized." She further remarks on the individual's ". . . education in the emotional lexicon of his society." She asserts that "the range and quality of emotional experience is potentially the same for all human beings: such terms as anxiety or hostility . . . refer to basically human—that is, universal—emotions." This last suggests to us that certain specific natural emotions exist in humans, forming a universe from which a society selects, emphasizing some, ignoring others. Otherwise, we cannot know how all humans may be thought to possess the same emotional potential. This idea certainly presents problems, but the point that each of us is educated in his society's "emotional lexicon" is an exceedingly useful one.

Also helpful in giving weight to this general point of view is Hallowell (1938:27). "With respect to the emotions, culture defines: (a) the situations that will arouse certain emotional responses and not others; (b) the degree to which the response is supported by custom or inhibitions demanded; (c) the particular form which emotional expression may take." An objection might be raised to the suggestions that situations, culturally defined, are responsible for the arousal of particular emotions from among those which, presumably, are available to be aroused. Thus, we may suppose, one society defines the death of a relative as a cause of rejoicing because the dead person now enjoys a far happier existence than his earthly one. Another society regards the death as reasonable inducement to violent and inconsolable grief because the loss cannot be compensated. Hallowell intimates that both grief and joy are present in the human psyche, waiting to be aroused and expressed. But it is not clear that such a kit of natural emotions is present in each of us, forming the spectrum of potential affective behavior from which a society picks and chooses.

Clifford Geertz (1973:80;81) tells us that "the achievement of a workable, well-ordered, clearly articulated emotional life in man . . . is a matter of giving specific, explicit, determinate form to the general, diffuse, ongoing flow of bodily sensations." Since this is not accomplished outside cultural systems he concludes that "not only ideas, but emotions too, are cultural artifacts in man."

But apart from a few useful and suggestive comments such as these we are left largely in the hands of the psychologist when we try to understand the emotional lives of humans. This essay is not a critique of psychological theories of emotion, but I will suggest that the several competing theories which are available, including a school of thought which considers that either the emotions do not exist in any way which permits them to be studied, or that the study would be of no value in any case, may make the choice of a particular one rather arbitrary.

One might go farther and conclude that there is a fundamental flaw in what psychology is trying to do. The failure to achieve significant agreement on the nature, origin, and functions of human emotions is the reasonable outcome of an insistence on the individual as the locus of emotional experience.

Kemper (1978:1) tells us that "emotions are highly appropriate for psychological analysis because the individual is both the unit of emotional expression and undeniably the locus of emotions at the psychological level." As a guide to the analysis of human behavior this statement is of limited value, although in a sense it is incontrovertible. Not only do individual humans, as individuals, express and experience emotions but everything that human beings do and experience, of whatever kind, is done by individuals. If this were taken at face value the social sciences would have to cease their work, for individuals are the units of social behavior and the locus of all things cultural. As nothing greater or smaller than the particular human exists or can exist, this reduction leaves psychology, the study of the individual, as the sole source of information about our species. Yet, humans are social creatures, and that dimension of reality cannot be slighted.

The difference between the psychologist and the social scientist lies in the questions each asks and the answers each is prepared to accept. The psychologist asks what are love, hate, joy, and fear to the human who experiences them. What events within or without the individual evoke or trigger them? What is the meaning of these feelings, thus summoned, to the particular human? Anthropologists and sociologists, on the other hand, ask what may be the meaning of emotional events to the community of which the individual is, after all, only a transient component. How do social circumstances create emotions in the group's constituent elements and how are they used to collective ends?

It is always the case that answers one gets depend on the questions one asks. We shall ask, not only what is fear to me, but what is it to the society of which I chance, by the merest accident of birth, to be a member? Not simply, what is the part that fear plays in my life but what is its function in the community's ongoing existence?

The difference is one of perspectives. In the social sciences the individual is displaced under the anthropological and sociological microscope by an aggregation of individuals. To the student of mankind the particular human must always be of engrossing interest but, paradoxically, the individual is not the level at which Homo sapiens can be most effectively studied. The psychologist abandons his inquiry at precisely the point at which humans commence to assume the special identity of their kind: when the individual disappears in the group and thereby ceases, from the point of view of analysis, to exist.

Additionally, discussion in psychology about the nature of emotion, the character of feelings, the connections between them, the origins of these phenomena, and their relationship to sensation and motivation is incomplete because it pays insufficient attention, if it notes it at all, to the dominating feature of human evolution: the emergence of the capacity to create, acquire, transmit, and depend upon culture.

It is as ineffectual to seek the nature of emotion in the individual as it is to look for the character of art in the ability of the human eye to see color, or to propose that the nature of music and its influence on our lives are explicated by a description of those qualities of our hearing which enable us to detect certain sounds but not others. It would not occur to us that a discussion of the anatomy and physiology of our reproductive systems constituted a satisfactory analysis of marriage and the family.

Here is a principle of great importance to our inquiry. In each case certain structural attributes of the human body are vital components of a complex and persistent set of behavior patterns. These patterns are of inestimable significance to the individual but they are not created by him. They are learned as part of his internalization of his community's customary behavior, its culture. While the behavior could not develop in the absence of the physical capacity, it is not fully explained or accounted for by that capacity.

So it is with emotions. We accept that fearing, hating, loving, rejoicing, and despairing do not exist in a physiological vacuum. There must be the material capability present in order for humans to do anything they do. All such capacities are the results of the evolutionary history of our kind. It will not stretch our imaginations too much to think that these capacities we discover in ourselves had important selective advantages in earlier times.

In the case of what are sometimes described as basic emotions this advantage may appear to be self-evident. If we fear something that is a threat to our safety we will be led to avoid it by running away. If we cannot run from the danger we will fight. We may think we can recreate the ancient survival role of other emotions, as well, but there are limits to this kind of reasoning and we will be misled if we depend on it heavily. On the surface it is an attractive solution to problems because it is so simple, but the number of such survival oriented emotions is probably small, while the current range of human emotional expression is great.

It is not our purpose here either to enumerate human emotions or classify them, even assuming that such enumeration and classification could be done. However, the possibility might suggest itself of separating them into two categories: survival-oriented emotions and all others. To the first group we would doubtless consign fear, anger, and love. One suspects that the second group would be very large, indeed. But to undertake such a task would require that we first identify all human emotions, and if, as I am convinced, emotions are cultural artifacts it is hard to imagine how such an enumeration could be done. As to such a category as survival emotions, that rubric merely proposes phylogenetic origins, not current functions.

The hazard remains that we may be persuaded to derive specific cultural functions from particular evolutionary events. This has the unfortunate effect of reducing human social behavior to biological terms.

Some psychologists demonstrate a fondness for conceiving of emotions on this level and seem reluctant to go beyond it. Plutchik (1962:151;170) observes, for example, that "emotions are typically . . . biological reactions." And further, ". . . the idea that learning affects emotions is true only in a very special sense."

A concentration on what we may call the organismic approach leaves us with a decorticated animal. Excessive emphasis on the basal mechanics of emotion and on a search for their "essential" nature has inhibited the development of a clear perception of what it is that emotions do. We will take for granted that we humans have an arousal capacity which is subsumed by chemical processes. As Solomon (1976:137) puts it, "it will simply be assumed that every emotion has its correlate in the physiology of the central nervous system." We may further take it for granted that this arousal capacity is, or at least at one time was, related to behavioral expressions some of which might usefully be interpreted as survival mechanisms.

In the lives of humans the somatic foundation upon which behavior rests is precisely that, a foundation. It must be understood to exist, but analysis that stops at that level not only fails to produce the understanding we seek but suggests that there is nothing more to understand. An examination of renaissance painting that went no farther than identifying the limits of the chromatic spectrum which the fifteenth century Italian eye could see would leave us woefully ill-informed about Leonardo's art.

The somatic is a point of departure, not the end of analysis. Societies depend upon these features and what they permit us to do; they use them in creating the complex fabric of social behavior by means of which humans survive. It is always illuminating to observe the interaction between the physical attributes of our species and the cultural behavior of its members. We shall accept that humans are able to experience emotions, whatever this may mean in the way of physiological mechanisms, and that these mechanisms have been historically derived and are genetically mediated. Beyond this point the question which we must answer is, what do human societies do with these abilities? What is their function in human life?

In answer to that I propose that this imperfectly defined and poorly described class of behavior we term the emotions can efficiently be understood as communication. Therefore, it serves cultural and social as well as individual purposes, as all communication does. This point has been effectively stated by Gerber (1975:2) in her unpublished dissertation, "emotion terms may be studied in a purely cultural manner, as a set of communicative symbols with shared meanings which are not directly dependent on individual experience."

When they are construed as techniques of communication some commonly held assumptions about them are contradicted. The emotions are not innate features of the humans who experience them, any more than language is. A more accurate formulation of the relationship between the emoting individual and his emotions would be to say that he performs them, rather than has them. One does not have communication, in the sense that the communication event is a necessary part of the communicator. The emotions are not, therefore, as they are so often portrayed, real entities or states of being. They are not submerged elements of our nature which arise and come forth when they are evoked or summoned by circumstance, somewhat after the manner in which the Witch of Endor evoked the shade of Samuel. Such metaphors are frequently employed in the psychological literature and although they may be intended as nothing more than metaphors, the vehicle by which an idea is communicated easily comes to be the idea. The container becomes the thing contained.

Emotions are events, not entities. Since they are events in an individual human's interaction experience we must bear in mind certain invariable features of that experience: events in our lives are set in a framework of social relations and these social relations and the circumstances which involve them are expressed, hence experienced, in cultural terms.

When emotions are understood virtually as elements of language a number of possibilities are presented. We may also understand why so much work has been done to so little purpose. Psychologists have been looking for the "real" nature of the emotions, on the assumption that the word, emotion, or the words for various presumed emotional states, e.g. fear, anger, joy, and grief, designated actual conditions of humans which could in some sense be found, isolated, classified, and analyzed. It became just a matter of digging deeply enough into our nature, or of performing subtle laboratory analyses of response reactions and blood chemistry.

This perception of the emotions might serve its purpose if they had real existences whose features and dimensions could be discovered and described. But if we adopt the view that they are not things but events we arrive at quite different conclusions. As well and as futilely might we seek the "real" nature of the family, or the "veritable" character of the state, or the "true" nature of art or religion.

Fear, joy, grief, anger, lust, hate, suspicion are all symbols by which we give order and meaning to portions of our existences. The experience achieves its status of real by being assigned a symbol which not only identifies and is associated with it but, in the only acceptable sense of the word, is it. In the beginning is the word.

The common error of the psychologist has been to assume that the symbol must be symbolic of some thing, that has an actual, palpable existence. That being thought to be the case it became their task to locate that thing, identify its chemical constituents, measure its intensity, describe how it affected the muscles, capillaries, and heart rate, and discover how it emerged from some deep reservoir within us. However, we should be aware that simply beause we have created a symbol it does not necessarily follow that the thing symbolized is fundamental to the character of life or even exists at all, outside the symbol, itself.

We can understand the problem which has arisen when efforts have been made to compare animal and human emotions. When we see a squirrel run from a dog, as we might run from a grizzly bear, we apply the same symbol to the rodent's behavior as to our own. We say that each is afraid, that each feels fear, and we suppose that each has had the same sensations—the same experience. The symbol becomes not only a reality in our personal lives but assumes a kind of supraspecies reality, as well. Fear becomes a quality of all life and is evoked in animals by life-threatening experiences. When we observe "fear" in the behavior of many creatures, from lowest to highest, it is only natural to identify it as an element of our collective evolution, the development in all forms of life of effective survival behavior.

I do not mean to imply that because the emotions may be efficiently conceptualized as instruments of communication, almost as elements of speech, they are therefore made irrelevant to our lives and play no part in our survival behavior. It would be absurd to separate them from our evolution. It is important, however, not to confuse their role in those lives, for only when we see clearly what they are will we be in a position to grasp the character of our emotional behavior. It is not the emotions that we must study, but emotional behavior. In order to follow this observation to its conclusion we will remind ourselves that the ability to communicate is a necessary, not an incidental, condition of human existence.

The human animal is obliged to live in those groups or collectivities, marked by certain definable principles of organization and structure, which we call societies. That only in them is human life possible is axiomatic, for this mode of existence is a necessary part of any definition of mankind. The reason for this is that only in society is it possible for life sustaining processes to be performed with predictable success.

These communities of humans are collectivities whose primary functional outcome is the survival of the species and the realization of human potentials. Life can be maintained in them not simply because a number of people are present who reflect the normal segmentation by age and sex, but because cooperative activities are undertaken and concluded which have as their results the support of those organisms. Among examples of these actions are such fundamental ones as food getting, reproduction, care of the immature members of the group, and defense against dangers. As individual humans cannot accomplish these tasks alone, society itself becomes the most basic of all human needs.

A necessary condition for those cooperative undertakings is effective communication among those who are involved in them. This may not be as critically important a requirement in various infrahuman species as it is with us, for the kinds and levels of cooperation required by many animals demand less extensive, complex, and efficient communication. In addition, it is often supposed that communication and cooperation among infrahumans may be partly or largely the results of genetic mediation of behavior.

However, in humans we have concluded that such genetic tendencies are lacking or are, at most, of limited directive strength. While some may not agree with this it seems wisest at this point to accept the consensus of social scientists, at least until sociobiology succeeds in demonstrating the contrary more persuasively than it has been able to do at this time. Humans must cooperate to live and must communicate to cooperate.

Various behavioral modes were developed in the course of our history by means of which essential communication among individuals might be accomplished. The most important of these, because it is the most efficient, flexible, and open-ended, is language. In the sense that it is at the root of virtually all that is human in our behavior a perceptive Martian taxonomist would doubtless define us as the symboling animal.

Language can be defined in many ways but Winnick's (1956:309) will do as well as another. "[Language is] a system of arbitrary vocal symbols, used to express communicable thoughts and feelings, and enabling the members of a social group or speech community to interact and cooperate." There are other means by which meanings can be conveyed, such as gestures, facial expressions, and nonsymbolic sounds. But merely to mention these is to realize how limited is their contribution to the ongoing tasks of life. Charade is no doubt a splendid parlor game but it is certainly inadequate to the purposes of effective conveyance of thoughts.

One of the intriguing features of language is the fact that, while it clearly reflects the phylogenetic development of a superior technique of achieving cooperation toward survival ends, it lends itself equally to other functions which have little or nothing to do with performances that can be associated with natural selection. As always in human affairs a trait whose origin and fixation in the species can be accounted for by natural selection may be employed *ad lib* for other ends which are unrelated to the primary historical one.

We have already referred to several cases in which certain organic features whose contribution to survival must be understood as their raison d'etre, have become fundamental to nonsurvival behavior systems. We could hardly find a better example than color vision. This faculty must be related to ancient primate arboreal experience, but it has been used by humans as, among other things, an essential element of systems of esthetics. The variety of uses to which we put color, uses which cannot have anything to do with staying alive, reminds us of this. Clothing, houses, art, entertainment, all these without color are literally drab and unsatisfying to us. By the same token we are able to use any or all of our communication techniques to express ourselves about whatever we wish, so long as we have created symbols for the purpose, and to cooperate for reasons which have nothing to do with surviving.

Inasmuch as humans must live in societies because they are unable to live outside them, that cooperation among their members is both the opportunity and the necessity afforded by life in these groups. Cooperation is accomplished through learned techniques of communicating knowledge, ideas, and feelings, of which techniques language is the most useful. Communication among humans can be understood as of two kinds, depending on who is the receiver. There are communication events in which we can distinguish between the sender and the receiver. This is interpersonal communication. There are also communication events in which we are unable to distinguish between a sender and a receiver because they are the same person. Communication of this type we shall describe as intrapersonal. This is communicating with oneself.

It is perhaps common to think of interpersonal communication as the primary function of language. While it is true that this exemplifies the importance of the phenomenon in our survival behavior because it permits cooperative interaction among individuals to take place, we make note of an interesting fact: intrapersonal communication is the more common communication event. Ordinary experience reminds us that humans communicate with themselves far more often than with others. In brief, intrapersonal communication may best be understood as equivalent to thinking. Whorf, quoted in Shibles (1974):22, asserts that "thinking is to a large extent linguistic." Watson, also in Shibles, says that "thinking is largely 'subvocal talking'" and Shibles himself states that ". . . one cannot have thought without language. . . . and this language usage is or constitutes most of what we usually mean by thought."

With these observations in mind we may now undertake the development of a social theory of emotion, considering the emotions to be cultural artifacts or constructions. They are instruments which permit the members of a society, joint participants in a cultural tradition, to exchange significant meanings with one another, and also each with himself. As such they can be construed in no other way than as elements of linguistic systems, which means, among other things, that they are constrained by the regular features of those systems. The meanings conveyed by emotions are important in helping people function in their society, which is as vital for the welfare of the group as it is for the individual's. At the individual level emotional experiences may be viewed as motivating behavior.

The following schematic presentation and its elucidation will clarify these proposals. Features of this model, or diagram, may be found in various authors, e.g. Shibles (1974), Solomon (1976), Izard (1977), and Coulter (1979).

Model of an Emotion

- first step: an experience
- second step: its interpretation
- third step: the evaluation/labeling
- fourth step: a feeling
- fifth step: its expression
- sixth step: an action

We commence with an individual human, recognizing that the individual is the irreducible unit of all human experience. This person, our Ego, has an experience—something happens to him, in him, about him. Ego experiences a stimulus which is brought to his attention through one or a combination of the senses. Or, the stimulus may simply be Ego's own thoughts. In any case, and by whatever means, he becomes conscious of something taking place.

The event cannot have meaning for this person until it has been interpreted and that meaning and its significance have been determined. This step in the sequence is accomplished as the essential elements of the transaction are identified, then compared against previous experience, knowledge, understandings, and habits. The events which take place during this stage represent a taxonomic evaluation. It is only as the elements of the experience are perceived by Ego to be equivalent to prior experiences that he is able to assign meaning to them. Otherwise, they are incomprehensible.

The process of element extraction, comparison with existing experiential taxa, and eventual determination of significance is one that is governed by Ego's life to that point. Since this life has been led within a society which is associated with a set of shared cultural understandings his interpretation is essentially a cultural one. No one can separate himself from his own past. Ego's life, of course, is not precisely like the life of any other member of his community. His experience of his culture is uniquely his own and his interpretation of the meaning and significance of his experiences will not be identical to that of any of his compatriots. Despite this, it can be expected to fall within certain limits which are imposed upon all members of the society through their exposure to a common culture, including its language; naturally, individuality of intepretation must be allowed for.

The mind extracts important elements from the experience and interprets them by comparing them with significant categories of prior, culturally mediated, experience. This leads to the next step in the emotion process. (We emphasize again that an emotion is not a thing but an event, an action which Ego performs.) This next step is the evaluation of the experience in qualitative terms. Here is a critical point in the emotion process because some experiences do not result in emotion action and others do. Ego interprets all experiences in order to discover their meaning for him but some of these interpretations justify emotion action while others do not.

The emotion process continues its development if Ego discovers from his evaluation of what has happened that he is able, or required, to apply to it a label, which is drawn from his lexicon of emotions. This lexicon is a subset of Ego's language and provides the terms by which emotions may be designated. It is important to stress that this lexicon is Ego's own set of terms only because he is a speaker of a certain language. If he is a speaker of English he will have available a variety of commonly recognized emotion words: good, bad, outrageous, disgusting, uplifting, joyful, cruel, evil, compassionate, immoral, hateful, ecstatic, anxious, fearful, irate, to name only a few. If Ego judges an experience in terms of one of these labels and acts accordingly the result is not only an emotion event, in the personal sense, but a social one as well.

Ego cannot, it follows, select as the labeling term an identifier which is not available to him—a term that is not part of his language. He cannot describe what he cannot say. To the question whether Ego can experience an emotion for which there is no term available in his emotion nomenclature, the answer may well be that he cannot. He cannot, I will argue, feel what he cannot say. This would hold true even if his society's language provided such terms but his familiarity with the language did not include them. For instance, let us suppose his linguistic experience has not equipped him with the emotion term, compassion, or some near equivalent. We question whether he is capable of that emotional experience.

It may be objected that Ego still has not "had" an emotion because he hasn't felt anything. Psychologists have wrestled long and earnestly with the relationship between emotion and feeling. There is little agreement. Some insist that feelings have nothing to do with emotions, while others are convinced that the feeling effectively is the emotion. One naturally hesitates to enter an arena in which so much conceptual dust has been raised and so much semantic blood shed. Where Shott (1979:1319) makes no distinction between the terms, proposing that feelings and emotions are semantic equivalents, Shibles (1974:17) argues that emotions are rational assessments which guide feelings and are therefore separate from them. Still others, such as Kemper (1978), do not appear to have any particular interest in feelings.

Can we have emotions without feelings? We can certainly speak of having an emotion although we are not experiencing any feelings appropriate to that emotion. Having won a tennis match I may tell my opponent I am sorry he lost. I am, of course, no such thing. My feelings are, in fact, very different from the ones I have announced. However, I do not consider that an emotion event can take place without feelings being involved. If we insist that emotions guide feelings but are separate from them; if we agree with Solomon (1976:187) that "an emotion is an evaluative (or 'normative') judgment, a judgment about my situation and about myself and/or about all other people," a formulation which otherwise has much to be said for it, we will find it difficult to separate emotions from other judgmental processes few will consider to be emotions. I may make a series of judgments relating to whether or not I should buy a new car and if so how it should be chosen, financed, and insured, but I decline to call the judgments emotion. Without the necessary presence of feelings our emotions disappear into the general background of judgment making, or rational assessing, as Shibles calls it. The word then ceases to have useful discriminating power and is no longer of much value.

I doubt if most people, queried about the character of their own emotions and emotional experiences, would hesitate before deciding that feelings have a great deal to do with them. Many might use the terms, emotions and feelings, interchangeably. Should this conventional usage guide us in thinking about the subject or should we ignore it? I see no compelling reason why we should reject out of hand an association between the two when that association is part of the customary experience of mankind. It is these human experiences that we are trying to analyze.

Therefore, we will regard feelings as significant elements of the sequence of events, that total experience that we term an emotion. To deny that they ought to be considered seems too much to fly in the face of life's realities. When we are angry we feel angry. Whether we feel some specific "anger" feeling is irrelevant to the fact that we feel, and we are angry. We certainly feel something and in the context of what is happening to us what we feel is indisputably anger. When I feel fear, on the other hand, I have certain sensations and I know they are feelings of fear because I have identified the situation as fear provoking. What I feel must be fear for that is the emotion which is appropriate to the circumstances. We identify the feelings with the situation in which they occur. This, of course, is the conclusion reached by Schachter and Singer in their celebrated experiment. They conclude (1962:398) that "cognitive factors appear to be indispensable elements in any formulation of emotions."

These feelings are real, in the sense that physiological events take place. Our hearts race, our mouths become dry, our breathing accelerates, our limbs tremble. But, although we have these feelings as parts of an emotion event they are not, themselves, the emotion, for that is a complex social event, albeit it does not rule out physical associations. The connection in humans between body and behavior requires no elaboration here.

So, by whatever mechanisms experience generates feelings. The feelings alone are not the emotion, for no single element of the process can claim to be. They are one of several components of that process. We have experiences that we label anger, fear, joy, apprehension, guilt, and we feel anger, fear, joy, apprehension, or guilt. We know that the feelings are appropriate to the emotion which we are having because we have identified them by the proper term.

The penultimate stage of the emotion event is its expression. We again are able to discern the powerful influence of the culture with which our social experience has been identified. We need not argue that the expression of our response to an experience is utterly controlled by the constraining influence of that culture, but we can assert that while it is necessary to allow for individual variation within a society in the mode of emotion expression, that variation is likely to fall within certain generally understood limits. Outside those limits a society will be inclined to regard an individual's behavior as eccentric, bizarre, even lunatic. (There are important implications here for an understanding of the nature of what we commonly, if rather unthinkingly, call emotional disorders.) This seems necessarily to be the case. If emotions are acts of communication, partaking of the nature of language, their expression to others must not be allowed to fall outside certain limits, for if that happens communication cannot occur.

It is easily documented that societies differ widely from each other in the encouraged or tolerated expression of emotions. One of the more interesting examples may be found among mourning customs. Thus, we find among the plains Indians an expression of grief on the death of a relative which would be thought unwarranted and excessive in our society. Wild crying out, slashing of one's arms and breast with knives, irrepressible and inconsolable grief are the marks of mourning among these people, with whom it is our habit to associate a stoic acceptance of pain, misfortune, and the general vicissitudes of life.

Grief, exultation, rage, love, these are emotions suitable to the occasion, but we believe their expression should be seemly and moderate. Our society, although it may exaggerate the actual condition in its native land, still thinks rather highly of the Englishman's stiff upper lip. Anglo-Saxon understatement of emotion remains a generally admired trait, although note should be made that many people appear to find satisfaction in the fact that American men are finally learning to weep in public.

And last, we must ask to what end this complex apparatus exists. What purpose does it serve? We are capable of emotions, feelings, language, but what do these mean to us? How does society use them? Are they simply a species of epiphenomenon, as Kemper intimates? If we do not reply satisfactorily to these questions we are left regarding the emotions almost as evolutionary vestiges and indeed, this attitude seems, implicitly, rather common.

The answer is not far to seek. Fisher (1979:100) observes that "emotions drive the intellect. The mind controls the body; the emotions control the mind; sometimes the emotions bypass the mind." We may find fault with much of this, especially when she speaks of "the deeper nerve centers, where emotion is commonly located. . . ." She falls into the common error of identifying the emotions as entities which can be located in a specific part of the organism. However, the implication of the comment coupled with a remark by Piaget, which she quotes: "There is no behavior without emotion," is worth considering. It is altogether unlikely that emotions can occur, be mediated as we have described, and have no results. On the contrary, emotions do have important consequences: they influence our behavior. They are means, in fact, through which a society accomplishes vital tasks, for they are instrumental in encouraging conformity to significant behavioral and attitudinal norms of that society. They provide individuals with approved and accepted response tendencies in situations which are judged to be important.

It is useful to compare this approach and its conclusions with the explicitly sociological theory of emotions developed by Kemper (1978:47;430). He defines emotion as ". . . a relatively short-term evaluative response essentially positive or negative in nature involving distinct somatic (and often cognitive) components." Many emotions are the results of ". . . real, imagined, or anticipated outcomes in social relationships."

This attitude is characteristic of much of the thinking about emotions by psychologists and, less often, by social scientists. It can be summarized in this way: what causes emotions? From what events, forces, elements, underlying mechanisms do they stem? The concern has been with what they are, in a descriptive sense, usually as concrete as possible, and in how they arise. The term, arise, can be used in two ways: metaphorically, in the sense of come into being or come to our attention, and concretely or materially, as it seems commonly to be assumed that the emotions are always in us, deep down, waiting to be awakened, much like the Kraken.

The preoccupation with what causes emotion has had the unfortunate effect of stultifying genuine understanding of them. The question which ought to guide us is not where do they lie, waiting to be aroused by some event that jolts them into consciousness so they percolate up from the depths of our psyches to the level of awareness, and cause our capillaries to dilate or constrict, our hearts to accelerate, our hands to tremble, and our stomachs to knot. The important, if infrequently asked, question is: what is their role in our lives? Their nature, once this is understood to be the critical issue, becomes operationally simple to determine: they are events that have outcomes.

And these outcomes, what are they? They are tendencies to behave, to act. But they are not tendencies to act in a random manner, dictated by the personal character of the emotion. On the contrary, they are inclinations to behave in such ways as to confirm the judgment of our society that certain kinds of social relationships and events are consistent with or contrary to the interests of society and the individual.

Hence, the cultural theory of emotions, in order to have cogency as an analytic device, must not only account for what is but must also show what its role is in our socialcultural lives. It is not enough to presume that by specifying that many emotions arise out of social relationships one has created a social theory of emotions, still less a cultural one. Social acts have social consequences in which the confirmation of cultural prescriptions, proscriptions, attitudes, and values occurs. This confirmation may be expressed through behavior, tendencies to behave, and attitudes toward real or potential events. We see the culmination of emotion processes in action, understanding action to include dynamics of thought as well as motor behavior. As such, emotions become members of a broad class of phenomena which, at the individual level, we may call motives. The particular feature of emotions-as-motives is their association with feelings. The inadequacy of some theories of emotion lies partly in their failure to grapple with the significance of the relationship between feelings and emotions. The arguments have generally been cast in the form of a question whether or not feelings and emotions are identical and whether emotions guide feelings, channeling them so to speak, or do not.

The issue is more complex than such questions suggest. We need to know what the role of feelings is in a complex social process. We are too often given static conceptions of emotions and feelings. Only when we comprehend that emotions are techniques of communication and that this communication does not take place idiosyncratically but follows rules which are the result of one's habituation to a cultural system can we confirm their function in our lives and their utility both for the individual and the community.

Humans—all creatures—are ceaselessly active. This constant behavior is ultimately a means to the end of individual and group survival. Every act has a cause, however trivial the former and inconsequential the latter; something does not proceed from nothing. Humans are quintessentially typical of those creatures whose behavior is the result of learned motives or is strongly influenced by them. Our society, through its cultural system, provides us with the corpus of motives which are both necessary and sufficient causes of our actions. We learn to act, and through acting to live. Emotions are part of that body of motives and as such are aspects of our communication system. They are simply those motives which have, as a vital element of their motivating force, feelings which we have learned to identify through cultural labeling.

Thus, if culture does not create feelings, if these sensations that we associate with anger, fear, joy, lust, rage, and the rest are physiological, culture nevertheless uses them, as well as our somatic capacities, for social purposes. Humanity is an animal which directs its inherited, evolution-derived capabilities toward socially determined ends. As we have said, every social habit and form is supported by structural attributes. The use by societies, through their traditional systems of behavior, of our capacity to feel, to identify the common qualities of experiences, to label them with terms which are linguistically available, and so to create emotions, is another example of the most characteristic of human features.

The reality of emotions is finally revealed to be almost commonplace. No longer mysterious, they are experiences which play roles in our lives we can readily understand, at least in principle. We can perceive the error of the psychologists for whom the emotions are mainly biological entities, little affected by life and learning. We can see how far from the mark Izard (1977:64) is, for example, when he says,

An emotion is a complex phenomenon having neurophysiological motor-expressive, and experiential components. The intraindividual process whereby these components interact *to produce the emotions* [emphasis mine] is an evolutionary-biogenetic phenomenon. For example, in the human being the expression of anger and the experiential phenomenon of anger are innate, pan cultural, universal phenomena.

His failure to specify the socialcultural setting in which this complex phenomenon occurs, and because of which it occurs, goes far to vitiate his observations. Failing to note that emotions are the means through which the collective sentiments and judgments of the community are felt, expressed, enforced, and preserved, means that his perceptions have no outcomes, hence no meanings.

Sociophobics

We have discussed at some length the general subject of human emotions, despite the fact that our subject is but a single one of them. As we pointed out, emotions must first be recognized as amenable to treatment by the social sciences, especially anthropology and sociology. We have noted that while there is some precedent for this, Coulter's (1979:125) comment that ". . . affective states have been allowed to fall exclusively within the province of psychology," reminds us that we usually depend on the attitudes, theories, methods, and techniques of that discipline to guide us in the study of emotions.

No fault can be found with psychologists studying human emotions as psychological phenomena, and it is hardly to be wondered that their results bear the characteristic imprint of their field. In this undertaking I have not argued that the social sciences can improve on psychology in the study of subjects that are essentially psychological. It may be suggestive, however, that psychologists have found it difficult to agree on what the emotions are, how they ought to be studied, how they came to be, and what they mean to us. We have quoted Scherer to the effect that emotion theorists agree that emotions are psychological constructs. However, Plutchik (1982:529) remarks that "although most people believe they know a great deal about emotions, psychologists have had difficulty in achieving consensus about what emotions are and how they work. . . ." Perhaps it would not be unfair to infer certain conceptual or procedural inadequacies, but it is not our task to correct these for we have different concerns.

It is only when we bring ourselves to view the emotional activity of the human animal as a variety of social behavior and to insist that such behavior is imbedded in the cultural matrix of experience that dominates the lives of humans, that we are in a position to ask and answer the sorts of questions we are interested in.

Psychologists should not be thought unaware of the fact that humans are socialcultural creatures (Averill 1976) but they seldom perceive the emotions as artifacts of cultural systems. Thus Maletesta (in Field & Fogel 1982:1) speaks of the emotions in this way:

> They [the emotions] make us feel good or terrible. They are powerful impeders or facilitators of interpersonal relationships. Consider the fact that every human culture has developed variously elaborate and subtle rituals for the regulation of emotional expressions. Rituals serve to restrain and refocus emotional energy. Certain rituals ensure that negative emotions be dampened or concealed to keep them from escalating and 'getting out of hand.' Other rituals serve to heighten or amplify positive feeling states and expressions. Because emotions can have both extremely positive and extremely negative consequences for individuals as well as social relationships, there is great personal and social pressure to bring feelings under control.

In this passage the attitude of much of psychology is clearly articulated and the differences between a psychological approach to the emotions and a genuinely socialcultural theory of affective experiences stand out in sharp relief. Despite the ostensible concern for the role of culture in "dealing" with the emotions Maletesta's position is clear. The motions are, in some unstated but unmistakable way, external to those who experience them. They are either outside us or else deeply but independently within us, so they can correctly be regarded as with or in, but not of us. Cultures try to cope with them, regulate them, restrain that mysterious energy with which they are thought to be imbued. Otherwise they may escape our control, get out of hand, and work no one knows what mischief. And, as is often the case, psychological discussion of the emotions depends heavily on the use of metaphors. This habit is unhappily responsible for a great deal of ambiguous discourse.

Of the various "basic" or "standard" emotions with which psychology deals none is more likely to lend itself to a perception of its potential power to disrupt than fear. We find ourselves in the grip of fear. We are paralyzed by it and reduced to impotence under its malign influence. Fear does not have a good press. It can be taken for granted that we would prefer not to be afraid or, perhaps more accurately, we would prefer not to find ourselves in circumstances which, in the classical view, will evoke this least desirable of emotions. It is often presented in the literature as a negative emotion (Geer 1965:45; Izard 1977:8). In our society negative is bad. When speakers of modern English label anything or any experience negative, we at once know they mean to damn it. Izard (1977:355-56) puts this view with unusual vehemence. "Fear affects every human being, and at one time or another it leaves its mark on each of us. It locks into our minds experiences that we can often easily recall and that sometimes erupt into consciousness through our dreams. *Fear is the most toxic of all emotions* [emphasis mine]." He further remarks that "an understanding of fear does not remove dangerous or frightening situations, but it may provide an added measure of control over this toxic emotion." Cole (1959:275) confirms this view. "Fear is destructive. Its only value is to prevent one from doing something that is dangerous or unwise. It is therefore useful for survival in moments of actual physical danger under primitive conditions."

This last is a little strange. One might be inclined to think that anything tending to preserve the individual from danger and foolish behavior, even under primitive conditions, cannot be entirely destructive. But in spite of these emphatic strictures on fear's effects Izard is not above finding a kind, if somewhat grudging, word to say on its behalf. ". . . Fear is not all bad. It can serve as a warning signal and redirect thought and action." This after the fact and reluctant admission that fear may not be altogether contrary to our interests is part of the conventional psychological wisdom, which derives from the assumed relationship between certain emotional states and survival behavior in the phylogenetic past of all animals, humans included. Hence, Izard (1977:83;90) can tell us that "each of the fundamental emotions has an inherently adaptive function." With respect to fear in particular he observes that "this emotion mobilizes energy and provides motivation for escape from danger."

The admission that fear may have a positive, life-sustaining function seems curiously at odds with his confident assertion that it possesses "great toxicity," and is, indeed, "the most toxic of emotions." One may be troubled by his use of the term toxic, for it intimates that foreign elements have intruded into the system, there producing symptoms of malaise. I assume, however, that he regards fear in small doses, so to speak, to have survival advantages through encouraging flight in the face of danger, but that in excess its potentially toxic effects may express themselves in destructive ways. He reminds us that death through fear is a real possibility.

We should not be surprised by this attitude toward fear. In one form or another it would very likely be echoed by most people. Nor are we surprised by the usual response of being afraid. Farley, *et al* (1978:17) remind us that "the study of human fears has usually in recent years been dominated by the therapeutic concerns of clinical and counseling psychology and psychiatry." Anything that is toxic or negative is hardly something we are likely to feel comfortable with. Most of us would doubtless prefer to lead lives free of fear if we could, although it might be more exact to say that we would wish to live free of exposure to situations that encourage a fear response.

An exception to these sentiments must be noted, for there are circumstances in which not only do we fail to object to experiencing fear but actually encourage it in ourselves. We sometimes deliberately seek fear for the excitement we find in it; that excitement is a form of pleasure. Unless I am a hopeless cynic I do not go to a horror movie to laugh or cry but to feel fear, indeed to revel in it. As any movie buff who is addicted to that genre knows, we judge the merit of such a film by its success in terrifying us. Of course, the fear is, in a sense, bogus because the circumstances are artificial, a fact well known to the audience. However, the audience is glad to suspend this knowledge for the sake of the thrill.

I have not tried to climb the north face of the Eiger, played chicken on a narrow country road at night, or spun the cylinder of a revolver in a round of Russian roulette. But people do these things and many others like them. The pursuit of an experience which we are usually happy to avoid opens some interesting opportunities for speculation and research. On the surface the existence of what we may call safe fears and the deliberate courting of real danger as a source of the fear thrill strongly suggest the intrusion of culture into the psychic life of the individual.

But to return to Izard's point about the adaptive value of fear, anthropologists are often partial to interpretations of human behavior which remind us of our prehuman antecedents, although we tend to fight shy of the event specific gene approach. I don't know if Izard has that in mind when he refers to fear's function as being "inherently adaptive." The phrase is susceptible of more than one interpretation and therefore suffers from ambiguity.

Lewis and Rosenblum (1974:9) are more explicit. "At least in infancy it is reasonable to discuss the possibility that there exists a series of events having the innate biological capacity to elicit fearful behavior." Presumably, they mean to say that there exists in the human infant an inherited, i.e. gene determined, tendency to interpret certain specific events in such a way as to lead it to respond by fearing, and by so doing to enhance its survival probabilities.

Similarly, Jeffrey Gray (1971:21) describes a class of fear experiences he calls "special evolutionary dangers." "Where a particular situation is repeatedly responsible for the death of a significantly large proportion of the members of a species over a sufficiently large . . . span of time, the individuals of that species may be expected to develop an innate (i.e. gene specific) fear of some of the stimuli characteristic of that situation and to avoid them." In this way he accounts for what he regards as the innate human fear of snakes, dead or mutilated bodies and, possibly, darkness. Without taking issue at this time with the examples Gray proposes of the phylogenetically derived advantages of fear we will take note of the presence in contemporary psychology of a number of inclinations in the approach to fear behavior.

Certainly, we agree that fear is very often an important part of our lives and that it is a useful objective to try to understand it better. If we choose to use that understanding to eliminate the experience of fear from those lives, well and good, although it is not difficult to raise certain practical objections to that goal. On the other hand, if we conclude that fear is something that has been built into us through the ages of experience of our species and has become as much a part of our nature as the color of our skin or the structure of our digestive system, so that we are stuck with it and can't really help ourselves when we recoil from the serpent, that is acceptable as well. Except that, given such a view of fear one wonders about the possible efficacy of fear therapy.

Sociophobics is committed to neither view. Its findings may or may not help us rid ourselves of our fears, or at least keep them under tighter control. Indeed, it may not even conclude that it would be wise to do so if we could. What sociophobics hopes to accomplish, in any case, is the realization that fearing has played quite a different role in our lives than the one which has so often been assigned to it.

In keeping with our discussion of the emotions in the previous section we suggest that fearing can most usefully be described as an act of intrapersonal and often interpersonal communication and, as is true of other such human transactions, this communication conveys significant cultural meanings. The techniques through which this is accomplished are of cultural origin, as is language, or are powerfully influenced by cultural habits and expectations, as in the case of the feelings which are part of the emotion event.

Such a perception of the character of fearing permits us to interpret its effects at various levels whereas the psychological approach tends to concentrate on the visceral level of the individual actor to the exclusion of others. From our vantage point we can understand fearing as a technique which enables an individual to avoid danger—some threat to his well-being, perhaps to his very life. This is consistent in its outcome with the common interpretation in which fear reactions are conceived as responses to threats to individuals. Perhaps we could call it the predator avoidance response. This is Izard's fear as inherently adaptative interpretation and Gray's fear of snakes, darkness, and dead bodies.

But there is nothing to prevent us from enjoying the analytical advantages of treating fear as adaptive without being compelled to have recourse to the gene specific explanation of it, as so often seems to be supposed. Indeed, in the interests of parsimonious explanation and in the absence of satisfactory evidence in support of such a theory of gene control, a nongenetic interpretation is to be preferred. It is instructive to examine the popular tradition that assigns to humans an innate fear of snakes. Gray (1971:15) comments on that theory.

> The evidence from humans suggests that the fear of snakes is innate, but does not develop until the child is several years old. In 1928 two psychologists . . . set a large, active, but harmless snake free in an enclosure with children of different ages. There were no signs of fear before the age of two; between three and four the children showed signs of cautiousness, and at four and over there were definite signs of fear which increased in frequency and intensity up to the age of about seventeen in people who had never been harmed by a snake. All this strongly suggests maturation process; but, of course, the results obtained may be due to the subjects' having read or heard about snakes. It is fortunate, therefore, that the question may be resolved by experiments on the chimpanzee.

It is jarring to the social scientist to learn that, although Gray raises the possibility that the children may have received some early fear training which could account for the increasing anxiety they displayed in the presence of snakes the possible role of learning is evidently not worth pursuing. On the other hand, he is content to make a leap of logic from the behavior of the chimpanzee to our own actions, using the ape as a psychological stand-in. While the chimpanzee is unquestionably among man's closest living relatives Gray's readiness to accept that primate as a suitable substitute for humans in determining the causes of human behavior is facile and thoroughly unsatisfactory. The proper study of mankind remains man, not the chimp.

Furthermore, following his own remarks about "special evolutionary dangers," he is presumably ready to assume the existence of prehistoric circumstances which we are in no position either to affirm or deny. He notes that in order for the fear of snakes to become innate a "significantly large proportion" of early humans must regularly have been killed by venomous serpents, over a great many generations and, one presumes, in many parts of the world. I do not believe we can say that this happened nor, for that matter, can we categorically deny that it did. The proposal is entirely speculative and the burden of persuasion rests on Gray.

From our perspective, the sociophobic point of view, the emotion transaction involving humans and snakes is an altogether different and simpler one which demands no acceptance of the undemonstrated and the undemonstrable. Human fears are situational, occurring when culturally defined situations appropriate to fear present themselves, under conditions which are understood to make fear a reasonable response.

As I walk in the desert in the early evening I perceive a rattlesnake in my path. I am afraid. The question which we must answer is why I have that particular emotion and not another. Let us proceed according to the principles we have already discussed. I have an experience; I see the snake and, if it rattles, hear it as well. The experience is conveyed to me through my eyes and ears and thus constitutes a potential stimulus which may produce a reaction.

First, however, I must interpret this perception. The information, we may say, is processed by the brain, which is not very satisfactory as a neurological description but it is unclear that our understanding of the social explanation of the event would profit even if we were able to be more exact. The important conclusion to which I have come is that this is a snake and, moreover, a dangerous one which is capable of inflicting serious injury if it bites me. I know it is a snake and do not require the memories of my long dead Pliocene ancestors to make that clear to me. I have learned something of snakes which allows me to extract the significant features from the example before me and compare them with the conception of snakes I have in my mind. From the previous information I conclude that it is a rattler, rather than a garter snake or a gopher snake or some other harmless variety.

From the interpretation of my perception I move to a judgment of its significance, which results in a qualitative label being attached to the experience. Since it is a dangerous snake the label alerts me to the importance of our encounter, and that label is fear. It is entirely reasonable for me to be afraid of the snake when I am in its environment instead of finding it in mine, in a glass case in the zoo. It would be foolish not to feel fear. Every parent wishes his offspring to fear the rattler.

I have feelings and I know that what I am experiencing is fear, rather than some other emotion. It is the fear feeling that makes my mouth dry, my heart race, my respiration accelerate. Under other circumstances the feeling might have been sexual passion or anger or something else, but it happens to be fear. There is no difficulty in concluding that this is what I feel because immediately before me is the object which is the cause of the sensation, and it is a fear inducing thing.

I express that fear. The feeling and the expression of it doubtless feed upon each other and part of the expression is internal as I tell myself, in effect, what I see, what it means, and how I feel about it.

But there are external indicators of the emotion, as well: I yell in surprise and fright, jump back out of reach, or simply stare at it, afraid to move for fear it will strike. This process of fear motivates action. I may run away, or poke at it with my walking stick, or look about for a rock to throw at it, or step back out of harm's way and wait for it to go on its way. These several reactions and the choice I make from among them are, themselves, influenced by cultural considerations. If I am a girl, I have probably been encouraged to react by running away, or screaming. A boy, anxious to present the appearance of indifference to danger, may choose a more aggressive response, while a dedicated environmentalist is shocked at the idea of injuring the animal for no reason.

How, then, does this process differ from a nonemotional one? The question is a critical one. The only element of consequence present here and lacking in a nonemotional situation of comparable character is the feeling component. There is nothing else. The feelings are the means by which I announce to myself the significance of the thing in front of me. These feelings confirm the brain's interpretation of it, which is that the creature is something worthy of being feared. I am prepared to believe that if I were an experienced herpetologist on an evening stroll looking for snakes I wouldn't be afraid of it at all. Respectful, perhaps, but not afraid. On the contrary, I would be delighted to happen upon such a splendid specimen, exceptionally large, nicely marked, and vigorous. My emotion would be a very different one.

On the other hand, if I see something else on that path—a flower growing among the rocks or a butterfly poised on a cactus—it is quite possible that I will have a feeling and experience an emotion, but it will certainly be a different one. I may feel joy or gratitude for being able to appreciate objects of such fragile beauty. Instead of recoiling I will approach in order to increase my agreeable sensations by a closer inspection.

Perhaps what lies before me is a wallet stuffed with large denomination bills. Beyond doubt, I will have an emotion. I will experience feelings, but they may variously be elation, excitement of a pleasurable sort, anticipation, and perhaps, alas! greed. These may be followed by guilt feelings if I resolve to appropriate the money for my own use without trying first to return it to its rightful owner. I may decide to keep it, salving my conscience by telling myself it was probably dropped by a drug dealer or a mafia courier. So my emotions vary with what is on the path, how I interpret it, how I label it, drawing on my society's lexicon of feeling terms, what my feelings tell me, how I express these, and what actions I am moved to take in consideration of the emotion.

My expression of fear in this case may also serve as a vehicle of interpersonal communication. When I shout in alarm, jump back on the path, I convey to my companion just behind me something about myself: my feeling. He will certainly interpret my behavior in the light of his experience with the expression of feelings in himself and others, as these have been learned by him in his society. He will perceive that I am startled and very likely that I am afraid of something. He will be alerted to fear, himself, and will cry out, "What's the matter?" He invites me to share my fear with him in more explicit detail. He is asking for guidance for his own emotions.

Therefore, I have communicated to him a significant if nonspecific meaning. He correctly understands my actions as meaning that there is danger or at least a situation which is upsetting to me, possibly threatening, albeit he does not yet know the details. My behavior has not communicated to him the cause of my fear, the source of my evident feelings. My actions are not object specific. However, the communication is fear specific and he is therefore prepared to fear and to act in an appropriate manner when the cause of my anxiety has been explained to him.

Two final points remain to complete our analysis of this little drama, but they have general application to sociophobic theory. The first is this: my fear of the snake is socially induced. I learn to fear this aspect of nature. My brain has been trained to tell me, via my feelings, that when the eye and ear bring it sensations that it classifies as rattlesnake I am to fear, for I am threatened by a very dangerous creature. It is quite possible that I have never before seen a living rattlesnake, and it is not necessary that I should have had any direct experience with one. I have learned about them through experience, of course, but the experience has not been with the snake at all; rather, it has been with other people. And they need not have had personal contact with rattlers, either. I react to their accounts of such animals and their meaning, and the way I should feel, and how I ought to react. The entire transaction is founded upon and made possible by shared symbols. That is the way humans live.

I, myself, as a child of eight or nine, stepped on a rattlesnake, quite accidentally. The emotion process, from perception of stimulus to final action, was marvelously compressed! The important point is that my experience of life included conditioning to a wide variety of stimuli many of which I had never encountered. Since this was my first meeting with one of the family *Crotalidae*, through no experience of my own could I have affirmed the potential danger of the snake upon which I unwittingly trod and the harmlessness of the nonvenomous reptiles with which I played from time to time. I didn't run away from garter snakes.

The second point has to do with the social function of this particular fear, which at first glance seems so natural and so personal as not to involve my society and its culture at all. That it is personally advantageous to feel a "healthy" fear of rattlesnakes is obvious. Although they may not be as deadly as many think, they are quite dangerous enough to justify fearing. But what does my society gain by my fear of them? How can that fear be construed as a culturally significant meaning? Why should the community take the trouble to engender this fear in me?

The answer to this does not require an unreasonable broadening of the principle of behavior utility. I have heretofore emphasized that the individual is a creature of his society, brought into being and mature fruition through the gradual absorption of that society's cultural knowledge, attitudes, skills, and understandings. To the extent that my fear is an advantage to me, the individual, my society also profits. We must not forget what a society of humans is and what it does: a group of animals living together and cooperating with one another for common purposes. This collective existence affords the individual members the opportunity of living, of surviving from day to day, which is clearly an advantage to those whose lives are thus sustained. But on another level it is also the means through which society, itself, is perpetuated.

The particular human is as important to the community as the group is to him. The two can, in fact, be distinguished from each other chiefly in principle rather than in practice. The group is but the individual writ large; the individual is the group reduced to unit level. If the community should fail it is the individual who is placed in jeopardy. On the other hand, if the individual fails it is the group which is placed at risk, to whatever degree. No society can accept with equanimity the loss of its members or a major reduction in the effectiveness of their contributions to the collective life effort, for the first obligation of any society is to preserve itself. In this sense, at least, Donne was perfectly correct. The death or otherwise removal from full participation in life of the individual diminishes the community. The elimination of an individual from the group deprives it of the performance with which his or her role was associated. The loss of an adult male or female is always of great importance to the group, for those are the cadre forming the core of task accomplishment. The loss of the immature, on the other hand, is the loss of a prospective cog in the survival machine.

Perhaps this seems an intolerably mechanical assessment of human worth. As individuals we may choose to take exception to the principle that we are of value mainly because of what we are actually or potentially able to contribute to the common weal, to the seemingly impersonal tasks which result in the survival of the species. But the correctness of this view becomes more clear when we remember that until quite recently humanity has lived in small groups and that during a great many years the hold these little communities had on life was probably marginal.

It is easy for us to forget, in this era of mammoth human populations from which the removal of a single person is of no consequence to the effective functioning of the group, how tentative mankind's hold was for a period to be measured only in millions of years. We cannot dispute that today there is no such person as the indispensable man, and in various ways it has always been true. In the fullness of time each is demonstrated to be one without whose presence life can still go on. But anything that contributed to the survival and well-being of humans in that endless time when our sort was very thinly distributed and whose survival chances were uncertain, was a positive advantage to the whole.

Therefore, it is as important for the group as it is for me, the individual, that I be trained in a variety of useful skills, and every society does that, as anthropologists know so well. After all, most of the first two decades of life is spent maturing, and only a part of that process is physical. The successful acquisition of the culture of one's society is as critical to adult performance as skeletal growth and physiological maturation. Learning to fear, learning what it means to understand a situation, label it accurately, feel the significance of it, express it accurately to self and others, and act upon it was, I suggest, as important a survival skill as learning to make fire, or chip flint. And the process, we may think, was not much different.

Humans are born capable of learning just about anything they can devise for themselves to learn. Not only are we possessed of this remarkable ability but we utterly depend on it. If we do not learn we do not live. The learning of some skills and techniques and attitudes seems to be unmistakably related to living. We take this learning for granted and understand that no one knows how to make a stone axe or an article of skin clothing or fire or a spear or a cradle board unless he has been trained to do those things. But it somehow seems to us that certain fundamental qualities of our nature must, in a quite mysterious manner, come with us as part of the package of our genetic inheritance, just as we bring with us our skin color, hair form, and blood groups. It is occasionally difficult for us to grasp the full extent of the fundamental fact of our lives: what we are is what we have learned.

We propose that humans are born with a fear potential, just as they are born with an anger potential, a joy potential, a grief potential, and a guilt potential. I will not say that we are born with latent fear, although it might seem to amount to much the same thing. It does not. Latent fear suggests the presence in us of certain predetermined fears, which have been part of us from the instant of conception and only await a suitable stimulus before they express themselves. Fears would thus amount to archetypal memories of our species' ancient experience, husbanded in the germ plasm.

Fear potential, on the contrary, is quite another matter. It means the capacity to learn fear but intimates nothing whatever about specific phylogenetic experiences and certainly nothing about slumbering reactions and feelings brought to life, as by the kiss of a passing prince. In order that our fear potential may be translated into active, or kinetic, fear a number of capabilities must be called on. Fear potential means the capacity to learn the speech patterns of a society. It means the ability to learn to distinguish between many sets of circumstances in the light of learned situational indicators. It means the capacity to label experiences, organize feelings, and channel the expression of these, both for one's own benefit and for that of others. It means the capacity to act in accordance with the chain of events and circumstances and, finally, it means the ability to teach this process to others that they, also, may profit from fearing.

Children learn to fear snakes as they learn to fear fire, the dangers inherent in venturing into the streets and highways, the hazards of accepting candy from strange men, and the danger of appearing in school without their homework assignment for the day. They learn to fear the dangers of entering a neighborhood where they are strangers, and of not doing their jobs well. The list of such learned fear reactions we could make up is literally without end. It is certainly not limited to things that long ago went bump in the night or hissed in the grass. How useless fear would be, if it only protected us against threats mainly experienced by humans who have been dead for untold millenia!

Even from contemplating making such a list of possible fear reactions one or two useful points emerge. Children do not learn to fear dangers which do not exist in their particular world, or are not believed to exist in that world. Our little prehistoric ancestor feared fire, but only after fire had been tamed and made a part of human life. He did not fear the streets and highways or strange men beckoning him to their cars with the promise of candy; the danger of being among strangers, very likely, but perhaps not the fear of public speaking, which afflicts so many of us.

Fears are situational, as we have pointed out, and until the situation occurs as part of life one does not fear it. The potential to fear anything is in us but this potential is only made actual when there is some reason for it. As we cannot die deaths not yet invented, so we cannot suffer fears not yet parts of our lives. The evolution of our fear experiences parallels the development of our culture. We adjust our fears to the worlds that we inhabit. This view is consistent with the anthropologist's repeated insistence that human behavior is flexible to a degree undreamed of by other animals. It would be passing strange if this observation did not include our fears, as well, for fear is a part of life as life is lived.

The second point is this: it is convenient to fall into the habit of associating fear with actual threats to life. This is especially true if one is enamoured of the interpretation of fear as an encouragement to flee from danger. It seems to offer a ready understanding of fear in historical, or at least pseudohistorical, terms. I do not mean to discount the importance of being able to fear as an element of the survival behavior of our remote ancestors, or of ourselves. Much fear alerts one to immediate life hazards, as our analysis of the rattlesnake episode suggests.

Still, it is doubtful if we could affirm that a majority of our fears are of that character. Nor, indeed, are we in a position to reconstruct such a majority for prehistoric times. Reasonably, sinanthropus, neanderthal, australopithecus, and the rest did fear what threatened their lives, whatever that may have been. Wild animals come immediately to mind, but are we in a position to judge the frequency with which members of those populations were actually in physical danger from predators? Perhaps more often than I imagine; perhaps less often than some others suppose.

But speaking for ourselves, with unusual exceptions it would be hard to say that humans are regularly and routinely in danger of some threat to life. Of course, we are always threatened by the possibility of disease carrying us away, or an automobile accident ending our lives, or an earthquake, or a mugger. But for the most part is it not true that our fears are expressive of social events and relations? I think we are more often than not fearful of circumstances that present no physical threat. The fear of loneliness, of rejection, of failure in some important enterprise, of making a serious social blunder, these are with us far more than the sudden fear of imminent death or destruction.

Furthermore, many of our fears are not simply concerns that arise from the fortuitous character of social relations, which suggests that they are incidental, not central, but are effectively created by society for its own purposes. No human society can tolerate unrestrained departure from normative behavior expectations. We must live and act within more or less clearly defined limits on what we are free to do. To venture outside those limits is to invite some kind of collective retribution. The character and severity of the retributive response will depend on a cultural definition of the event and its significance as well, perhaps, as on the social features of the one who strays. But in general terms, members of a society are encouraged to be afraid of departing from what is expected of them and what is tolerated. Societies of humans are self-sustaining survival instruments, and there is no human community which does not take some pains to specify what behavior is not permitted and what is likely to happen if one ignores prohibitions. Fear is useful to the group for its members are encouraged to behave properly lest they have cause to fear. It is equally useful to the individual, for his fear alerts him to the possibility that he may incur his society's resentment.

Perhaps this sounds rather depressing. We shall begin to think that we all live in a world of fear, a world in which life must be dominated and consumed by numberless fears arising from the innumerable sources of threat of one kind or another. No one, surely, wishes to live such a life as that. By understanding fear should we not be able to overcome and conquer it, rid our lives of it and thus live in blessed freedom from its icy fingers at our throats? Hence, the psychologist's frequent concern with fear therapy.

Impossible. Fear is our society speaking to us through our own voice, insistently reminding us of what it means to live in the world—the real world. The world is a place where there are threats that face us from without and hazards which our own behavior and inclinations create. We cannot ignore these for they are present, whether we will or won't. If we somehow succeeded in eliminating our fearing we should have deprived ourselves of one of the chief instruments through which we deal with life's problems. Would we have preferred that the little neanderthal child not be taught to fear the cave bear? For his sake and for the sake of those who loved him, I hope no one tried to do that. Should we avoid encouraging our children to feel fear of the consequences of misbehavior? For the sake of crime statistics we will not want to do that. If we did not learn to fear disease and its results we would not try to develop means of treating it. The results of such fearlessness would be disastrous for the individual and destructive of the interests of the community. If I do not learn to fear the tornado why should I take the trouble to dig a storm cellar? If I don't fear the cold blasts of winter will I bother to collect wood in anticipation of it? I will suffer for my lack of fearing and my society will also suffer. The fearless man, in the face of natural hazards, is a foolish man for reasonable fear is as vital a defense against these threats as fire, clothing, knowledge, and tools.

By the same token I must learn to fear the results of ill-advised behavior toward my fellows. I must learn to fear the consequences of failing to obey properly constituted authority, whatever that authority may be. The fear is not of authority itself, but of the outcome of ignoring its rightful demands. That fear may be of punishment, of ridicule, of ostracism, or rejection. Whatever form it takes, it is to be feared by reasonable people. But the effects of wrong behavior must not only be rationally judged, they must also be felt in order to be of maximum usefulness.

It was not enough simply to proclaim to the Israelites that they ought not kill one another because the functional efficiency of the community would thereby be diminished and the balance of survival probabilities perhaps upset. That was true enough, but it required a qualitative stimulus to increase the likelihood that killing would not occur. We must fear the outcome of killing. We must be afraid of the hot displeasure of Jehovah, who instructed us what we were not to do. That this fear was situationally defined is made clear by the approval of socially valued killing, as when Philistines were the victims. Then, the young women went out of the city to welcome home those who had killed, and Jehovah rejoiced with them.

How vital it is for the community that our fear potential be translated into fear reality under the correct circumstances. We must not fear randomly or mistakenly. We must know how to fear, what to fear, when to fear, how to express fear in order to make it a more effective instrument of social purpose, and how to behave in response to it. Fears which are not heeded, or are responded to in the wrong way, or are responses to inappropriate circumstances are counter productive. There is an art to fearing and learning this social skill is a vital part of an individual's preparation for life. It is part of learning to perceive the nature of reality.

To this discussion of fear it may be worth adding that what has been said of one emotion might also be said of others. Anger, joy, hate, remorse, grief, that roster of the "standard" or "basic" emotions could all be treated in the same fashion. The principle that begins to emerge is an interesting and instructive one. It helps to enlighten us about the extent to which we are shaped into our humanity.

Emotions are instruments and adjuncts of social life. They are the expressions of collective interests. If we discover basic, which is merely to say pancultural, emotions as we examine the behavior of people in different societies, we may be encouraged to postulate the organic unity of mankind in order to account for them. We may easily find ourselves arguing that these seemingly fundamental emotional events are innate in our form of life. We will perhaps seek their genesis in the ancient past of our species, deriving their evident universality from our common descent.

While this is an alluring prospect an alternative interpretation is, to my mind, both more satisfying and more useful as an analytical device.

The universality of anything human can, in the context of our discussion, imply organic cause. These abilities or tendencies or capacities or inclinations are "caused" by our common inheritance which, in specific terms can only mean that there is a particular genetic mechanism which accounts for each emotional response.

On the other hand, if we accept the common capacity of humans to learn symbolic systems and all that this implies we can, and I believe we must, account for the basic emotions in a different way. We can do this without straining at the gnat or easily passing the elephant. The worlds which humans inhabit present similar problems, including hazards, everywhere. Basic emotions are basic simply because they are the learned techniques of dealing with basic, which is to say common, problems. These are the great issues of human life and they arise from the necessity each faces of adjusting to himself, to other humans, and to the natural world.

Fear is but a specific method of using the human capacity to symbolize and to feel in order to cope with problems that arise from living. Anger is another technique, as are joy, love, hate, guilt, and remorse. Each is an appropriate and useful response to different sets of problems. What announces our common humanity is not the possession of a set of innate emotions but the common circumstances we face and the fact that these conditions must be faced, because they can only be thus faced, through the medium of learned behavior, and from the inescapable fact that we do exist and can only exist within the confines of organized groups.

The Individual and His Emotions

We have concentrated on the emotions as features of a society's culture. We have urged that they can most usefully be understood as important elements of the set of techniques by which that society, through the gradual induction of its immature members into a universe of shared symbols and their meanings, develops and maintains conformity to the crucial attitudes, values, sentiments, and behavioral norms that underlie and make possible collective action. We contend that emotions, thus perceived, are aspects of a group's survival behavior and should be interpreted in that light.

However, this emphasis may leave the impression that the individual human has had too little attention paid to what he himself is likely to regard as the essential character of his own emotional life. We can expect that most people will insist that their emotions are private, internal parts of their lives and that their feelings do not, so to speak, belong to the community. Indeed, we might expect to find it argued that it is through these very emotions, these innermost feelings, that people oftentimes escape from or relieve the pressures and demands of society, and the exigencies of that collective action through which their lives are sustained.

Nevertheless, that emphasis has reflected what I believe to be the case with our emotions and has also been intended as a reasonable corrective to the usual attitude of psychologists and philosophers. Thus, in his excellent book, *The Passions*, Solomon (1976:188;199;245) tells us that "emotions are self-involved and relatively *intense* evaluative judgments." "The judgments and objects that constitute our emotions are those which are especially important to us, meaningful to us, concerning matters in which we have invested our Selves." "Every emotion," he further remarks, "is . . . a personal ideology" and "ultimately, all emotions have a common goal—the maximization of self-esteem."

Not all are committed entirely to a perception of emotions as internal. Shibles (1974:10;37;23;29), for example, speaks of them as including "behavior, judgment, feeling, context, and intention." This strongly intimates the involvement of emotions in the world of experience external to the individual, but one in which he participates. That world, of course, is a socialcultural one. However, he also observes: "'What is the purpose of an emotion?' and 'What is an emotion for?' can now be answered. Traditionally it was regarded as a mechanism for survival. It seems rather that negative emotions are forms of self-destruction. On the other hand, positive emotions can lead to physical well-being and long life." Hence, although he persuasively develops the theme of the connection between emotion and language: "It is not clear that language and emotions . . . are two separate things." "Emotion is largely a verbal skill," and "emotion is inseparable from emotion words," he does not make the crucial connection between this verbal aptitude and the linguistic community, i.e. the society with its characteristic culture, which alone can give this skill meaning. So he ends by confirming the significance of emotions in personal terms.

(At some point in our discussion of the emotions and language some readers may have found themselves wondering what is the fate of emotions in nonhuman animals. The emphasis in sociophobics on the central role of language in emotion transactions and the comments here of Solomon and Shibles appear to leave little room for nonhuman emotional experience. Although I cannot speak for the two philosophers, for my own part I am convinced that what we are saying about humans cannot be repeated for infrahumans. This certainly does not deny to other animals something akin to human emotions but it does reject emphatically the notion that the emotional lives of humans and nonhumans are comparable. Any suggestion to the contrary runs the risk of overlooking the development in our hominid ancestors of a capacity for and dependence on symbols. A failure to make that development the central feature of any interpretation of human behavior dooms such an interpretation.)

Having registered these objections to the shortcomings of the conventional view of the emotions there remain some things to be said on the subject. First, we are not obliged to deal with the individual and his emotions. As we noted, one of the hallmarks of the social sciences is the disappearance of the individual, as an individual, from his central position as conceptualized by psychological sciences. In the social sciences he and his behavior are replaced by the group and the collective behavior of that aggregate of humans. It is precisely because the process of growing up in a society of people, marked by its historically derived cultural aparatus, gives evidence of orienting the nondirectional behavior potentials of the individual toward culturally directed proclivities, that we are able to make any general statements about humans, beyond the purely physical level. In this essay we have undertaken to look at the individual as an exemplar of his community and his behavior as the consequence and expression of the systematic imposition upon him of its modes of life, thought, and action.

But, and this is the second point, we are still left with the indisputable fact that the individual is the locus of emotional action, as he is also the irreducible minimum of every cultural event. It is he, as an individual human, who rages, fears, rejoices, hopes, and despairs. This may occur when he is alone or it may happen in groups, as when a great concourse of people is said to be swept by a wave of emotion at a religious ritual, a political rally, a lynching, or a rock festival. And it may be that we humans feel those feelings at that time and in that place because we are brought together for a common purpose and are profoundly and intensely conscious of that common bond. But we are, nonetheless, individual persons.

What may seem to be a paradox, that the emotions are felt by individuals yet are not, ultimately, of the individual, perhaps does not really exist. In order to resolve the problem we must turn once again to language and what we may call its dual role in human life. To the extent that a clear distinction can be made between the individual and his society, instead of regarding the particular human simply as the norms, attitudes, tendencies, and habits of that society made manifest in the flesh, this distinction can be attributed to the power of language not only to communicate reality but also to create it.

The principle which we have sought to establish is that emotions are best described as aspects of human interpersonal and intrapersonal communication. Through them significant meanings are transmitted, both to self and to others. What separates the emotions from nonemotional communication is the necessary involvement of feelings. Otherwise they are indistinguishable from any other acts of communication through which significant meanings are also transmitted. These meanings, thus transmitted, are conspicuously devoted to the establishment and confirmation of cultural meanings which are shared by the speakers of an emotional language, who share a lexicon of feeling terms. They are techniques by which we affirm to ourselves and to others our involvement in, acceptance of, and commitment to cultural judgments. The peculiar feature of the emotions is that this affirmation takes the form of feelings.

So, when I feel indignation at the mistreatment of someone who cannot defend himself I am reminding myself, through that feeling, of my cultural bias in favor of fair play and against the strong violating the norms and expectations which are intended to protect the weak. In a society in which such norms did not exist I could hardly be expected to be indignant. Finally, I am likely to express this feeling to others through culturally designed idioms of behavior which announce to anyone familiar with my society's habits that I am, in fact, experiencing this feeling and sharing these principles. On the other hand, when I feel elation because my team has won an athletic contest I confirm to myself the culturally established rightness of vigorous competition conducted according to precise and well-understood rules, and the importance of winning graciously or, if need be, of losing gracefully.

When my heart soars in patriotic fervor at a national political convention I am committing myself to the cultural conclusion that it is right and proper to revere the state and to express that exalted feeling through tears and cheers. I may even, ultimately, embrace the principle that it is right and fitting to accept death with fortitude in exemplification and demonstration of that deep conviction, perhaps even carrying the principle to the extreme of lamenting that I can die only once for my country.

When I feel jealous of another, envious of his success, I affirm my society's decision that not only do I exist for the group but also for myself. I wish to excel, to get ahead, to succeed, and triumph over others who likewise strive, for my society has taught me that by the success of my efforts I will be significantly judged and should, therefore, judge myself accordingly. Jealousy of another is a reminder that he has met his community's expectations and I have not.

But is there not some point at which the individual human can be utterly private? Does he never march to the beat of a drum that no one else hears? Does he never, in effect, communicate to himself significant meanings which are not derived from his culture? Are our emotions, in fine, never really our own? Perhaps there is no satisfactory answer to that question. Perhaps, in fact, it is a nonquestion, for it appears to set up conditions which do not, indeed cannot, exist: the independence of a human being from the milieu in which he lives and which, in a very real sense, has created him. Of all the aspects of this milieu none is so important in its formative power as language. Not only, as we observed, does it convey reality but it effectively creates reality, as well. It seems, in the end, that it is impossible to separate the container from the thing contained.

However, insofar as there is a cultural lexicon of emotions which is peculiar to a society; insofar as there are the ties we propose between language and emotion; insofar as societies use our feeling-communication capacity to direct our attitudes, hence our behavior; in short, insofar as we are, as individuals, the offspring of our socialcultural systems, our theory has usefulness in accounting for behavior, and that is the task which was given it to do.

We can turn to the linguistic analogy to understand this better, and envision the articulation between the Individual as individual and the Individual as community.

- No speaker of a language ever learns the whole of that language.
- No person ever understands his language precisely as another speaker of the "same" language does.
- No member of a society, even the most perfectly integrated one, ever lives the life of another member of that same society.
- No person, it may be, has exactly the same arousal or feeling capacity as another—the same physiology.

Therefore we must, surely, allow that members of the same society have at least as much emotional individuality as they have linguistic, life history, and physiological individuality. It appears, in consequence, that no two members of the same society speak, i.e. feel, exactly the same emotion. It follows that one's emotional life must be as particular as these other traits we have mentioned; no more, but certainly no less.

However, the cultural theory of emotion does not stand or fall on the point of the individual uniqueness of emotional experience, any more than it does on the issue of linguistic uniqueness. The speakers of a language do not have to be, and are never presumed to be, linguistically identical. They must share enough of their language so that it can do for them what languages do, which is permit effective symbolic communication.

The fact that I have a private linguistic life, that I use my language not only to tell others what I think but also to talk to myself and to think, an act understandably regarded as private, does not prevent my language from being a cultural construct, designed to accomplish collective ends. Nor, in reverse, does the essential groupness of language interfere with its use for personal ends.

Then it must be likewise for the emotions. Private they are, without doubt, in the sense that they are felt privately, in the sense that they convey to the self certain meanings which are the results of the unique experiences the self has had, and the unique integration of those experiences to form a person. Nevertheless, the emotions which serve these personal and private ends are culturally created, derived, and used. Like language, they serve collective ends.

3
Measurement in Research on Sociophobics

William H. Key

What Has Been Done?

The goal of this chapter is two-fold. First, it will provide an overview of the instruments and techniques which have been used in research on fear in a variety of fields, the data gathering strategies with which such instruments have been associated, and the research designs which have been employed. Second, I shall evaluate those instruments and approaches for their potential utility in pursuing sociophobic studies and suggest possible strategies which can be useful to the social scientist. I shall avoid as much as possible duplicating the substantive and theoretical discussions which form the focus of other chapters, though a discussion of strategies for answering theoretical questions makes unavoidable a certain amount of overlap.

The material on which this chapter is based was gathered by a computer search of sociological and psychological abstracts for the last ten years using "method" as the key descriptor, a library catalog review of books in social psychology which seemed to promise some, at least tangential, relationship to the topic, an unsystematic review of a number of catalogs of scales used in the areas of social psychology and mental health, and a "hands on" review of every issue from the last ten years of most of the major publications in sociology and anthropology to identify articles which might throw some light on the topic, but which might not have been uncovered by the computer search.

As was indicated above, the narrowly defined goal was to uncover reports of empirical research which had operationalized the definition of fear in some data gathering instrument. Of the hundreds of references collected, only 49 included enough information on data gathering methods to be useful for the purpose of this chapter.

My search of the literature, buttressed by the reports of research detailed elsewhere in this book, confirms Scruton's assertion in the introductory chapter that social scientists have paid little attention to the emotions in general and fear in particular. That may be due to the widely held view that emotions are somehow biologically based or at least buried in the unconscious part of the human psyche and that pursuit of the topic would force the social scientist into psychological reductionism. If social scientists have paid very little attention to the topic at all it is not surprising that even fewer efforts have been expended on the task of precisely defining and measuring fear. There are, as one would imagine, some conceptual definitions to be found in the theoretical literature; however, attempts to operationalize those concepts are scarce. The only formal attention to definition I uncovered was by Bamber (1979:13), who, after devoting a chapter to the meaning of fear, concluded with the following definition: "the positive reaction an individual makes to a verbal stimulus on a questionnaire when he is asked to identify those items which he thinks he might find frightening or unpleasant. . . ."

Empirical studies of fear have been dominated by psychologists, and within their discipline by clinical practitioners interested in the identification of fear objects to be used in planning and implementing behavior therapy threatment for patients (Turner 1978; Grossberg and Wilson 1965; Wolpe and Lang 1964).

The techniques which have been used to study fear can be grouped into five categories: 1) observation by the researcher; 2) the use of informants, e.g. parents' reports of the fears of their children; 3) the listing of fears by subjects; 4) the use of interviews, primarily by clinicians; and 5) the use of questionnaires. The use of questionnaires has become the dominant technique in a majority of empirical studies.

In situ observation is limited by both practical and ethical considerations and has been used infrequently (MacFarlane, Allen, and Hunzik 1951). Observation in the laboratory offers more possibilities and has been used both to test the validity of other measures and as a technique to generate substantive results (Greer 1965; Lanyon and Manosevitz 1966). Studies using parents as informants of their children's fears show a low correlation between the child's self-report and what the parent reports (Lapousse and Monk 1959; Yarrow, Campbell, and Burton 1968, reported in Croake and Hinkley 1976). The technique of asking subjects to list their fears has been used, but primarily among children. Asking subjects via an open-ended question to recall fears (or any material) always raises the question of how complete is the recall. Therefore, the technique has been used sparingly (Angelino, Dallins, and Mech 1956; Pratt 1945).

Personal interviews have been employed in a variety of studies but most frequently by psychiatrists and clinical psychologists. Interviews have also been used in conjunction with self-report scales or listing techniques.

Interviews are, for the most part, unstandardized and lack the apparent virtues of the Fear Survey Schedules described below. Clinicians have focused on their traditional categories of information, e.g. childhood experiences related to the resolution of an oedipal complex (Haldipur et al 1982).

Self-report questionnaires which are converted into scales have become increasingly popular. They have the apparent virtue of being objective and offer the possibility of standardization which facilitates comparisons across samples. The most frequently used scales are known as Fear Survey Schedules I, II, and III. These scales share a common origin in an unpublished doctoral dissertation at the University of Pittsburgh (Akutagawa 1956). Greer (1965) presents a succinct chronology of the main developments of these schedules (FSSs) in the following paragraphs:

> Akutagawa (1956) developed a Fear Survey that was constructed by selecting 50 items that he felt covered most commonly occurring fears. Lang and Lazovick (1963) used that scale in a study evaluating systematic desensitization therapy and reported that the scale correlated with standard anxiety scales. The scale presented in this paper is patterned after Akutagawa's scale and is called the Fear Survey Schedule II (FSS II).
>
> In a recent paper, Wolpe and Lang (1964) presented a fear scale that was developed following the initial work on the FSS II. Their scale, developed on the basis of clinical observation and theoretical conceptualization has been labeled the Fear Survey Schedule III. Wolpe and Lang suggest that their scale be used as an adjunct to behavior therapy.

The Fear Survey Schedules are paper and pencil self-report check lists composed of stimuli (words) which stand for potential fear provoking objects or situations. The intensity of the subject's reactions is indicated on a Likert type scale usually involving five or seven gradations ranging from no fear to very much fear or terrors, or some similar label. Scores are summarized by adding the scale values of individual items. Thus, on an instrument utilizing 50 items and a five point Likert scale, the scores could range from a minimum of 50 to a maximum of 250. The number of items actually included in the various Fear Survey Schedules has ranged from 50 to over 100. The Fear Survey Schedule used by Wolpe and Lazarus (1966) is described in Appendix A as one example of such instruments. As one might expect, there have been other modifications of the FSS for specific studies but none has found the acceptance of FSS I, II, and III.

Most users have divided the schedules into subscales by employing either logic or statistics. For example, Wolpe and Lang (1964) divided their schedule into six logically (theoretically?) derived subclasses: classical phobias, fear of animals, tissue damage or illness, social stimuli, noises, and miscellaneous objects. In an earlier study using a different self-report technique Angelino et al (1956) defined ten sub-classes: safety, school, natural phenomenon, animals, health, economic and political, personal appearance, social relations, personal conduct, and the super-natural.

In addition, the Fear Survey Schedules have been subjected to factor analysis by a number of researchers. (See Bernstein and Allen 1969; Merbaum and Stricker 1972; Rubin et al 1968; Braun and Reynolds 1969; Landy and Gaupp 1971). These factor analytic studies have identified from five to twenty-one factors. A comparison of these studies demonstrates some overlap in the factors identified, particularly with respect to two factors. These are fear of animals and fear of some version of social interaction (or interpersonal anxiety). The first factor, fear of animals, is composed of approximately the same items. The fear of social interaction, or interpersonal anxiety, is also reasonably consistent. These scales have been rather widely adopted for research purposes by a number of scholars, including Greer (1965), Manosevitz and Lanyon (1965, 1966), Farley et al (1978), Landy and Gaupp (1971), Brown and Reynolds (1969), Merbaum and Stricker (1972), Bernstein and Allen (1969), Fischer and Turner (1978), Bamber (1974), and Last and Blanchard (1982). Minor changes, such as increasing the number of items, have been made but such changes do not alter the basic approach.

A scale similar to the Fear Survey Schedules was developed by Dixon, de Monchaux, and Sandler (1957) who used twenty-six items of the Tavistock Self-Assessment Inventory. Wolpe and Lang (1964) credit this study with starting the trend toward attempting to determine anxiety stimuli through the use of an inventory. Dixon and his colleagues, focusing exclusively on social anxieties, identified five factors: 1) general social anxiety (e.g. feeling uncomfortable in a crowd of strangers, being the center of attention, not knowing what is expected, speaking to someone in authority, etc), 2) social timidity (e.g. feeling awkward with strangers, speaking to someone in authority, difficulty in asking other people for information, eating and drinking in front of others), 3) fear of loss of control (e.g., vomiting or being sick in public, fainting, wanting to pass water at an inconvenient time), 4) fear of exhibitionism (being the center of attention, arriving late, performing, etc.), and 5) fear of revealing inferiority or being judged critically by others.

The research designs have consisted primarily of "one-shot" surveys frequently using college or younger students as subjects. Bamber (1979) has perhaps the most exhaustive inventory of studies of fear among children. Not all of those references are included here since Bamber was not focusing on method, but the reader who is interested in the substantive results can consult the Bamber volume. Saish (1982) developed a Lebanese version of the Fear Survey Schedule to study war-related anxieties.

In general, little attention has been given to the measurement of socio-cultural factors, except in a few studies involving age groups, rural and urban residents, family structure, socio-economic classes, and differences between Israeli and American men and women.

Problems and Criticisms

The perennial questions of reliability and validity are largely unanswered. Some researchers who used the Fear Survey Schedules have attempted to measure reliability and validity. Researchers who have used the other techniques reported above have not explicitly considered the questions of reliability and validity.

For the Fear Survey Schedules, reliability is usually reported as satisfactory (Greer 1965; Bamber 1979). Validity, as usual, is more troublesome. Validity has been studied primarily by correlating total scores on FSSs with various measures of anxiety and personality (Greer 1965; Manosevitz and Lanyon 1965; Husen 1971). Some researchers have also tested the ability to predict behavior in laboratory settings from total scores of a Fear Survey Schedule and from certain subsets of items. The experiments have followed a typical pattern of administering the Fear Survey Schedule to identify the specific objects or situations feared, e.g. spiders, dogs, snakes, etc, exposing the subjects to those stimuli in a controlled situation, and then comparing the laboratory reactions of subjects to their responses on the Fear Survey Schedule. The results of the various tests of validity have been inconsistent.

From this brief review it is clear that no tested and sophisticated methodology is available which social scientists might adopt and use in the investigations of problems. At this point, let me summarize the methodological issues touched upon above as well as others which are not associated with specific data gathering techniques. The following summary and discussion borrows heavily from Croake and Hinkley (1976) who identified the major methodological issues.

Definition. The design difficulties begin with defining fear and especially differentiating it from anxiety. As indicated above, few researchers bother defining the term. However, there is some attempt to distinguish between fear and anxiety on the basis of the degree of concreteness of the stimuli. Fear is thought of as the emotional reaction to concrete or clearly in-focus objects, e.g. spiders, snakes, etc. Anxiety, on the other hand, is described as an emotional reaction when the object or situation is vague or not clearly in focus, e.g. fear of failure or of criticism. Notice that the Fear Survey Schedules include both types of items which may be the basis of some of their difficulties. Bamber (1979) has an extended discussion of this topic in his Chapter I.

Reliability and Validity. See the discussion of this topic above and Croake and Hinkley (1976) and Bamber (1979).

Methods of Reporting. The various methods produce different quantitative and qualitative results. The sub-issues are as follows:

a. Results seem to depend on whether the subject perceives that it is socially acceptable to identify a specific fear.

b. If one uses a version of the Fear Survey Schedule, there are some specific issues, e.g. the longer the list, the greater the number of fears reported. Also, categories (see discussion of Categorization below) often have an unequal number of specific fears which may require a weighting scheme.

Categorization. Is it desirable to subdivide fears into a set of classes? If so, is it preferable to derive a set of classes using some logical/theoretical criteria or is it preferable to use some empirical/mechanical techniques such as factor analysis?

How should social scientists proceed in their study of fear? What is an adequate methodology? Obviously, that question is not answerable as it is posed. One cannot specify an adequate methodology in the absence of a specification of the research questions to be answered and the research tasks to be accomplished.

The Fear Survey Schedules have been the most widely used instruments for studying fear. Croake and Hinkley (1976) and Bamber (1979) after extensive reviews of the literature conclude that the Fear Survey Schedules are the instruments of choice for pursuing the study of fear. That conclusion may be valid for psychologists but my conclusion is that the Fear Survey Schedules show only modest promise for use by social scientists in understanding this complex subject. I reached that conclusion for the following reasons:

1. The Fear Survey Schedules successfully address only one of the four methodological issues (reliability) listed above.

2. Item selection has been unguided by theory. Except for the early work by Akutagawa who developed his initial scale from material gathered in psychotherapeutic encounters, the selection of items has appeared to be without theoretical rationale. Therefore, it is difficult to fit the results into any explanatory schema. One possible value to social scientists might be the use of Fear Survey Schedules as an exploratory instrument

to describe the distribution of fear stimuli among various categories of the population.

3. The factor analyses reported raise more questions than they can answer. What can account for the constellations of specific items in any given study? How does one explain the variety of factors reported by the various studies? While this may be a problem of the overuse of factor analysis, the results do not promise answers to the questions raised elsewhere in this book.

4. Finally, the technique produces results which are time and space bound. It appears that cultural or social interactional questions could be approached only with difficulty using Fear Survey Schedules.

It would be arrogant and probably foolish to suggest that thirty years of research should be abandoned. As indicated above, Bamber (1979) and Croake and Hinkley (1976) felt that continuing the use of Fear Survey Schedules offered the greatest possibility of payoff. For example, Bamber, after a thorough review of the same research, came to the conclusion that the Fear Survey Schedules were acceptable and used them in his study of fear among adolescents. After Croake and Hinkley (1976) reviewed the methodological issues in the study of fear, they came to the conclusion that progress in the solution of problems in instrumentation will be greatest if we stay with the existing instruments. They suggest continuing refinement by borrowing from all of the inventories, constructing a synthetic one, readministration, factor analyzing the results, dropping items which are checked infrequently, readministration, dropping, etc. They suggest following the same practice with categories. This may be a wise direction for someone to pursue because there is a thirty to forty year history of development of these measures and evidence of some clinical utility. However, I would not advise social scientists to spend any major amount of their research time on improving these scales beyond the uses suggested below.

Proposed Strategies for Future Research

This brings us back to the question of what techniques promise the greatest payoff for social scientists in the absence of some guiding theory. The task of developing theory is beyond the scope of this chapter, but is being addressed elsewhere in this volume. However, there are some social science research areas which, on the basis of past experience, offer a prospect of advancing our understanding even in the absence of coherent theory. Below is my list of examples of social science issues which might be explored based on the perspective outlined in Scruton's initial chapter. That perspective is summarized by Hallowell's (1938) succinct statement quoted by Scruton which places the study of emotions in a cultural context and suggests some of the early research tasks to be pursued. "Culture defines: (a) the situation that will arouse certain emotional responses and not others; (b) the degree to which the response is supported by customs or inhibition demanded; [and] (c) the particular forms which emotional expression may take."

My reading of Hallowell's statement and Scruton's expansion of the perspective suggests the following specific research tasks or questions.

1. We need to explore whether the existing lists exhaust the specific manifestations of fear.

2. We need to explore how the kinetic fears are distributed among familiar social science cohorts: sex, age, socio-economic groups, rural-urban, etc., and whether current fears are the same as those reported in the past.

3. We need to begin the exploration of the more difficult question of the source of fears. That is, we need to identify the social interactional event(s) which lead to kinetic fear. So far, most studies have been primarily descriptive of specific stimuli which evoke fear reactions.

4. We need to explore the question of whether fear is a general social psychological characteristic or is stimulus and/or situationally specific.

5. We need to explore the question of whether the networks to which an individual belongs affect the incidence and type of fear. For example, do highly mobile people who do not remain long in any network display a greater number or different types of fear?

6. We need to identify what culturally standardized techniques of supporting the individual and mitigating his fears are available.

If the above is a list, admittedly incomplete, of some of the research tasks to be accomplished, what techniques seem most likely to help us in our efforts to find the answers? The steps suggested below should be seen as only preliminary. Multiple methodologies are likely to yield superior results at this early stage, so we should not be restrictive in our choices. My suggestion is to rely on exploratory and "soft" techniques in the initial stages. For example:

1. Explore the subject with open-ended interviews carried out by a variety of interviewers whose only direction is to identify fears—then share the results, examine the overlaps, sharpen the definition and then interview another sample.

2. Use the techniques of content analysis to insure some degreee of consistency either initially or following the initial interviews. (I am indebted for most of the content of this section to Ms. Nancy Miller, a Ph.D. candidate in the Department of Sociology, University of Denver. The material is taken from a Doctoral Paper presented to satisfy a qualifying examination.) Content analysis has most frequently been used as an unobtrusive research techniques to analyze documents for which

the researcher has provided no direct stimulus and exercised no control. Recently, content analysis has also been applied to unstructured interviews and open-ended questionnaires. In the field of psychology, a primary application of content analysis is the data gathered through open-ended questionnaires, verbal tests and the Thematic Apperception Test (Krippendorff 1980).

In the case of open-ended questions, respondents are aware of being measured; the researcher provides the stimulus but no structure is provided for the reply.

> Open-ended questions are called for when the issue is complex, when the relevant dimensions are not known, or when the interest of the research lies in the explanation of a process or of the individual's formulation of an issue. . . . The flexibility of the unstructured interview helps to bring out the affective and value laden aspects of respondent's responses and to determine the personal significance of their attitudes. It should also elicit the personal and social context of beliefs and feelings (Sellitz et al 1976).

I did not find a reference to any work on fear that used content analysis or formalized the use of open-ended questions beyond those previously reported. However, groups headquartered at Northwestern University and the University of Denver are studying emotional development using a questionnaire composed of open-ended questions and are using content analysis to code and analyze the completed questionnaire. While their instruments and codes are specific to their research questions, the technique appears to be useful in studying emotions and adaptable to the study of fear (Personal communication from Dr. Frank Falk and Ms. Nancy Miller).

3. Finally, someone should examine the studies using the Fear Survey Schedules to try and understand and explain the results. For example, why would dirt and nude women appear in the same factor? Or why do some studies report twenty factors and others many fewer? I do not agree with Croake and Hinkley that social scientists, or indeed anyone, should expend a major effort on refining the Fear Survey Schedules at this stage of development. However, there is a body of data gathered over thirty or more years which might yield some useful insights if the results were examined from the social science perspectives outlined in this book.

Summary

A review of research on fear conducted over the last three or four decades has demonstrated a movement from interviews to more formalized and structured instruments. The empirical research has focused primarily on identifying the various stimuli which elicit fear reactions in subjects. Since fear research has been performed primarily by psychologists, very little attention has been paid to questions which interest social scientists. Unresolved issues and questions which have been raised by various authors about existing research include definition of fear, reliability, validity, the methods of reporting, and categorization.

The use of objective tests seems inappropriate for the preliminary stage in which we find social science research into fear. The "soft" techniques of unstructured interviews, open-ended questionnaires and content analysis were suggested as the most appropriate techniques at this stage. As research proceeds, the interplay of theory and research should lead to more structured instruments and to the use of more modern and sophisticated analytic techniques such as modelling through the use of Partial Least Squares or Lisrel. For now, however, the application of advanced statistical or quantitative techniques seems premature.

4
Sociophobic Data and the Cross-Cultural Perspective

Enya P. Flores-Meiser

Introduction:
Sociophobics and Anthropology

One of the tasks before us, as we launch this collective endeavor, is to identify the nature of our data and eventually to locate them. Following on the heels of psychologists, who by no means are of uniform persuasion but who for quite some time have been engaged in the study of fear and related concepts, we commence, in one sense, at an advantage. The volume of data and paradigms stemming from this sister discipline is enormous and available at our disposal. From it we can take direction; to it we may take exception. With regard to the latter, we must recognize, and we do, the intrinsic limitation of much of their data as they bear proximate relevance to the individual, largely as organism and very little else beyond it. In other words, the relative neglect of the role of the sociocultural sphere in the analysis and understanding of fear is notable and justification enough to draw our attention to that fact. Even when comparative psychology attempts to consider the cultural dimension, the latter is nothing more than a weak background. In that particular effort what has been essentially accomplished is replication of research designs directed at different populations. The tools, almost exclusively in the form of the questionnaire, are initially tested in the American samples and then translated into the language appropriate for the cultural group. (See Spielberger and Diaz-Guerrero 1973). Thus against the enormous quantity of statistical data and the large number of theories generated by psychology, what anthropology can propose to offer on the subject of fear is, at the very least, a particular perspective.

The anthropological perspective as we have come to recognize it has been fashioned around intensive ethnographic fieldwork in small and relatively self-contained groups. And as Plotnicov (1973) rightly reminds us, the basic premise upon which this disciplinary approach has rested, involves the notion of holistic culture. In the face of complex trends in the development of the groups traditionally studied by anthropologists, and at the prospect of a rapidly evolving world system, Plotnicov's (Ibid:254) point is well taken, to wit:

> If holism once meant knowing everything about a people, it no longer does; it now refers, first of all, to a cognitive assumption that any cultural trait or social pattern may only be understood and defined in terms of its own context.

Of course, the foundation of meritorious contextual analysis lies in disciplined ethnography itself, toward which Geertz' (1973:6;9-10) instructions remain indisputable and deserve reiteration. He said:

> In anthropology, or anyway social anthropology, what practitioners do is ethnography. And it is in understanding what ethnography is, or more exactly *what doing* ethnography is, that a start can be made toward grasping what anthropological analysis amounts to as a form of knowledge.

> . . . what defines it is the kind of intellectual effort it is: an elaborate venture in, to borrow a notion from Gilbert Ryle, "thick description."

> . . . The point for now is only that ethnography is thick description. What the ethnographer is in fact faced with . . . is a multiplicity of complex conceptual structures, many of them superimposed upon or knotted into one another, which are at once strange, irregular, and inexplicit, and which he must contrive somehow first to grasp and then to render. . . . Doing ethnography is like trying to read . . . a manuscript—foreign, faded, full of elipses, incoherencies, suspicious emendations, and tendentious commentaries but written not in conventionalized graphs of sounds but in transient examples of shaped behavior.[1]

To date the ethnographic accounts directed to fear analysis are few (Geertz 1959; Robarcheck 1979), if not residual. This observation is based on the scrutiny of two sets of ethnographic sources. One is a sample[2] from the *Human Relations Area Files*, the largest repertory of ethnographic data; the other, Whiting et al's (1963) *Child Rearing in Six Cultures*. Both sources have been controlled, to the extent that is possible, for comparability and uniform reporting. As expected, both exhibit paucity of relevant data leading us to the conclusion that fear has not been a subject that has had much interest for anthropologists. This fact, while readily understood in conjunction with the traditional "division of labor" within the academic disciplines, has interesting implications and consequences. For one thing, despite our implicit subscription to the assumption that fear as well as other emotions are pan human traits, without ethnographies the cross-cultural dimension of sociophobics is bound to be slighted. Thus even if fear were reduced to an event, as Scruton (1985) contends, the diversity in the structuring of this human attribute offers a wide area of investigation.

The anthropological or ethnographic inquiry into the phenomenon of inner states has been at best, marginal. However, more recent interest in the cross-cultural notions of self and personhood[3] may yet prove crucial to a significant systematization of data and theory appropriate to sociophobics. Until then, the conceptualization, identification, and operational definition of fear vis-à-vis other forms of inner states or emotions, e.g. anger, fury, loneliness, etc, remain problematic. Even in Rosaldo's (1980) masterful analysis and interpretation of the Ilongot's passion, reference to fear, per se is merely passing, while Gerber (1975:253-257) allotted a few more pages to discussing this emotion. This observation necessarily leads us to a hypothetical consideration for which we must remember that what psychology has so far accomplished is a body of fear data and theory which is significantly instrument-bound (questionnaire) and also culture-bound, i.e. Western or more precisely Euro-American.

Thus at the risk of oversimplification, a dichotomy between Western and non-Western societies may be proposed to the effect that "fear" in the latter may not be as readily identified or even inferred, either as thought or behavior or both. The opposite is more the case for the former. Framed on the premise that ethnography typically depicts the normative more than the idiosyncratic, the noted absence of fear data in ethnographical sources mentioned above makes the hypothesis plausible. In a paper in this volume, Parkin similarly points to a direction of fundamental contrast between these two types of societies as follows:

> I might surprise readers by suggesting that the Western concept of fear both occupies a more focal role in our thinking and has a larger number of associated concepts than among a number of African societies of my acquaintance, principally the Giriama of Kenya and some related Bantu peoples, and the East African southern Luo and other Nilotic peoples. I do not mean to say that, in such African societies, people feel less fear. Rather, I contend that fear, as concept translatable into the Western equivalent as best it can be, does not figure so largely in people's minds and talk.

Yet within the broad spectrum of non-Western societies, variation in the cultural significance attached to fear and other emotions is further presumed to occur at various loci in diverse manners and at different levels of embeddedness in the normal sociocultural life. As such, the main task of the anthropologist is to delineate the complex connection between fear-related dynamics and the supporting institutions as larger units for sociophobic analysis permitting as it may a wider taxonomy and understanding of these units. This goal will not only require more focused ethnographies, but most decidedly require also a recasting of the earlier ones.

In the *Landscapes of Fear*, Tuan (1979), a geographer, did precisely that and identified what I would call fear configurations or profiles, which he attributed expectedly to types of habitat and subsistence modes. Interpreting the classic ethnographies of the Semai, Mbuti, Eskimos, Aztecs, and Navahos, to name a few, Tuan's analysis is a historical one, describing the likely transition of one type of fear to another against the changing background of man's adaptation. If nothing else, the work reminds us of the potential significance of a rigorous cross-cultural examination of fear that indeed awaits us. In this endeavor anthroplogy must join psychology with which it has enjoyed both collaboration and disputation at various points of their respective histories: at first, in culture and personality studies, then in cross-cultural child rearing practices and socialization, and later in ethnopsychology. That this long interdisciplinary association would inevitably lead anthropology to fear studies, as proposed in two symposia,[4] is an understandable extension.

Fear and Shame Among Tagalogs[5]

The contextual recasting/remolding of early ethnographic information into the subject of sociophobics is bound to be an arbitrary process that is slightly more than a random search for fear data.[6] In attempting to delineate the sphere of sociophobics among Philippine Tagalogs, I suggest that one aspect or locus of it may be sought in the culture's fear-shame complex. I am guided in doing so by standard concepts from psychology which I find not only helpful but worth exploring, particularly for cross-cultural comparison. The commonly held assertion from psychologists that fear and anxiety are closely linked as aspects of each other seems to be a reasonable place to start.

Commonly encountered in the literature on fear are such notions as: "Fear is focused, anxiety is not"; "fear is specific, anxiety, generalized"; or as Epstein (1976:197) put it, "anxiety is a state of undirected arousal following the perception of threat, or as an unresolved fear." However, Averill's description (1980:123) of fear and fear-related systems which takes a broader scale is far more instructive when he said:

An experience of dread, fear, or terror is one of the most consistently reported features of anxiety (in the emotional as opposed to the formal sense of anxiety). What is the source of this experience? In most instances, the emotion we call fear is largely a social product. Such socially constructed fears are not aspects of anxiety, except perhaps in a formal sense (i.e., standard fear reactions may be used as defenses against the threat of cognitive disintegration). There are, however, a variety of fear-like responses which are closely related to biological systems. Among these, fear of the unknown may play an especially prominent role in anxiety because of its close association with intellectual functioning.

Taken as a complex, fear and anxiety are further juxtaposed as follows (Ibid:118-119):

> Anxiety . . . entails a disintegration or disruption of cognitive systems related to personal identity in the absence of any supporting frame of reference (which may or may not be consciously articulated).
>
> When used in a formal sense, "anxiety" does not refer to a specific emotion among other emotions. Rather, it has a function somewhat analogous to the concept of illness. . . . In short, anxiety can be—and often is—used only in a general sense to refer to any of a variety of potential reactions resulting from a threat to a person's sense of identity and worth. As such, it does not refer to a particular initial response but rather to a formal property (threat to personal identity) of a number of quite different emotional and defensive reactions. [parenthetical additions, mine]

In this framework, therefore, and at this level (a social psychological one), fear can be viewed as constituting a response to ongoing dynamics of anxiety at once combining or competing with other emotional responses and arousals, e.g. anger, panic, etc.

Among the Tagalogs, the concept, *hiya* [throughout this book, native words and phrases will only appear in italics on their first use.—ed.] demarcates and touches upon, if not translates directly into the notion of anxiety as described above. Possessing linguistic equivalence in other Philippine groups, hiya in Cebuano is *ulao*; Hiligaynon, *huya*, Iloko, *bain*, Kapangpangan, *dine*, and Pangasinan, *baeng* (Bulatao 1964:324). Often treated as synonymous with embarrassment, shyness, or shame, hiya has been generally described as the fundamental psychological aspect of all Philippine interpersonal behavior.

Drawing from a wide range of behaviors and situations, Bulatao's (1964) treatment of hiya takes one into various spectra of meanings: from losing face, to feeling oneself slowly dissolving; from a sense of inadequacy, to utter failure in meeting expectations of conformity in conjunction with personal goals, but more appropriately, group ones as well; or from being sensitive to others' concerns, to having an intense capacity for empathy. At once a feeling, an emotion, a sanction, and a value, hiya is a versatile psychocultural mechanism,[7] a flexibly organized device to protect the ego whenever deemed necessary.

Rooted in what Bulatao called the "unindividuated ego," which is in turn based on childrearing practices (1964:428-431;427) the following tentative definition was offered as he wrote:

> Hiya may be defined as a painful emotion arising from a relationship with an authority figure or with society, inhibiting self-assertion in a situation which is perceived as dangerous to one's ego. It is a kind of anxiety, *a fear of being left exposed, unprotected, and unaccepted*. It is *a fear* of abandonment, or "loss of soul," a loss not only of one's possession or even of one's life, but of something perceived as more valuable than life itself, namely the ego, the self. [Emphasis mine]

In hiya dynamics, Bulatao further noted the exclusion of guilt as appeared below:

> Guilt, the consciousness that one had done moral wrong, is outside the concept of *hiya*. Even, as in illustration 7 when the girl is revealed as having done a socially unacceptable act by eating peanuts in class, the hiya is not over the wrong done but its revelation.

Thus recalling the one-time controversy between guilt and shame (Piers and Singer 1971; Ausubel 1955; Benedict 1946; Leighton and Kluckhohn 1947; Mead 1949, 1950), hiya appears to lie closer on the side of shame about which more will be said.

In the analytical delineation of the Tagalog fear-anxiety complex, the socialization process is examined for possible clues to the structuring of this complex. During early socialization, the Tagalog fear-anxiety or perhaps more appropriately, fear-shame (*takot*-hiya) complex begins to be set in place.

Mediated through the language which the child at two may begin to understand, if not verbally articulate with precision, takot (fear) and hiya (shame) are semantically drawn, though not clearly so in the responsive behaviors elicited. To instill takot (fear) and hiya (shame) in a young child is not only coeval and deliberate but also parallel in objectives. Designed to cultivate obedience and overt conformity, both fear-arousing and shame-generating techniques involve repeated subjection of the child to threats of exposure to (or confrontation with) real or imagined entities. Be the latter, a *sipay* (bogeyman), an *aswang* (witch), *Mamang Saro* (a real person), or the *mumu* (an abstract, vague, supernatural agent used mainly to scare children), their reality is bounded by the quality of threat associated and the anticipated potential danger perceived to bear upon the very person of ego and his immediate world. Typical threats are as follows: the sipay is coming, with the rest of the threat left suspended; the aswang will get you; or we will ask Mamang Saro to come and take your toys away. During the fear and shame conditioning, a child is often coaxed to look at a person, an object, or a blank space, forcing him to apprehend the same. Overpowered, the child may cover his face with his hands, bury it in his mother's lap, run away, or burst into tears. Consider, for instance, the following observation:

Junior (age 3) refused to share his candies with sister, Sylvia (age 6). Unable to persuade, Sylvia went to her father to complain and solicit support. Not quite ready to interfere, Nicolas (the father) made a suggestion.

Nicolas:Takutin mo si Junior (Go ahead and frighten Junior.)

Sylvia:Papaano po? Ano po ang aking ipapanakot? (How, Sir? With what shall I frighten him?)

Nicolas: Sabihin mo ay isasauli sa inyong tiya ang ibinigay sa kanyang laruan. (Tell him that his toy cart shall be returned to your aunt.)

The latter had brought it the previous day. Junior was not impressed; Sylvia seemed unconvincing. So at her own initiative, Sylvia tricked her brother into entering a bedroom, turned off the lights, and locked the door behind her, leaving him alone. Gripped by terror, Junior's reaction was unmistakable as he pounded at the door; wailed at the top of his lungs; and clung to his father's legs after the door sprang open. He cried for a whole hour. He did not share his candies after all; and even got Sylvia scolded for having undertaken what was construed as a more severe measure. (Fieldnotes, May 31, 1983).

The above incident seems to suggest that an unsettling situation is created in part because the ultimate source of authority, the parent, delegates his legitimate task to a subordinate. Also, in part there is a lack of clarity in the specific techniques to be employed. In any event, the merit of learning "how to fear" is given positive value among Tagalogs, an observation which appears not correspondingly encouraged in the American culture, for example. Thus an occasional comment such as "frighten so-and-so to make sure he does not eat bad foods, loiter in the wrong places, or get into mischiefs" suggests the very functional attribute of this human trait. That is, to demarcate the collectively perceived zones of potential danger, physical and symbolical.

Fear-arousal in the Tagalog child does not inhere in a particular object or entity, but rather in the chronically sustained threats about potential actions/activities caused by human and nonhuman agents toward ego. Unlike in the Semai whose fear-conditioning is initially staged by the cycles of severe thunderstorms, and reinforced later by encounters with strangers (Robarchek 1979;558), or contrary to psychoanalytic theories which posit germinal or original fear to develop first in connection with humans, and then extended subsequently to nonhumans, Tagalogs learn early to fear humans and nonhumans at once. In the growing up process, specific threats occur in succession or substitution in the sense that some are outgrown after a time. Fear of mumu and sipay is understood to be effective and appropriate usage in connection with small children, but not for the older ones, and certainly not adults.

As increasing immersion in social life proceeds, fear in nonhumans becomes less discussed or employed in threats. To the extent that this development is countered by a corresponding increase in fear of humans, the fear becomes moot. At some point in the socialization I suggest that the two classes of feared entities, humans and nonhumans, are somehow sorted out in such a way that fear (takot) particularly of humans either directly transforms itself into a more generalized and/or institutionalized form of anxiety (hiya), or converges with it. In such a stage, hiya, whose application almost invariably pertains to persons or human agents, dominates or spills over as it were, on fear. As such, fear of humans appears to become submerged, muted, or even refashioned within hiya. But fear of nonhumans remains quite contained, if not quiescent most of the time, and isomorphous. In a sense this kind of fear is comparable to the sort of "raw" fear Parkin describes. In the world of the adults such fears bear limited or specialized relevance, i.e. in the context of organismic or biological survival. This experience is brought to consciousness by events of war and natural disasters—volcanic eruptions, severe typhoons and earthquakes. Sometimes fear of ghosts are precipitated by recent deaths of relatives and friends.

This is not to say, however, that humans may no longer become feared as shame(ing) becomes the major sanction. To the contrary, parents continue to be feared at the prospect of physical punishment, especially beating, which they mete out for wrongdoing. At the time when physical sanctions are no longer brought to bear on a socializee, the mechanism of hiya is expected to take its role in social control. This point of transition suggests the completion of personhood, arrival at maturity, and readiness to assume appropriate obligations. Besides parents, certain individuals may become feared either as a result of their reputation—real or imagined. In case of the latter such a person casts no more mystery than a suspected witch might do in many tribal societies, just as a stranger may become equally threatening. Thus in the nexus of human relationships those who are feared or causing shame are typically avoided, leaving a wide spectrum of interactive systems of which a general sense of uncertainty about all others is characteristic, and toward whom encounter must be always guarded and cautious.

Although it is logically feasible to think in terms of having hiya toward spirits, mumu and the like, this sort of relationship was not noted or heard verbalized. However, in the world of the adults respective associations between the notion of God and hiya or between God and takot as in the following semantic forms perfectly makes sense and assumes definite meanings. *Mahiya ka sa Diyos* (be ashamed toward God) not only connotes milder sanctions than *matakot ka sa Diyos* (fear God), but their comparative application further suggests a relative difference in the seriousness of the situation. In the first usage, mahiya ka Diyos warns the individual to submit to God's criticism in the same way that one might be treated by a neighbor resulting, in effect, in the devaluation of self and status (Lebra 1971:246-250); in the second, to God's wrath and punishment. Whereas the latter, within the context of Christian ideology may be interpreted as ultimately ending in hell, or an exaction emanating from the highest form of authority, the absolute nature of the threat poses greater severity. On the other hand, if one were to feel shamed before God, the situation is quite mitigated in the sense that the God-Ego relationship in this exclusive context lacks a third party as audience (Lebra Ibid:250). However, in practical terms, whether or not hiya toward God rather than toward man is truly provoked in any given triadic situation becomes analytically problematic. Otherwise, hiya with relation to God is a little more than a metaphor, and might be interpreted as a prologue to what could be a more serious state. Along the same vein when mahiya ka sa sarili mo is used, which translates literally as "to be shamed by one's own self," it is in effect an appeal to the Ego-Ideal. Definitely an internalized aspect of shame, the process in this case does not appear to require an audience.

Even in the delivery of these threats, the emphasis as communicated verbally or bodily is projected with greater strength when speaking of "fear of God." Here probably lies an area in which the subtle differentiation between shame and guilt in this particular cultural group may be pursued. It is consistent with Piers and Singer's theory (Ibid:23-24) that shame obtains in conjunction with a sense of abandonment, a fear of separation; and guilt with annihilation, whose prototype is fear of castration. Thus for reasons already noted, hiya relative to God may weakly apply to the first; while takot in connection with God suggests conformity to the second. According to this model, the manner in which both kinds of fears may combine or differentiate from each other in the organization of selves and cultural forms of social control offers potential areas of inquiry. Perhaps by concentrating on fear as a major ingredient of sanction, either as guilt or shame, that we might further clarify and assist in the precise distinction between them. Admittedly, the shame-guilt analysis is not only complex but remains tentative upon which Lebra's (1971:242) comments are appropriately directed, to wit:

> While accepting the critics' contention that no culture can be characterized exclusively in terms of guilt or shame, I want to argue that these terms are conceptually distinguishable, and that there is cultural variation in the usage of them.

Conclusion

Viewed from a theory of anxiety, the fear-shame (takot-hiya) complex of the Tagalog as has been noted is structured early in socialization, but at some point undergoes divergent emphasis and functional relevance. In due course, the semantic form, takot, rarely applies to people, but is often reserved for nonhumans, events, and summarily, for the unknown. Whereas in counterpoint, hiya (shame) is almost strictly employed with reference to persons, seldom with nonpersons. The reshaping, as it were, of fear of humans into the structure of shame in this group is presumably a necessity of the social life. That is to say, no cultural group can afford prolonged and exaggerated emphasis on "fear of others" without risking the potential perversion not only in individual personalities but of social life itself. On this account alone we should be able to explain the general lack of fear-related ethnographies as noted in the early part of this paper.

Having pursued the subject of fear as an analytical correlate of shame, a number of considerations have emerged. Proposed as if it were an unstable chemical element or one that is structurally dependent, fear is viewed here as having the natural proclivity either to transmutate into or to coalesce with something more socially functional.[8] As such, the fear-shame complex described here is suggested to constitute one possible version of the linkage and the dynamics involved. The implication, of course, is that other comparable complexes such as "fear-authority," "fear-anger," or "fear-respect" do form, merit proper identification, and eventually may lead us to a general taxonomy of such complexes.

Cast in the broader picture, the Tagalog fear-shame (takot-hiya) association is further proposed here as a subclass under the fear-shame phenomenon that appears to characterize the Oceanic culture area, if not Asiatic cultures as well. Occasional ethnographic reference to this linkage has been already mentioned in certain Oceanic groups (Gerber

1975; Levy 1974; Strathern 1975) to the extent that a "genetic" connection between these concepts is proposed. Rosaldo (Ibid), for one, did as much for the Ilongots but offers no further clarification. However, from Gerber's work (Ibid) on componential and behavioral analysis of the emotions in a Samoan group such a probability is inferred.

Thus in the making of sociophobics, we will no doubt discover various ways to examine the subject in the ethnographic field, in the review of dust-covered field notes, or in the reinterpretation of old data. In the process, we may choose to be bound by concepts and notions well established in psychology; or we may not. Not only that, we must anticipate cultural variation in the organization of inner states, and likewise in their articulation to the external world. Regardless of how anthropology may successfully direct this endeavor, what it promises to achieve is a complementary perspective to what psychology has already accomplished, and an expanded framework that is cross-cultural. Even when we may clumsily resort to semantic translations and conceptual equivalencies across cultural boundaries, there are commonalities from which premise our task may be made clearer. One such given is the attribute of the self and its genesis to which Hallowell (1967) accords the evolutionary threshold of our species, and on which ultimately hinge the basic operations of social life.

Notes

1. Geertz made the point that anthropology, particularly ethnography, is an interpretive discipline whose goal is to search for meanings, thereby contrasting it to an experimental science that is in search of law. Since psychology has done a great deal of the latter, anthropology's role in the study of fear should prove at once to be both complementary and supplementary.

2. In my cursory attempt to identify references to fear on a cross-cultural level, I chose a subsample of eight societies out of the 60-society sample which Narrol et al have supposedly perfected for controlled comparison. Each society, described in the ethnographic present, represents a major geographical region in the world and are, respectively, identified in the files as: Korea (AA1), Ifugao (OA19), Kurds (MA11), Serbs (EF6), Dogon (FA16), Yakut (RV2), Tlingit (NA12) and Cuna (SB5). For no other consideration, societies were chosen for being at the top in each regional list. Against this mass of ethnographic data, the blind search for any reference to fear was, to say the least, excruciating and tedious, and on the whole not commensurately productive. In the Ifugao, for example, no object or idea was specifically noted as being feared, and therefore fear is not focused; yet, Barton (HRAF) in his voluminous reports managed to describe the Ifugao as "a people who are generally fearful of everything." Just where and how fear is articulated in this cultural system was not clear.

3. Hallowell is probably the main pioneer in this endeavor and whose work has recently received greater attention under the impetus of ethnoscience and cognitive anthropology.

4. The first symposium on sociophobics was held at Ball State University in October, 1981; the second, during the XIth International Congress of Anthropological and Ethnological Sciences in Vancouver, British Columbia, Canada, August 20-24, 1983. From two separate papers given respectively during these occasions, the present paper is the result of combining both.

5. This group lives in a provincial city of about 120,000 people in Luzon island where this anthropologist was born and raised. A systematic ethnography on fear has yet to be done, but some isolated observations in the course of several field trips have provided minimum insight into the subject at hand.

6. For each of the cultural groups chosen from the HRAF, the following summary of fear data was obtained and extracted from the texts:

1. Korea: the father is the most feared object (person) against the background of society with extremely severe punishments for private and public crimes;

2. Ifugao: fear is unfocused;

3. Kurds: the evil eye and inappropriate etiquette produce anxiety;

4. Serbs: while they fear corpses culminating in the fear of the vampires and graveyards, they do not fear death per se. Other fears were mentioned in relation to envy, evil eye, and recently, the nationalization of farm lands;

5. Dogon: fear of unpopularity particularly from the vantage point of an aging man, fear of punishment, fear of error in ritual performance, fear of the magician, and fear of uttering names of dead ancestors were among those noted;

6. Yakuts: fear of sick people who are facing death, but not fear of death or the dead;

7. Tlingit: fear of the dead as among the Serbs, but not death itself; fear of sorcery and witchcraft; fear of necrophilia; fear of the shaman's ghost, and in their recent history, fear of disease, particularly smallpox;

8. Cuna: fear of disease and magician who controls bad and good medicines. Said Nordenskiold: "The Cunas do not fear the soul of a deceased magician. It is while he is alive that he is deemed dangerous." (430)

7. A more incisive interpretation of hiya vis-à-vis other Tagalog concepts, for example, *utang na loob*, has been the focus of a doctoral dissertation at Cornell University which was to be available from the University of Michigan Microfilms. SEASSI Conference, August 2, 1984.

8. Perhaps the structural merit of what Durkheim (1972) termed social sentiments may need reexamination as potential points of departure in the analysis. Taking emotions per se as private and subjective states, he distinguished them from sentiments, the latter being culturally constructed patterns. Of sentiments, Durkheim said: ". . . there are two sorts of social sentiments. The first bind each individual to the person of his fellow citizens: these are manifest

within the community, in the day-to-day relationships of life. These include the sentiments of honor, respect, affection and fear which we may feel towards one another. The second are those which bind me to the social entity as a whole; these manifest themselves primarily in the relationships of the society with other societies, and could be called intersocial" (1972:219–220).

5
Foci of Fear
in Two African Societies

Colby R. Hatfield, Jr.

Introduction

Even the intrepid Maasai warrior ventures into situations of uncertainty supplied with an impressive armory of tools and techniques. In undertaking the immense task of exploring fear in two East African societies, I feel it important to inform the reader about what sort of experiential and conceptual armament I felt it necessary to bear so that he can better assess how effective they are in such a pursuit.[1]

I have had long experience with both the WaSukuma (called Sukuma henceforth) and the Maasai, who are somewhat hostile neighbors in northcentral Tanzania, but in ethnographic and theoretical contexts quite different from the one I venture into in this essay. In beginning this journey, I felt as if, like a Maasai warrior, I had only visited a place by day and am now called upon to return to it by night, where the knowledge I had gained is challenged and where what appeared in one context certainly cannot be taken for granted in another. It is not that I was innocently protected from situations of fear in either experience. I did observe fear, and sometimes people discussed fear. But devising a "lexicon of the emotions," as Geertz has so aptly called it, which would be the first step in understanding what any one category of emotion is, was not a part of my orientation. Indeed, on my first field trip, of the two "bibles" of research I carried, *Notes and Queries in Anthropology* and *Outline of Cultural Materials*, only the latter made but passing reference to "emotional states." I did have some acquaintance with the Radcliffe-Brown/Malinowski controversy over the primacy of basic human needs and society's demands and other such anthropological debate as well as another set of arguments concerning whether societies feared the supernatural or not, and, as my first research was in the functions of witchcraft among the Sukuma, I did have the idea that emotional states had some relevance for investigation. Nonetheless, I was more concerned with how individuals acted as members of social units and the notion of emotions was too greatly tied with individual psychology to be useful. Therefore my understanding of how the Sukuma and Maasai pattern emotions came about implicitly, occuring almost by osmosis as I attempted to learn more about and become more intimate with them. One of the personal challenges of this retrospective adventure has been to bring this implicit understanding to consciousness.

There is another component to my experience. In Sukumaland I witnessed or identified emotions other than fear or anxiety more frequently: pleasure, love, boredom, ridicule, shame, embarrassment, suspicion, anger, and hate. Perhaps fear was a category like witchcraft, something grown-ups did not discuss, or rather revealed in ways which might have proven too subtle for a young anthropologist to identify. Among the Maasai, I was preconditioned to look for bravery, independence, courage, so when I did see or hear of fear, I was always surprised and took note.

The task I have set for myself is to explore how fear is culturally patterned among these two societies. I am making an assumption that like almost all other aspects of the human person, emotions are not exempt from the intervention of tradition in molding them, defining them, contextualizing them, promoting them, denying them, associating them with patterns related to age, sex, and status, isolating them in special categories, and infusing them with meaning and relationships.

As far as I have been able to discover, the Sukuma have no term for "emotion," although I suspect they might borrow from KiSwahili or share a similar form. *Maono* is the generic term for emotion in KiSwahili. Derived from *ku ona*, to see or perceive, it associates perception, thought, and feeling together (Johnson 1967:354-55). The Maasai term is curious, for it derives from *a push*, used specifically to describe warriors in a dissociated state of trembling and shaking called *empushuna*, and from *a pushu*, which describes animals in rut (Tucker and Ole Mpaayei 1955:273; Mol n.d.:61). Maasai emphasize loss of control in emotional states, an orientation very much in keeping with conditioning against fear among warriors. Western tradition tends to separate perceptual and cognitive from affective consciousness, and while it does introduce physical states of agitation, these are not carried to quite the extreme of the Maasai.

In her review of theory and research on emotions, Arnold (1960:194) expands on our emic understanding. "Emotions," she writes, "are actions, tendencies, felt impulses to action." As the action which is set in motion becomes more difficult to achieve, so increases the "degree of impulsion" until the action arrives as "an urge to contend for anything that is difficult to reach and to contend against anything that is difficult to avoid." Although we may find considerable room for profitable discussion as to the advisability of employing a concept so caught up with a particular cultural tradition's orientation, we can see from the brief comparison of Sukuma and Maasai views of emotions that there appear to be at least two not always separable components, the latter of which Arnold emphasizes: an affective internal state or response deriving from an external stimulus and the behavior to which it gives rise. The value of understanding the coexistence of these two components at the onset is immense when we realize that more often than not the observer has only the latter as clues to the existence of the former.

In a recent review, specifically devoted to fear states in animals and humans, Thomson (1979:8) reports three conditions, one of which must be present to identify fear: dangerous and threatening circumstances in the human environment, physical symptoms of fear, and action taken in relation to the object of fear. He also goes on to stress the importance of context and interpretation in determining courses of action. From an anthropological perspective, we would consider it important to determine whose view is dominant in determining which circumstances in the human environment are dangerous and threatening. Outsiders would create a very different catalogue of fearful circumstances in Maasailand than would the Maasai. I might think that the presence of a lion near my path provides a universal source of danger; however, Maasai warriors boast that such proximity is harmless under certain circumstances. Similarly, a western observer might wonder why the Sukuma take so many precautions against witches and the Sukuma wonder how Europeans can be so naive and foolish. Once a satisfactory arrangement is made between the emic and etic views of a situation, this condition provides a valuable resource for the cross-cultural researcher. The second condition provides an interesting challenge to cross-cultural research, focusing on the question of whether emotional states take on universal physical manifestations. In terms of externally visible reactions—sweating, loss of bladder control, etc.—the researcher, sensitized to look for such manifestations, might be greatly rewarded. (Seeking less immediately observable reactions, heart beat, galvanic skin response, etc., would require a rather imaginative research design in the field and might not produce much of value as some of these reactions apparently are incited by different emotional stimuli. See Thomson 1979:2).

Once the first set of conditions are identified, they can provide a context for exploring courses of action. For purposes of my exploration into fear states among the Maasai and Sukuma, I have found focusing on circumstances and actions to be effective means of understanding what its dynamics are.

The last piece of conceptual armament I have employed is related to employing a ready-made model to assist in identifying situations of fear and understanding what kinds of responses to look for. Mary Douglas (1966), although more concerned with analyzing pollution states in cultures, provides an employable framework based on Steiner's studies of taboo. She suggests one should examine situations which a society defines as dangerous or threatening and then note the precautions which it develops around them. Fundamental to this view is the notion that danger situations highlight areas where social relations and benefits are ambiguous, competitive, contradictory, or unresolved, where a structure or pattern itself is weak or missing. By surrounding these areas of a society's experience, it announces danger. Threats, dangers, precautions, and defense become markers of circumstances where fear is, or should be, present and actions or beliefs developed to prevent the threat or resolve the danger. Where one cannot easily find fear expressed—and in reality fear, as it is manifest in individual members of a society, may be more deeply felt than spoken of—these markers become signposts for the explorer of emotions as well as signposts of danger to members of the society.

I have chosen three sets of circumstances which the Sukuma and Maasai have surrounded by precautions or defense structures either physical or conceptual. In doing so I have not acted democratically by randomly choosing three from all possible foci of fear in the societies. Instead, I have chosen them because each represents a somewhat different way of approaching circumstances of fear and a somewhat different challenge for analysis. Once I had selected the areas, I attempted to approach my material with a certain amount of "ethnographic innocence," even though the reader will readily perceive some of my biases. It is an innocence in that, aside from my general understanding of "what kind of people these are," one which only partly conforms to classic distinctions between pastoralist and farmer, and some opinions as to the functions and operations of certain institutions and beliefs—witchcraft, for example—I did not know where approaching the data from the view of dangers and precautions associated with fear would actually lead me. Nor could I anticipate what new meanings and insights I would gain from this adventure. It was analogous to returning to a place only known by day, from one perspective. That in many instances the analysis led me back to a previous understanding may be indicative of the success of the venture, but it might also reveal the unconscious persistence of my own views.

I began searching for foci of fear within the context of Douglas' four broad circumstances of danger: from the implications of internal structures, from the margins or transitional states in the social body, from the clash of institutions or orientations in conflict or contradiction, and from the dangers pressing in on the boundaries of society (1966:122). But I was not able to employ these points of reference satisfactorily, partly because as I proceeded in the analysis of one set of circumstances, it began to spill over into other categories. I have kept Douglas' metaphor of society being analogous to a body within which and against which exist real and perceived dangers, but I have not consistently adhered to her four points of danger.

The first focus of fear concerns orientations, values, and practices associated with the institution of marriage, whose collision under certain circumstances form pockets of threat and danger primarily to women. Marriage provides an example of a situation where threats appear to result as consequences of the interplay of ideals and structures, none of which in themselves are marked as circumstances of fear; however, we will have the opportunity to briefly discuss the relationship between fear and respect. The analysis raises a challenging question concerning the relative absence of markers of danger in spite of its presence and forces us to look more carefully at the results of a male dominated orientation determining what is danger and what is not. The second focus came almost naturally out of the peculiar situation of the Maasai warrior. Here we have the opportunity to examine how and why a society deliberately conditions a segment of its population not to fear. The broader question which this analysis raises concerns implications of the conditioning for the warrior and his community. We will also have the chance to see similar forces at work among the Sukuma, particularly in dance societies. The third focus of fear is on enemies, those who are believed to destroy from within the safety zones of the social body, witches and other evil doers, and those who threaten the societies from without.

We will learn more about specific characteristics of both groups in the essay itself, but brief introductions are in order here. The Sukuma are the largest ethnic group in Tanzania, inhabiting a deep semicircle of about 64,000 square miles around the southern and eastern shores of Lake Victoria. Sukumaland displays some topographical variation, but it is generally savannah lands which become drier and less suited for farming as one moves further from the lake. Predominantly agriculturalists, the Sukuma do keep livestock as a kind of living bank account. For many years they have been involved in growing cash crops, among which cotton is dominant. Before resettlement they lived in "parishes" or villages called *gunguli*, which were composed of well-spaced homesteads, *kaya*, surrounded by family fields. A kaya normally consisted of a patrilineal extended family which sometimes included an affine or two or an unrelated dependent or laborer. Each family in a kaya had only partial responsibility over its affairs, for its members were considered to be under the authority of the resident senior elder and his paternal ancestors.

Maasai number approximately 100,000 individuals in Tanzania. Most belong to the Kissongo Section, which was divided upon the partition of Tanganyika from Kenya at the turn of the century. They occupy about 30,000 square miles of high country called the Maasai steppe, which runs roughly south from the Kenya border to the boundaries of Arusha Region. The area is topographically quite varied, ranging from high altitude areas around Ngorongoro Crater, through the depression of the Rift Valley, to heavy areas of bush in the more southern sections. The area is dry with few permanent water points and is most suited for the kind of extensive mixed livestock keeping that the Maasai employ. Some parts of the territory are heavily infested with tsetse fly and not usable. Throughout the area Maasai share their pastures with game animals, many of whom are dangerous to stock and human alike.

As pastoralists, they have a tradition of physical mobility arising from the needs of extensive livestock keeping; however, unless under very severe stress, they do not move entire residences much more than fifty miles at the most. More often each *enkang* has a wet and dry season residence. In spite of intensive efforts to reestablish livestock markets and establish ranching schemes, Maasai do not routinely market their stock. They are also still firmly entrenched dairy farmers rather than beef producers. The equivalent of the kaya is the enkang, which Jacobs calls a "kraal camp" (1965). These days it is composed of a wide variety of residents ranging from an extended family similar to the Sukuma type to a group of unrelated families camping together for convenience. Although the elders of an enkang do form a loosely cooperative group, each head of household treasures his own freedom of action and independence and maintains complete authority over his family. The extended family forms an exception, where a man retains fairly tight control over his sons, married or not, and their livestock (Hatfield 1976:8ff).

Marriage: Fear Through Clashes in Rights and Identities

Although I am using marriage as an example of how otherwise positive values, obligations, and relationships, when juxtaposed or in collision, can give rise to situations of danger and threat, it must be admitted at the onset that fear is acknowledged by both Sukuma and Maasai as a foundation for the institution itself. This kind of fear is inextricable from notions of respect and authority, values which of course extend beyond the conjugal and into every relationship which is hierarchical. In the specific instance of marriage this kind of fear is crystallized into rules determining what obligations and rights exist between spouses and in attitudinal issues supporting authority which assume ritualized behavior (Sukuma women curtsying to men in Sukumaland, for example). On this level, the use of the term "fear" is somewhat like our own use of "fear of the Lord." It is not intended to incite emotional response, but assumes a powerful symbol calling attention to the paramount importance of adhering to authority. There is, however, another, more personal side to this emotional foundation of marriage in that in both societies authority of the husband is supported by custom which tends correspondingly to minimize rights of his wife, so that when he abuses his authority there is often little recourse for her. It is here, in these situations when things go wrong, that a different, more personal, fear is aroused.

Democracy then is not a foundation for marriage either among the Sukuma or Maasai. There are other structural commonalities. Both societies are patrilineal, having exogamous clans. Both encourage polygynous marriages. Both emphasize virilocality, although many Sukuma begin marriage with residence at the girl's parents' household. A common goal of marriage is to produce many children, especially sons, who will inherit their father's property and provide an important domestic labor force. Women in Maasailand cannot inherit property. In Sukumaland women can inherit under some circumstances. Both societies normally arrange marriages for their children, a transaction sealed with payment of brideprice.

Beyond these commonalities a world of difference characterizes each society. Of relevance to this discussion are differences concerning what are proper spheres of male and female action. Maasai adhere to a rigid separation of what they consider appropriate behavior and activities for either sex. Women's work is not to be done by men, save under the most unusual and disastrous circumstances, and the work of men excludes women. (See Ole Kulet 1972 for a poignant fictional account of a Maasai widower.) The division of labor extends beyond physical work into all sectors of life. Women do not speak out in public meetings of Maasai. Decisions are the prerogative of adult males alone. Males also have responsibilities to "control" women, but not vice versa. Such responsibilities not only include determination of whom a daughter is to marry, but any situation in which a woman's person is to be used. As Llewelyn-Davies (1981:341) put it, women ". . . do not have the rights of disposal over themselves." Women are always under the jurisdiction of men—fathers, husbands, and eventually sons—and it is only through the authority of men and customary laws related to men that they gain authority and have recourse to redress for wrongs.[2]

In spite of the authoritarian basis of Sukuma marriage, the realities may be quite different. As farmers, both sexes often do the same kinds of work together. Although a woman is expected to do most domestic tasks, a man does not feel shame and anger when a situation arises in which he must assist. The Sukuma tend to blur male-female distinctions in the sphere of work and to some extent in the realm of authority. So also exists a softening of rules dictating rights of men over women. Sukuma customary law operates to protect women to a certain extent from fathers and spouses. Also, each community has a relatively powerful women's organization which acts to promote female interests and counter misuses of male authority. Jellicoe (n.d.) summarizes the role of Sukuma women thusly: "The position of women is extremely ambiguous. In theory they are strictly subordinate to men, but in fact they have great influence which neither sex will acknowledge openly." Sukuma women overtly maintain that attitude of humbleness which accompanies respect for authority of husbands and fathers, but in reality they have many more options for independent action than their Maasai sisters.

Given this basic difference in the institution of marriage, we would expect to find fundamental differences in response to the common dangers which common structures in marriage encourage. I have chosen four areas within marriage which are potential foci of fear for women in both societies: physical abuse and neglect, polygyny, children, and widowhood. In most instances we shall find that once the threat is identified, a woman is provided with acceptable courses of action to prevent the danger from being realized, but in at least one instance the system appears to have reached impasse in extricating her from the danger without challenging the institution itself and perhaps the very basis of social cohesion.

Physical Abuse and Neglect

> . . . you are now a person to be relied on, and we expect you to give rather than to receive. You must respect your husband and follow his dictates. If you don't he will beat you and we give him that permission. . . . (Ole Saitoti 1980:182).

Saitoti describes this as one of the injunctions Maasai parents give to their daughters upon marriage. It summarizes the official role of a wife: to serve her husband and others in authority over her and to adhere to the fundamental value of respect for authority vested in him and to put it into practice. A woman who deviates from this ideal can be punished by beating. In fact the injunction goes on to warn her that she cannot come running home every time her husband is cruel to her.

Physical abuse of wives is quite common among the Maasai and is present among the Sukuma. It is the bottom line of the fear/respect alliance and therefore should only be used as an expression of anger that a wife (or child) has not shown proper respect. So long as the cause is considered justified (by custom), there is nothing a woman can do but endure it. A parent will not be sympathetic to daughters' complaints about abusive husbands if they consider them to have deserved punishment. In many ways physical beating is a given part of life's unpleasantness for all those in subordinate statuses. It may be feared because of the pain, shame, and embarrassment it reveals, but it is an inevitable consequence for some who dare break rules. Both groups consider adultery an especially appropriate reason for punishment. So also are being a bad housewife, a lazy worker, child neglecter, or domestic nuisance justifications for physical abuse.

One would think that fear of being publicly beaten would be a powerful disincentive towards breaking rules in the first place, but it is not. Maasai women, in spite of the fact that their husbands consider themselves to have absolute control over their bodies, are encouraged to take lovers (Llewelyn-Davies 1981:337; Sankan 1973:xii). So long as she keeps them discreet and within the appropriate age group, a wife follows a powerful age set value of share and share alike and cannot formally incite her husband's wrath because she is following a rule he himself is supposed to value highly. All too often, however, she is tempted to enter into a romantic liaison with someone outside the proper age set, particularly a warrior, who epitomizes all that is thrilling, beautiful, and masculine in Maasai life. Considering that a woman before marriage has had considerable opportunity to develop romantic attachments with warriors and may be married to a man much older than she, it is not surprising that she would willingly affront the dignity of her husband. Such cases indeed incur husbandly and age set rage. The wife is severely beaten and the lover heavily fined. Her punishment, however, only confirms her knowledge that love indeed triumphs over duty and possibly also that the revealing of the deed is a statement of rebellion to those who attempt to exercise authority over her. Affairs between warriors and married women form the stuff of romance among the Maasai.

Punishment for breaches of respect are predictable, the result of taking chances (a Maasai trait) and risking exposure and disaster (also a Maasai trait). But physical abuse often goes beyond the predictable and legitimate. As in our own society, men often take out their frustrations on their wives, beating them viciously for minor breaches of respect or for no other reason than their tempers, which with peers and others must be kept in check. Maasai women, then, become victims of frustrations their husbands may experience outside the home but have no outlet for. No Maasai would, I think, agree that this form of abuse is proper, but they appear to have devised no effective measures to save the situation. A woman trapped in such a relationship has good reason for fear and very deep resentment. If the first form of physical abuse at least carries with it a bitter triumph, this form incites only extreme anxiety, fear, and frustration.

Neglect operates in a similar fashion to unjustified beating. It is considered by the Maasai an abuse of rights vested in male authority in marriage. A wife who is physically neglected would find a more sympathetic ear at her natal home, and probably her father or brothers would look into the situation and appeal to her husband's age set for assistance. In theory brideprice could be returned and the relationship severed, but divorce is a most uncommon solution for marital problems among the Maasai. (See Ole Saitoti 1980:184). More than likely the situation would have to continue for a very long time until the husband had completely exhausted his resources and was reduced to the status of a dependent himself before so drastic a solution was taken. In the meanwhile his wife would have to suffer through it with him.[3]

The situation in Sukumaland begins with similar values: authority and rights of husbands to abuse wives physically when the cause is "just." Adultery is not uncommon among the Sukuma for probably much the same reasons as among the Maasai: young women are often wed to much older men, and also adultery is a form of assertion that in spite of what authority dictates, a woman has rights over her own body. Unjustified abuse, like a husband's physical neglect, breaks legitimate authority, so a man who refuses to or cannot support his wife is not keeping his part of the bargain. She can return to her natal home in disgust. And like the Maasai, the Sukuma have the option of dissolving such a marriage by returning the brideprice. This is probably more common among the Sukuma, for divorce itself is more frequent, but it would involve long and protracted debate over how much should be returned, so that the families involved would be more prone to attempt to preserve the marriage no matter how difficult it is for the wife than to have to enter into negotiations for divorce.

Under such circumstances, a woman in both societies only has one other option: to abandon home, husband, and children to live in concubinage with a lover. In doing so, she runs serious risk of being apprehended and returned to her husband. But also in taking this course she relinquishes whatever purchase she had in her future security, for a concubine is without brideprice and is consequently safeguarded by few personal rights and protecting agencies.

What kinds of assistance do these societies offer women caught in so unjust and personally dangerous dilemmas? We have already noted the possibility of elders and peers attempting to get a husband to change his ways. The problem here for the Maasai is that age mates and elders and in-laws have only theoretical powers of influence over a violent or neglectful husband. In reality this form of pressure may not be very effective. Maasai are most protective about their own affairs, so that even friends might be considered prying into too deeply personal issues to have much impact.

With no viable recourse to secular and male supported structures of authority to resolve such problems, a wife can appeal to the collective power of women. Such a community group gathers specifically for the purpose of attacking the malfeasor, beating him with impunity, impounding his stock and even casting a curse on him and his possessions. I have the sense that Maasai women would only engage in action of this sort if a domestic situation had become so chronically serious and unresolvable by other means that it was life-endangering. A Sukuma wife in a similar situation would have in contrast a more enduring female organization to which she could appeal for assistance.

Both societies depend more heavily on precautions to ensure that abuse and neglect do not occur in marriage before it takes place than in providing viable solutions to marital discord. Separating love from marriage eliminates what is felt to be a less durable basis for its creation. Both Sukuma and Maasai fathers are supposed to seek out the most compatible and successful husbands for their daughters, which inevitably leads to an older man who is already established. But more often it seems that a man selects husbands for daughters more in keeping with his own social, political, and economic needs than theirs. Sukuma fathers are reputed to be more responsive to children's opinions, but ultimately daughters (and sons) must trust in fathers' judgments and to fathers' personal vested interests, not theirs. Again, husbands and fathers appear to reap greater advantage in preserving difficult marriages than wives and daughters.

Another precaution is brideprice, for it operates to seal transfer of rights in and over a woman. Ideally brideprice insures a bride against her husband's misuse of authority over her, but as we have seen, in reality the insurance seems to work more to keep the marriage intact and protect interests of the males involved. I would think a wife's threat to her abusive husband that she will return home to her father and insist that the brideprice be returned would be met less with concern on his part than amusement as her naiveté. Llewelyn-Davies (1981:340-

1) concludes for the Maasai that brideprice expresses "a commitment to a relationship in which the transactibility of women is taken for granted." If this is the situation, then brideprice is meager insurance for a bride indeed.

Physical abuse and neglect in marriage appear in both societies to fall between the cracks of custom. On the whole the difficulties that these ambiguities and contradictions create for women do not find easy solution through most traditional precautions and modes of reconciling conflicts in marriage. Structures are present, but they appear mainly ineffective. The Sukuma at least have moved beyond trust in good intentions and actions of fathers, husbands, and in-laws to provide their women with access to other more objective institutions of dispute settlement. Maasai society operates primarily on the former level, assuming that a woman's protection lies in adherence to socially sanctioned expectations of what a good husband is and does, and that fathers, husbands, and in-laws will act justly. When inevitable marital discord erupts, women have few effective mechanisms to alleviate the danger they face other than escape, which carries its own great burdens, appeal to the collective power of feminity in the area, or endurance. A Maasai woman does have greater cause to fear, for she seems at this point to be abandoned by the system in order that the edifice of male authority and respect for male independence be supported. I suspect her fears are exacerbated in these situations by the realization that she possesses almost no means for self-protection within the confines of her own society.

Polygyny

The economic and social advantages which are served by polygyny have their counterpoint in one of its unintended consequences: endemic competition among wives. Conflict here can take the form of jealousy when a husband demonstrates more attention to one wife than another, but in a polygynous household where love is not a necessary cohesive force among partners differential displays of affection are accepted facts of life. A sensible husband, of course, attempts to minimize this form of domestic discord by being somewhat democratic in gifts and being consistent in his sexual responsibilities. The real issue at stake is resources. Polygyny encourages women to compete with each other through children to get as great access to a husband's property as possible. Especially among the Maasai sons are a woman's path to ultimate independence, informal power, and long term security. A family's resources can become objects of long almost visible maneuverings by wives whose covert competition is masked by an aura of domestic cooperation and concord.[4]

A great danger inheres in the playing out of vested interests within the same social unit, not only to women who might lose in the contest, but to the security and advancement of the household itself. Although women might be blamed for destroying domestic tranquility, the situation is not one of their creation. Nonetheless, both societies think of women as being innocent of the cooperative ideals which form the basis of formal male relationships.

The dangers inherent in co-wife conflict are partly averted by structure. Both the Sukuma and Maasai give preeminence to the first wife, for she becomes the caretaker of her husband's domestic affairs, the manager of a sometimes rather complex organization. Both societies also anticipate that a man will obtain a favorite wife as he gets older, an event which the rest of the household observes with some dismay, for in this doting love affair, a formerly parsimonious head of household may throw caution and their patrimony to the wind. Maasai carry structure a step farther by grouping wives' houses on either side of a homestead's gate, thereby forming the nucleus of a left and right side, each possessed of its own internal esprit de corps.

Another precaution having some force is that rule associated with proper exercise of respect and authority: a man is responsible for the welfare of his wives and children. We have already seen that infraction of this rule can incite actions by wives to protect themselves and their children. Reckless mishandling of property through spending or foolish favoritism calls attention to a man's inability to live up to what is expected of him. In Sukuma households such irresponsible behavior can become a rallying point for a collective wifely strike.

A woman's fear of retaliation from co-wives also forms a strong disincentive for unfair promotion of her vested interests in the household. Sukuma wives often share the same house. They work together in family fields. Thus, in many ways theirs is a much more constrained cooperation and it is not surprising that deep hostilities ferment under overt calm. To the contrary, Maasai women always have their own houses, one of the few things that they can control on their own terms. They have their own herds (their children's) for their own use. It would seem that in this virtually possessionless condition, what they do possess is much more clearly marked than among the Sukuma. Nevertheless, that witchcraft accusations among the Sukuma and the curse among the Maasai do occur among co-wives, reveals the limits of these secular constraining devices. There are conflicts in co-wife relationships which cannot be expressed or resolved easily. Witchcraft and the curse stand as ultimate weapons for aggression and defense when direct action is not possible.

Children

Co-wife competition may prove a minor fear in the lexicon of marriage-induced threats for a woman, but it assumes intensified meaning when associated with children, who are major reasons why competition arises in the first place. Among both Sukuma and Maasai women who bear no children or bear no sons are placed in dangerous positions. Just as children are a woman's insurance, so also are they in part her validation as a productive, worthy, respected member of the community. If she produces no children, she has not fulfilled her family's part of the contract represented by the brideprice, and she runs the risk of being sent back in shame while her father and brothers have to re-collect the animals given for her. Certainly it is not the prospect of returning home itself which creates anxiety in such a woman, but what the event will mean for her future. In neither Sukumaland nor Massailand would a man's family permit brideprice to be paid for a known barren woman. A desperate father might renegotiate for a very small sum, but when brideprice and bride gifts in Maasailand are indicators of one's worth, the worth of such a woman is publicly acknowledged to be very low indeed. Should she remain with her own family, she is doomed to become a kind of promiscuous spinster, or she may elect concubinage.

Remaining with her husband, as sometimes may happen, she is unsubtly thrust into a different relationship with other members of the household. Although now out of the conflict-because-of-children threat, she is now placed in the unfulfilled-person-ruled-by-jealousy role. She must watch her step even more carefully than before, lest when misfortune befalls her stepchildren and co-wives it be attributed to her.

A woman without sons faces a related problem. Where relatively high brideprice is commanded for Sukuma girls and men acknowledge that their sisters and daughters make them rich, I find it puzzling that a family does not formally rejoice over a multitude of daughters. Moreover, each girl means another potential link in the sociopolitical arena through her marriage. A man with only sons may be hard put to gather enough stock and money to marry them off properly. The answer, aside from the general higher worth placed on males, from a female perspective is associated with the unfortunate reality that daughters have relatively little share in their father's wealth. A Maasai woman with only daughters may have a strong domestic labor force, but she builds up little security, faces the prospect of living with a son-in-law at his sufferance, and is only an onlooker at all the great ceremonies which mark a son's journey into manhood. Her husband looks upon sons as labor for the household, but ultimately clones of himself. A man without sons amasses wealth for others' children.

With such emphasis placed on fertility and on male offspring, both the Sukuma and Maasai have invested considerable energy in finding ways of controlling infertility. A Sukuma would first attempt to discover the cause of the problem, because it is seldom considered purely physical. Moreover, misfortune often comes not from something his wife did but rather from the action of evildoers, like witches, or his own ancestors determined to require some special act of piety from him. In the latter case, his wife is the victim. Once cause is revealed and appropriate religious duties are carried out, they seek physical assistance. In some cases escape from the power of witches accompanies a cure at a healer's household. When I was in Sukumaland, a successful cure for infertility warranted payment of two cows. A cure may never be effected, but the process can take so long that the wife is so imbedded in the household that there might be moral pressure from it and the community to keep her there, especially if the cause of her misfortune is somehow or other placed on the shoulders of the husband or his kin group. So she remains, still a valued member of the household, for she provides everything other wives provide, but children. In a Sukuma household she remains a helpmate, careful, cooperative, tolerant, peripheral.

The Maasai take a somewhat more practical approach to the matter. They too would seek cause, for it could be a curse. But a childless woman may be given a child by a woman who has many. In such a manner will a woman gain a son if she has only daughters or a daughter if she has only sons. By doing this, the Massai acknowledge and avert the potentials of real tragedy arising from expectations they have imposed on women's fertility, which not all can meet.[5]

Widowhood

Despite many roadblocks to communal bliss in these two societies, some of which have been explored above, spouses usually build up long term relationships consisting of respect, affection, and sometimes love. Widowhood, when it comes, can be met with sorrow, but it is also the beginning of a woman's freedom. Many mothers end up happily being informal matriarchs of their sons' households. Some Sukuma women assume control of their husbands' households. Widowhood itself is not a time of danger but of opportunity; however, premature widowhood is fraught with difficulties and threats for women in both societies.

Both Maasai and Sukuma women marry at a much younger age than their husbands. In theory a Maasai male is not officially wed until he becomes a junior elder, at his middle thirties at the youngest. This does not seem to have been the case for a long time (see Fosbrooke 1948:45), for some warriors do marry before the changing of their age set.

Nevertheless, most Maasai girls are married shortly after puberty. Sukuma males labor under no age set requirements of celibacy, but young men often are reluctant to relinquish their bachelor status. Before they reach thirty, sons are usually informed by fathers that the time to settle down has come and an appropriate marriage is being arranged for them. The girls they marry can be quite young, but not usually just post-puberty. Recently education of girls in both societies is postponing age of marriage. In general, however, both among the Sukuma and Maasai a very young girl may find herself married to a very old man. Thus early widowhood is an inevitability.

The investment in a bride through the payment of brideprice and bride gifts is a collective one. As her husband's kin have contributed to the transaction, they have an interest in preserving their investment after his death. Both societies have developed mechanisms which deal with the humane problem of finding new support for the woman while preserving their interests in her children and their patrimony. The difficulty is that sometimes these mechanisms don't work as they should, the result being that the kin group—or someone in it—profits, while the children and mother lose. Premature widowhood is fraught with threats and insecurities as to the future of a woman and her children in the clutches of her in-laws.

The danger in both groups is the same, although the structures in which it is found are somewhat different: squandering or usurpation of a ward's inheritance by a guardian who is his paternal kinsman. When sons are too young to be given responsibility for their own property, a paternal uncle is often selected by the male elders of the kin group as their guardians. In Sukumaland this can involve a leviratic marriage (Kirwen 1979). In this manner the property and interests of the deceased are kept within family and patrilineage. Levirate among the Maasai, to my knowledge, does not occur; however, a widow, children, and livestock become wards of one of her husband's brothers.

Once this transfer occurs, the guardian has as complete control over them as did the husband, although a senior relative might keep a periodic eye on the situation. It would be a rare guardian who would take real interest in advancing his wards' fortunes. Thus even in Maasailand and Sukumaland, greed for personal gain can occasionally supersede social responsibilities. Being part of a somewhat viable lineage system, but at least a strong extended family structure, a Sukuma woman who senses that her guardian or new husband is misusing her children's wealth has easy access to his elder kinsmen. She can also appeal to the elders of the community. A Maasai widow has less access to appeal to effective agents for help. She may have moved some distance away from members of the kin group who made the decision, and, besides, the independence with which a man carries out his affairs often precludes any effective interference by others, even relatives. We must also realize that embezzlement can be a rather quiet event, taking place over many years. A woman may only suspect that the worst is happening, but may have little evidence to prosecute.

Premature widows sometimes have to plot alternatives. A Sukuma can refuse to marry her brother-in-law and return home to her father, but doing so forces her to leave her children's wealth behind. She could also remarry someone not within her husband's kin group (which would incite complex negotiations over return of brideprice), but that also serves less to preserve her children's inheritance than to serve her personal choice of another or fear of the man chosen for her. That the Sukuma have a number of locally powerful agencies to which a woman can appeal for help may obviate the need for more formal arrangements to preserve her children's patrimony.

The Maasai take a very direct means of resolving threats to widows with sons too young to be circumcised. As warriors are considered in theory to have control over their herds, the eldest of a woman's underage sons is circumcised and made a warrior, thus involving him in a powerful cohesive organization of young men who will look after his interests. The boy is protected further by the age set's *ol piron* elders, its sponsoring elder age set which had to give its consent for the operation to take place. The boy is doubly protected, as are his mother, younger brothers, and wealth.

Issues

The analysis of fear arising from threatening situations associated with marriage raises some difficult questions centered in my mind around the relative lack of markers associating this institution with dangers. Perhaps, as I suggested above, the concern with arrangements of who marries whom and the binding power of brideprice can be considered precautions. But, if they are designed to avert danger, I wonder for whom. Although in theory these two devices are supposed to ensure rights and protection of women once they enter into the respect/authority structures of their husbands' homes, marriage arrangements and brideprice seem to work more towards ensuring fathers' and husbands' investments than in protecting wives. Traditional marriage in neither society is marked with the pomp and circumstance of other transitions. At first I thought the answer lay in the lack of concepts of sex pollution, which would, in Douglas' view, remove the necessity to mark the event as dangerous. But, indeed, the transition is dangerous for women, not because of ritual pollution but because of the one-sidedness of the official orientation towards marriage. In a polygynous system a woman may only be married once, but a man hopes to be married many times. The transition itself becomes less important to him because it contains a different meaning and purpose. If women had written the rules for marriage, I would guess that the institution would be replete with traditional cautions and ritual calling attention to the inherent dangers it conceals.

That both societies have devised escape mechanisms indicates that there is indeed awareness of some of the dangers we have discussed and a need to resolve them, but both the Sukuma and Maasai fail to construct internal checks on physical abuse which are effective. To be sure Sukuma women do have more opportunities to deal constructively with an abusive husband, but these resources lie outside marriage itself: appeal to law and community organizations. Maasai women appear to have almost no recourse at all save to enlist the collective power of feminine outrage supported by divine mandate. Perhaps in both these societies issues of physical abuse of wives touches too deeply the sensitive spots within the respect/authority equation, upon which so much of the structure of order in human relations is built. And in the case of the Maasai, it also threatens the dominant male value of personal independence and freedom of action too much to permit any formal means of remedying the situation to have any effectiveness.

One last note. When one chooses to discuss fear and danger, there is a tendency to inadvertantly overemphasize its presence in a situation. I believe this to be the case in this particular analysis. Most marriages among the Sukuma and the Maasai are not fraught with the kinds of threats and discord which have been revealed here. Nevertheless, there is no guarantee in a marriage that they will not occur, and when they do, there appears to be little guarantee that they will be resolved.

The Fearless

The Maasai institution of *e murano* introduces a situation in which expression of fear is deliberately suppressed in young men. The equivalent age group among the Sukuma, *basumba batale*, although serving somewhat similar functions in the community, has no such component. It is not crucial that the Sukuma insist on fearlessness in their young men to the extent to which Maasai do. The Maasai appear to have founded the entire ethos of warriorhood on means of achieving and maintaining this state.

Following Douglas' notion of loci of fear in danger situations which are marked by precautions, the Maasai case conforms nicely as an example of dangers surrounding marginality or transition. The Sukuma in contrast, placing few markers here, reveal what little importance they place on this period, roughly corresponding to adolescence and young adulthood (somewhat older among the Maasai). I am not certain why this is the case. Sukuma youth experience domestic difficulties in achieving independence similar to Maasai. Their new identities as men are as important to them as to the Maasai. Certainly they do not face the daily physical dangers which are supposed to inhere in their Maasai brothers' world, yet bravery is valued and Sukuma youths are not cowards. The basumba batale may not emphasize this part of growing up, but other organizations exist in Sukumaland which contain characteristics more in keeping with e murano: strong markers of independence, competition, marginality of members, visibility and cultivation of fearlessness in dangerous situations. Consideration of one type, the *mbina*, dance society, will also reveal that like e murano it too is marked by ritual and social precautions.

There is a final portion of this particular analysis related to another of Douglas' categories of danger, a system turned against itself (1966: Ch. 9), for it raises the challenge of social control. If fear can serve as an inducement for conformity, what happens when a culture conditions a segment of its population to block out fear and act as if it did not exist? I suggest that the positive contributions such an ethos makes to the social body is counterbalanced by potential dangers resulting from the loss of control over those who are freed from fear. The problem of uncontrollable youth seems to be a necessary result of the freedoms with which Maasai culture burdens its youth. I hope to explore this notion below.

E murano and Its Discontents

Sometime after puberty a rather ragged, undistinguished, almost invisible Maasai boy undergoes an amazing metamorphosis. He becomes, via circumcision and entrance into an exclusive age set, a warrior, *ol murrani*. This former drudge, who sat on the periphery of meat feasts, to whom scraps were tossed by elders, who collected water and firewood, spent long and tiresome days herding livestock, has now become a "glamorous, semisacred" being. He becomes the symbol of "the elegance of Maasai life and the aesthetic excellence of Maasai culture in general" (Llewelyn-Davies 1981:348). He dresses, walks, talks, and possibly thinks in a manner different from all around him. Older girls vie for his attention. Young wives anticipate tabooed liaisons, older women recall their own warrior lovers. To them the warrior is touted as a culture hero. However, the older members of his age set, the seniors with whom he will have innumerable conflicts, view him with scorn. They think of him with more ambiguous feelings, for he is the manifestation of their pride and hope but also an agent of potential frustration and trouble. They know from their own experience that there is a long bumpy road ahead until the age set moves up another grade and passes its disruptive, uncontrollable, and parasitic character on to another set of youth waiting in the wings.

A murrani is characterized by the term *api*, sharp, which carries with it a cluster of similar meanings: courageous and self-reliant (Jacobs 1979), brave, bold, strong (Mol n.d.). Api is a term also used to describe important accoutrements of a warrior, his spear and stabbing sword. Just as he hones his weapons to be api, so must he also hone himself. He is also considered *ogol*, strong or hard. The opposite of this ideal is *ol kuret*, the coward, derived from the verb, *a-ure*, to fear. Mol (personal communication) describes a coward with reference to this period in life as "a warrior who fears and runs away from battle or who turns his back to a charging animal."

Another study of Maasai personality characteristics finds common relationships between warriors and small children: disobedient, playful, avoiding work, not clever (meaning being open and direct and not devious), having a sense of realism, respectful, successful and brave. (Kirk and Burton 1977). Men on the other hand are closely allied with uncircumcised boys. This connection more than hints at similarities along the lines of social responsibility. Small children are not expected to engage in proper social behavior as they are just beginning to learn what their responsibilities will be in life. Warriors are permitted to abandon their formerly responsible roles and revert to unsocialized beings. It appears necessary that a warrior must be removed from society in order for him to develop into what it expects of him.

Creation of the Fearless

Warriors do not have a monopoly on fearless actions. Despite general notions that women and children run away from danger, in reality it is not true for either. All Maasai are suffused with this ethos of courage and high assertiveness. Uncircumcised boys spend long hours of arduous work caring for livestock in places of physical danger. Safety is not easily guaranteed anywhere in Maasailand. No matter what happens, they are expected to remain with their stock (Jacobs 1979:38). But fearlessness of the warrior sort is not the dominant concern of their lives. Rather, as is characteristic of their elders, boys should demonstrate conscientiousness and prudence.

Through initiation into and membership in an age set, a warrior experiences a powerful set of incentives for this metamorphosis and its enhancement. The first comes with entry itself. A youth undergoing circumcision is impressed with the absolute necessity that he demonstrate his courage by keeping expression of pain hidden during the operation.

Warriors are expected to disregard pain, fear of pain, and hardship. He must pass this first test, passively accepting what to me seemed an interminable operation. His reactions are keenly and anxiously observed, for failure on his part means not only disgrace for him but also for his parents.

Newly circumcised boys form the local seed of an age set, which has been formally opened by a religious specialist, mandated by a senior age set with whom it establishes a friendly and protective relationship, and given a name. One cannot emphasize enough the power of this peer group, for it becomes the most important social reference the boy will ever have in Maasailand. All relationships are redefined through it.

As soon as his wounds heal, he begins the process of breaking away from his family's authority through adherence to a new set of rules for warriors all designed to intensify his exemption from the normal round of social life. For example, he follows rules dictating what he can eat, with whom, where, from whom he can accept food, etc. At the same time these new boundaries between him and his community enforce his identification with and dependence on his peers.

A fourth mechanism in his metamorphosis involves breaking down distinctions between "civilized" and "wild." Maasai have very definite notions about where the cosmos of order and predictability end and the world of the untamed begins. For the most part they avoid these places. But warriors deliberately venture into the bush and places of danger, in a sense testing out their conquest of fear or rehearsing scenarios when they will be called upon to court danger either in pursuit of lost animals, a hunt for dangerous predators or thieves, or on raids in unfamiliar territory.[6] It is not surprising that one of the fabled periods in warrior life is held deep in the bush. *Olpul* is nominally a meat feast which might last a month or longer. Warriors and uncircumcised girls take animals from their fathers' herds and set up housekeeping. But it is more than an extended orgy, for it is a period of learning the Maasai Way, and with its juxaposition of absolute relaxation and calm within the confines of the wild, it exemplifies what a warrior must be. It also indicates the contradiction which the warrior experiences of living in two worlds and under two sets of rules. Rigby (1976:339) comes essentially to the same conclusion concerning the meaning of olpul among the Il Baraguyu, Maa-speaking southern neighbors of the Maasai. They are in a sense "wild," associated with "nature, danger, bravery and death."

Warriors also have reinforcement in the creation and continuance of their image through ritual and blessings of the *laibon*, the religious leader, who gave supernatural approbation to the age set's formation. In the more secular sphere, they have a variety of barks and roots, the ingestion of which heighten their excitability. Warriors are forbidden tobacco and alcohol, but not these. Under their influence, a warrior gives the impression of being constantly on edge, never letting his persona drop for an instant. A Maasai friend told me that under their influence he felt a "terrible sensitivity" to everything around him. Another described the experience as an immense calm coupled with a feeling of power and strength so great that "even God couldn't interfere."

Intimate acquaintance with pain and hardship, forays into areas of cultural phobia, adherence to a rigid code of behavior within a highly cohesive face-to-face organization in intimate contact, supported by supernatural sanctions and drugs to intensify states of consciousness—all these form a powerful set of mechanisms to create and sustain the warrior image. The last, a warrior's intense preoccupation with self, unites them all. Warriors spend hours decorating their bodies and those of their friends, plaiting hair, adjusting ornaments with which they are gravured from head to ankle, gazing into mirrors, practicing dances and songs, usually surrounded by an admiring covey of uncircumcised girls. An onlooker is struck by the luxurious indolence and self-centeredness of a murrani, but these are yet another way of announcing and preserving that separateness which api and ogol symbolize.

Contradictions

Indolence of warriors is only an ephemeral state. The high social visibility and freedoms allowed warriors are compensations for their sacrifice to danger. Warriors are trained to be well-oiled but sometimes unpredictable and uncontrollable war machines. Their communities have to tolerate warriors' lack of adherence to the rules of normal social life, their consistent challenging of authority, their internal squabbles, and external troublesomeness. These are the price communities pay for a standing army which also forms the apex of its ideals. But the warrior also pays a price for these freedoms. As I have argued elsewhere (Hatfield 1983), an inevitable result of such conditioning to fight rather than flee or temporize when threats arise can be likened to short-circuiting an organism's defense mechanisms. Among warriors breakdown occurs in an epileptic-like seizure called empushuna rising in situations where, in spite of their apparent exemption from social rules, they cannot act as they have been trained to do—with direct force. Empushuna also occurs in other situations of stress in which powerful feelings dominate, as if the warrior becomes defenseless against them. Selye (1956:1975) claims that chronic responses of this sort will lead to exhaustion and death, but empushuna does not dominate a warrior's daily life and disappears once he enters into elder status. The other price a warrior pays of course is that he is always forced to be close to danger both within the community and outside it (see Tignor 1972). Internally patterned antagonisms between junior and senior arms of an age set are continuous cause for alertness to affront and quick revenge. Inherent conflicts between adjacent age sets are always manifest in demands for and challenges to respect. During e murano there would seem to be few times or places of safety and tranquility for the warrior.

The charter of e murano is built on contradictory expectations. A warrior is charged to defend and maintain Maasailand and its institutions as well as to advance the interests of his age set (and himself). Accomplishing both involves different approaches to authority and respectful relationships. This will become more evident if we briefly examine what warriors are to fear and not fear. From the above, we can guess that warriors are not to fear pain, deprivation, danger, death, the "wild" and its denizens, the night and its dangers, and pressures from outside the confines of the age set.

What warriors fear form the converse of the above: cowardice, shame and any behavior which blasts the fragile image they have assumed; routine, which forces them back into the everyday world and by demeaning their glamour erodes it; usurpation of their independence by outsiders over whom they have no control. The first fear seems to have effective baffles within the training and conditions of internal operations of the age set. But the second two do not. No matter how liminal the Maasai may consider this period, its occupants are required to enter in and out of it with great frequency simply by virtue of the tasks which they are expected to perform for their community. Defense of Maasailand and its institutions means more than the excitement of battle. It also involves tracking lost animals, seeking out thieves, arduous labor in some places to bring water from deep wells to livestock, long hours spent overseeing their younger brothers herding stock in dangerous areas, and treks to bring stock to grass, water, and minerals. Now and then there might be a chance to hunt a lion or leopard, where the sense of danger is heightened, but more often than not their noble charge becomes translated into less invigorating responsibilities. These homely tasks, however, are the means by which a warrior will ultimately advance himself as an elder. By his participation the warrior is ensuring the safety and advancement of his ultimate inheritance. Given this reality of Maasai labor requirements, we can see how the ideal glories of e murano seldom are realized. More often they become translated into petty local conflicts over abuse of its symbols.

That warriors fear loss of their independence of action also brings them to another dilemma. Just as they are only occasionally extruded physically from society, so also are they confronted with the realization that in many ways their lives are still controlled by its structure of authority. For example, livestock which is nominally theirs to use as they please, is still very much controlled by their fathers. In order to claim what a father should give, a warrior often has to snatch. He will also snatch other people's livestock, but if he's caught, his father pays the fine (doubtless from his son's part of the herd). Warriors are always confronted by attempts of elders to influence what they do. At this point who really has jurisdiction over whom is not always clear-cut, so that issues of authority become contests contaminated by the hegemony of respect and independent ideals of warriorhood. As a warrior moves through the later stages of his career, this conflict with fathers and other elders mellows somewhat, for he becomes more closely tied into domestic affairs and shares more points of common interest with them. Eventually at *Olng'esher*, his age set accepts its new position of elderhood and he removes the gravure of warriorhood, its taboos and discards the persona of fearless paragon of Maasai virtue in order to get on with the business of living as a real person in a whole community.

Basumba Batale Among the Sukuma

Perhaps this organization was more powerful and spectacular at the turn of the century—certainly reports of Sukuma warriors protecting the territory from outsiders (especially slave traders) parallel reports from Maasailand around the same time. In the middle part of this century it appears to have assumed a much more modest profile. Basumba Batale, "big boys," today are pallid shadows of the complex ambiguous glamour of Maasai warriors. Where warriorhood is at the apex of Maasai culture, this organization is considered just another step in the process of growing up among the Sukuma. Being an *nsumba ntale* (singular) does involve a youth in a certain amount of style and image making, but it is hardly equivalent to the efforts taken to create the warrior mystique. Rather than being thrust into a world betwixt and between, bounded by taboo and visible signs of separation, Sukuma youth join the basumba within the context of village life. And rather than be characterized by independence and fearlessness, they are considered self-reliant and reliable. Being a member of the organization does soften that often raw edge of discord between father and son over authority and self-determination, but conflict in parent/child relations never seems to reach the kinds of dramatic peaks found among the Maasai.

The organization of basumba batale follows a generic blueprint for all Sukuma common interest groups. Within the village it is part of a triumvirate of associations which monitor community affairs (the other two being the Old Women's and Old Men's societies). It has a leader, an inner circle, a modest amount of internal cohesion and esprit de corps, and is invested with responsibilities to deal with disputes and other problems arising within the age group and arbitrate issues between its members and the community. Its main public purpose in existing, however, is to provide the village with a well-organized labor force, capable of mobilization, whose services are contracted for pay. Profits are saved up for periodic feasts for the membership. Work consists of helping new arrivals get settled, building houses, clearing bush, and providing a village peace-keeping force.

Basumba Batale has some age set characteristics without its being an age set. Its members tend to be adolescent to young adult, share in common interests and activities, but there is no requirement that all youth of a certain age must join the association. Nor do members move as a group into the next status, marriage and elderhood, as is the case with the Maasai.

Although there are many common basal characteristics in basumba batale and e murano, the two organizations have different structures and somewhat different charters. The Sukuma organization is not formed for the pursuit of danger and cultivation of fearlessness, although it is to serve the social body just as its Maasai equivalent. Nor is it structured so as to exist on the margins of the social scene, rife with conflicts over responsibilities, respect and authority. Like members of any community body, its members are expected to conform to general expectations of proper social intercourse. The basumba batale, then, would seem to fulfill only one part of its Maasai equivalent: community service. To view the other part we need to examine another kind of association found among the Sukuma. Before doing that, it is valuable here to digress briefly and elaborate on fear and Sukuma youth.

What do young men in Sukumaland fear? In many ways the categories are variations on the Maasai theme. Routine, which involves most of the cycles of agricultural work which a youth has known since childhood. Men aren't exempt from these burdens either, but have responsibilities and opportunities which remove them from the drudgery of daily labor occasionally. A young man's approaching maturity is acknowledged by allowing him some freedom from these burdens either granted by his father or snatched when possible by the boy. Just as Maasai fathers characterize warriors as dangerous and uncontrollable, Sukuma fathers think of sons at this age as lazy and irresponsible when it comes to domestic work. The basumba batale affords Sukuma youth some respite from parental authority and a measure of peer group cohesion.

We have noted that Sukuma youth are not required to pay so much attention to promoting notions of their bravery as they are to developing and demonstrating their skills at organization, cooperation, and nego- tiations. Nevertheless, bravery is an ideal male trait. The Sukuma have a number of terms denoting bravery *bukali, bugimuu, budimu,* the first of which is related less to the notion of fearlessness than to anger. Sukuma males may have fewer occasions for involvement in dangerous acts than the Maasai, but they have many opportunities for anger. Confrontation with and courting of physical danger does not form an essential part of the basumba batale.

Similarly with shame and ridicule. All Sukuma fear having their faults aired in public, but the basumba batale do not have the monopoly of concern over this form of personal affront.

Fear of usurpation of authority might be more appropriately translated for Sukuma youth into fear of not achieving independence. In their hierarchical society with its many layers of authority, chances of being caught under someone's thumb are much greater than among the Maasai. Authority relationships in Sukumaland appear to be well-defined, but in action they are not. Perhaps the most articulated of them all lies within the kin structure. Most Sukuma youth are under a patrilineal thumb for most of their lives until middle age, although most aim to set up an independent household before their father's death, a goal not easily accomplished within the powerful grips of an extended family, whose leader controls everyone's resources. A Sukuma youth then must strive to achieve his eventual autonomy; a Maasai youth must strive to maintain the autonomy which in theory was granted him at circumcision.

Associated with independence is identity. We have seen that a Maasai warrior is given a powerful ready-made identity. A Sukuma youth does not have so well-articulated a persona to assume during this period of his life through the busumba batale. With few wars to fight and overt conflict considered bad form, he does not have many foci of masculine adventure to guide him. A basumba batale does not enjoy the status of a semisacred being, but he is also exempt somewhat from having to live an impossible ideal. His identity then is more of a developmental issue rather than conformity to a set of rigid characteristics which a Maasai warrior almost assumes overnight.

Dance Societies

The organization of youth in Sukumaland seems to contain one aspect of the Maasai e murano. Yet, there are associations among the Sukuma which in structure and function appear to provide excitement, glamour, and danger. The mbina, dance society, aesthetically is the most splendid expression of Sukuma life. These voluntary associations align all of Sukumaland into a network of hierarchical structures and competition. That they also involve courting physical danger gives us reason for viewing them as the missing pieces in a Sukuma youth's coming of age.

The mbina is also modeled on the generic Sukuma organization. It has a cohesive membership and a hierarchy of leaders and councils. But unlike a voluntary association it assumes a strong sense of fictive kinship among the members, the head being regarded as a surrogate father just as the *ise buhemba* among traditional religious specialists (Hatfield 1968). The mbina also operates with a quasi cult-like aura of supernatural protection, ritual, and beliefs which serves to unite membership even more. A Sukuma youth who joins such an organization is inducted into a situation paralleling that of his Maasai peer. He too becomes part of a pan-tribal organization based on rules of internal cooperation and brotherhood whose local groups provide powerful structures for activity and orientation. In becoming a member of a dance society, a Sukuma youth initiates his own journey socially and psychologically away from his family's household. Through initiation and visible marks of his new achievement, he gains a new identity. Within the inner sanctum of the organization he begins to master its esoterica, sacred and secular. He begins to obtain powerful "medicines" believed necessary to protect and advance a man in his journey through life but which have special importance, given the dangers which surround the society from outside competitors and evil-doers. Most of the public visibility of the mbina comes through carefully planned dance and song competitions, where participants are plumed as spectacularly as Maasai warriors and display feats of skill and amazement. The impact of such a performer on the young women of the community is certainly positive and perhaps even mildly charismatic.

Many dance societies have had their origins in activities which pose threat, uncertainty, and danger to Sukuma affairs. One mbina began from periodic Sukuma expeditions to Lake Eyasi in search of salt, a trip requiring planning, leadership, and an ample supply of supernatural and physical safeguards. Another group originated in attempts to eradicate porcupines from cultivated fields. African porcupines are rather large and can do great damage to crops. The Sukuma method of dealing with them was to crawl into their holes and flush them out. Sometimes the holes would be inhabited by poisonous snakes instead of porcupines. From this dangerous but mundane beginning two dance societies developed, each replete with practical techniques for handling snakes and porcupines as well as a host of powerful supernatural aids. The "Snake" society is perhaps the most spectacular of the mbina, for in its dance competitions, participants entertain and frighten audiences by their calm and fearless handling of large and very dangerous animals from snakes to crocodiles. Although much of this is pure showmanship, the element of real danger is ever-present, and favorite stories associated with this society always have at least one mention of a *ningi*, dance society performer, who died because he didn't take the proper precautions with his show animals. Here in these displays of skill dance society members juxtapose dissimilar and antagonistic arenas of life with absolute confidence. They are parallels to the Maasai warrior's merging of civilization with the untamed and wild. The Sukuma youth participating in one of these societies is given the same opportunity as his Maasai peer to investigate those ambiguous areas of life where unknown dangers and threats lurk and from them develop his own sense of confidence and courage.

Dance societies do not focus on the preservation of Sukumaland and its ideals—that's the task of the basumba batale—but they operate much in the same manner as warrior age sets to create powerful and cohesive organizations which exist outside the ken of everyday life. Like e murano, the mbina exists on the margins of society, but unlike e murano its members do not experience the kinds of problems and contradictions which confront warriors moving in and out of the secular world. Under normal circumstances the mbina poses no threat to the Sukuma. The marks of its separateness and the nature of its activities keep it from entering into and contaminating the orderly affairs of everyday life. Sukuma society does not make contradictory demands of its members, for it accepts their marginality so long as it remains within the context of dance competitions. A youth's often brief association with a mbina does not estrange him unduly from his community or family, but it can serve to allay some of his fears about dependency and help him mold an identity, enough at least to tide him over into marriage. He relinquishes his ties with a mbina slowly, as the duties of an adult take him more and more into the affairs of home and community once again. Here is another parallel with the transition from Maasai warrior to elder, but in typical Sukuma fashion there is no formal marker to announce the change. Unlike e murano, the mbina is truly peripheral to Sukuma life, and he who emerges from it does not have to bear the burden of resolving contradictory identities.[7]

Issues

In this section we have looked at what happens when a society insists on institutionalized fearlessness in some of its members. In order to preserve a way of life, the Maasai must create a force of warriors, but the method they choose involves their drastic separation from the community, physically and psychologically. This technique may be successful in creating such a person and such an organization, but in the Maasai instance separation from the normal routine of life is more illusory than real. A warrior is forced to return to the community. There he encounters the dilution of the image for which he has been so carefully conditioned. The entire edifice of e murano is fraught with contradictions, localized in the disjunction between the real and ideal spheres of activity and responsibility of warriors. The result is conflict on many levels. At the same time much of the Maasai image is constructed on conflict, so in a sense the contradictions tend to reinforce an image of that society's reality, albeit skewed heavily. Is it also possible that these very contradictions which could be considered the stuff of cognitive dissonance, create even greater reinforcement in commitment and resolve to continue in a life-threatening and emotionally exhausting state? It appears to me that the Maasai have not found effective means to contain the dangers that they let loose in creating and maintaining the warrior image.[8]

The Sukuma occupy the other end of the spectrum. The basumba batale works quite well to harness youthful energies into social use within the framework of village life. Even its complement to e murano, the dance society, with its exclusiveness, marginality, and "semisacred" parallels, is able to keep its power contained. Precautions in the liminal state of the mbina work because there is little conflict between one's duties and one's ideals. Sukuma can pursue adventures in the dangerous nooks and crannies of the Sukuma universe because these are indeed removed from everyday Sukuma life. Although, I began with the question of dangers arising from an overemphasis on fearlessness which leads to challenges of authority and anti-social tendencies, it would seem that, aside from some personal problems like empushuna, the real issue is not in insisting on a monopoly of fearlessness but on maintaining a consistent definition of where and when it is to operate.

Enemies Within; Danger Without

If a culture can structure emotions and institutions in such ways that in certain contexts individuals are conditioned to act as if fear did not exist, then it would also seem that cultures can create institutions supported by fear and situations defined by fear, actions to be feared, persons to be feared, and events to be feared. In this section we consider two areas of life which are marked by culturally sanctioned fear and precautions: enemies within and contamination from without. We will focus on comparisons of witchcraft and the curse as internal mechanisms inciting fear and on issues related to maintenance of external boundaries—physical, ideological and sociological. The Sukuma and Maasai do not have similar orientations on these matters, so we will be given the opportunity to consider why they take different approaches.

Space and Time

We should begin by exploring a geography of fear related to the physical settings in which the Sukuma and Maasai live. Both societies occupy an immense territory in Tanzania. The Sukuma have virtually filled their land with people and fields. The Maasai appear to have made modest dents in the landscape with homesteads and pastures. Physical worlds of safety can be considered a series of enclosed spaces such as house, homestead, encampment, community, while others, such as age set and association become safety points of orientation. As the space between these enclosures gets wider and wider, so do opportunities for ambiguity, uncertainty, strangeness, disorder, and danger become greater. The culmination of danger is identified where "civilization" and "culture" reach the untamed and wild, places where the half-human and superhuman dwell, where mysterious and unpredictable events happen, where normal patterns of action and caution are not effective. The other boundary is that of territory, beyond which lies an alien and threatening world of different ways of life, language, and beliefs.

Fear is also related to time. We would expect to find all occasions of uncertainty to be fear-inducing: childbirth, when rains refuse to fructify the land, when antagonistic groups of warriors encounter each other at a public ceremony. But fear is also given to the night and darkness. Evil deeds are often nightime deeds. Where the above juxtapose technology against nature and institutional limitations, night has the uncanny property of bringing the unknown geographically closer to those circles of comfort and familiarity, imposing on them a different and threatening order.

These geographical and temporal loci of fear have more than ideological significance. Danger really does lurk outside and the night only intensifies its threat. Maasai share their land with the great game animals of East Africa, many of whom are predators, most of whom are dangerous. The Sukuma have less reason to fear predators than the Maasai, although hyena and leopard are common. But there are still areas of bush and thicket in Sukumaland. Night is a particularly dangerous time for Sukuma, as we shall see below.

Another set of hazards come from human enemies. The Maasai fear livestock raids, and the Sukuma fear livestock thefts by the Maasai. Sukuma also have a great fear of thieves, individuals who are believed sometimes to possess special invisibility magic or the skill to move about a household without sound, taking whatever they wish.

A third set of predators are mystically empowered evildoers—witches. The problem with witches is that there are not many precautions against them which can be taken physically in defense of home and family.

Against some of the above dangers physical precautions are considered effective. Both the Maasai enkang and the Sukuma kaya, consisting of houses, stock corrals, out buildings, storage areas, etc., are nicely enclosed within a protective fence. In Maasailand this fence amounts to a virtually impenetratable thicket of thorn bush (and in a few areas a wooden stockade). Traditionally the Sukuma have used strong minala hedges which can literally hide the kaya from view, but today frequently a token fence surrounds a kaya. Gates and entrances take on ritual significance in both groups, for through them can pass both evil and good. Fences, gates, locks are all important physical precautions against dangers lurking outside a homestead.

To counter the threat of external mystical powers, which are not affected by locks and fences, the Sukuma and Maasai use charms. The Sukuma have a special category of protective medicines called *lukago* with which every family head literally knots his kaya in a web of protective safety. (Members of dance societies also obtain personal lukago from their leaders). Neither fences nor medicines are effective against enemies who live within these circles of safety. Thus, it is not only the horror which the image of witch can conjure up which becomes a focus for fear but the belief that the witch operates subversively within the very sanctity of household and community. The nice distinctions in the geography of danger are shattered by this person who is free to wander where he/she wishes.

> Witches are the social equivalents of beetles and spiders who live in the cracks of the walls . . . they attract the fears and dislikes which other ambiguities and contradictions attract in other thought structures, and the kinds of powers attributed to them symbolize their ambiguous, inarticulated status (Douglas 1966:102).

Although the image of evil creatures living in the interstices of safety zones makes a good metaphor, spiders and beetles might in Sukumaland be better represented by the termite. Most of the time the termite is invisible, but its handiwork is always evident. Sukuma traditionally construct houses of thatch and poles, which even while construction takes place are inexorably attacked by these creatures, who tear down, eat up, and carry away its substances until eventually the house collapses, its strength hollowed out. A constant reminder of this remarkable reflection on the transitoriness of human affairs and frustrations of human effort is the just audible clicking sounds of termites busy above and around one and the incessant gentle rain of dust from the roof. Witches are like this. They live within the edifice of the social body and are constantly laboring to destroy it.

It is important to distinguish briefly two aspects of witchcraft among the Sukuma, who appear to have much more interest in the subject than the Maasai. A Sukuma witch, *nogi*, is first the focus of a body of beliefs concerning human possession of marvelous and fearful powers. He/she delights in darkness, consorts with its creatures—hyena and owls—has the power to change into a mouse or fly and slip unnoticed into the most heavily protected kaya. A nogi can steal people, turning them into zombies who work in the fields by night and are hidden in the rafters of her house by day. Witches belong to clubs which meet in darkness in abandoned houses for orgies of feasting on purloined food. By day these witches are identified as the proud, the rich, those unwilling to adhere to rules of neighborliness, the stingy, or at the other end of the social spectrum, a person who is poor, without family or resources, who always allows neighbors to demonstrate their good will by sharing food and assistance.

In the anthropological literature this person is commonly called the "nightmare" witch, a creature embodying all that is the opposite of normalcy and goodness. People who should be like everyone else but who have achieved sudden visibility in the community or who refuse to act as good people should are suspects. But the nogi of nightmares is not psychologically complex. He/she is simply considered to have an overwhelming greed supported by a powerful supernatural gift from ancestors. As far as I know no one has ever captured such a witch, and those who are identified as witches in Sukumaland lack most of the spectacular abilities which they are supposed to possess. The revealed witch, however, is the more dangerous, for the partying, thefts of goats, and general nocturnal mayhem do minimal damage to Sukuma circles of safety. The revealed witch does her damage within the kaya itself and indeed may be one of its residents. Moreover, she possesses no distinguishing marks to warn the unwary, for until the deed is done, when a series of personal misfortunes occur, someone—especially a child—dies, and an elder takes his fears to a diviner for elucidation, she remains invisible like the termite. Sukuma have good reasons to fear and hate both refractions of the nogi. She embodies all that is secret and unpredictable, she possesses extraordinary powers to harm and destroy, and she is consumed by insatiable greed and hatred which all the rules of social life cannot dampen. Moreover, she has free access to the very hubs of safety and concord by posing as a co-wife or neighbor.

Sukuma are not completely at the mercy of witches. We have already mentioned the net of protective medicines which are considered to strengthen a household against all sorts of intrusions. These plus ancestors should help protect a family. A second precaution is simply to keep out of a witch's way by remaining at home at night and by "being good." The revealed witch is not capricious, her victim is not chosen at random, nor is the cause of her attack unprovoked, for she acts with cause. But she is quick to take offense and persistent in punishing. When her identity is revealed, so is the cause of her action, usually a breach of neighborliness by someone in the victim's family (Hatfield 1973). In spite of the consensus that revealed witches act with cause, most Sukuma prefer to depend on lukago and trust to luck, just as they do in adultery. Perhaps, like us, they find that "being good" is not only boring, but that sometimes in the context of real social interaction it is virtually impossible.[9]

The last two defenses against a nogi only occur once personal disaster occurs or is looming. A family which is diagnosed as being objects of a witch's wrath sometimes escapes by night to another community. A person can also move to the homestead of a religious specialist whose extra collection of lukago helps to prevent the witch from operating. A nogi can also be driven away from the community. Sometimes the suspect's family is informed that the village is "too hot," a phrase also used for victims, and that the family had better emigrate or risk public wrath. Eventually witches are purged from the village by an outraged posse of men who chase them to the boundaries with sticks. Few witches survive this purge. This revealed witch is always a woman, always in a socially peripheral role or else an unwitting victim caught in a skein of internicine power struggles. She is far from that ideal image of evil envisaged in the nightmare witch, who could turn herself into a hyena and lope away to freedom and revenge. It is not profitable to attempt to smooth out the rough edges and inconsistencies in Sukuma beliefs about the nogi. Sukuma, like the Navajo, have very little to say about these persons, fearing that they be considered witches for knowing too much. My sense is that this category of internal evil-doer must remain amorphous, ambiguous, and only partly defined so that the lines of characterization remain vague enough to provide a repository for all the internal dangers for which there are no viable mechanisms of prevention. That the power of witches diminishes with distance indicates the greater locus of tension and unresolvable danger residing at home and not abroad.

My understanding of Maasai parallels to the nogi is much less complete. On the whole, East African pastoralists prefer to deal with discrepancies in human affairs through direct action rather than fill up interpersonal relationships with threats of indirect harm from supernatural powers. Being physically more mobile with fewer enduring social arrangements, and more permissive of the use of physical force to deal with problems, the Maasai have less danger of getting enmeshed in a fabric of formal outward friendliness and cooperation matched by internal frustration and rage. Nevertheless, the Maasai do allow their world to be populated by agents of supernatural power which have evil intent: *onyek*, the evil eye, and *e sakutore*, witchcraft. (There is another use of supernatural power to harm in the curse, *ol deket*, but it operates in a different set of circumstances.) Witchcraft is also termed *e setan* (Mol n.d.:172), a borrowing from the ki-Swahili *shetani*, a devil or Satan, which might indicate that the concept is relatively new to the Maasai. The evil eye and witchcraft operate in ways similar to Sukuma witch beliefs with less emphasis on perpetrators being female: evil persons live within otherwise safe circles of social life in order to destroy others. That such persons are feared is evidenced by the fact that suspects are shunned and isolated, a terrible sanction for the Maasai who have precious few means of maintaining enduring social relationships and for whom, in spite of independent spirit and mobility, a singular existence could prove to be a death sentence (Ole Kuney, personal communication). As in the case of the nogi, this concatenation of beliefs becomes redefined as dangerous, fostering suspicion, exacerbating discord, and in some instances inciting murder. No one is exempt from this contamination.

Curses

My impression is that Maasai may identify categories of evilly empowered individuals as present in their society, but that they do not make much use of them. More frequent in my experience has been the employment of curses to deal with interpersonal problems which for some reason cannot be dealt with directly. The Sukuma also use curses for similar purposes. Curses appear in three contexts: when a supernatural seal of authority is placed to bind a collective decision; when an otherwise powerless group protests a course of action by the powerful; and when individuals cannot resolve personal disputes through direct action or arbitration. The curse, then, among the Maasai, is quite unlike witchcraft in that its wielders are not capricious or evil and that the objects of the curse are always guilty of some serious delict. As *Ng'ai*, God, is the supreme authority lying behind the power of the curse, its employment has to be justified or its power will revert and destroy the user.

The curse appears to have as much power in threat as in deed. Maasai elders of an area may set aside a grazing reserve or establish a pattern of watering livestock during the dry season. They will seal the decision with a curse. Women, infuriated by a leader's unjust or unconsidered action may publicly declare that they will curse him, wipe out his livestock, kill his children, and reduce him to penury. They may emphasize their intent by marching en masse to his homestead and forcibly take one of his animals. As individuals, women have little formal power, but as collective furies, backed by the power of Ng'ai, they are a force to be dealt with carefully. Similarly with curses between individuals, mothers often threaten to curse sons who do not follow their wishes. Recently mothers have been free with their threats when boys want to continue in school, but a curse can be incited by any action which she deplores.

The Sukuma equivalent is only found in the last category of curses. Physical punishment becomes difficult when a son is mature in both societies. Sukuma parents certainly would not employ sorcery against a son, and a mother would not bewitch him either. The curse is a parent's last resort for its use disenfranchises a child. By reciting the proper words and performing a public ritual the father officially removes family, patri-kin, and wealth ties to his son. He also takes away all the supernatural support which has sustained his son through ancestors. A man so cursed is doomed socially and spiritually. There is no place of safety remaining for him anywhere in Sukuma territory. This forms a powerful sanction and I am not even certain that it is ever used. Nonetheless, it remains like the Maasai curse as a powerful disincentive for sons to exceed the limits of abuse of parental authority and respect.

In calling attention to dangers which exist within society the Sukuma and Maasai are indirectly being as realistic about them as they are in acknowledging times and places of fear. For these are indeed pressure points where different orders collide and the defects in human endeavors are revealed. The curse, which takes a positive, admonishing, stance vis-à-vis its potential "victims" accepts the inevitability that human action cannot resolve all inequities and deviations by calling on a higher, more consistent authority to impose punishment on those who insist on flaunting the rules of social life. How successful a mechanism for justice it is in its sphere of operations is indicated by the power of its threat. In the curse we have an ultimate weapon against a different enemy within than in the witch, but nevertheless a danger to the safety of the social body.

The witch is at the center of a set of more complex issues, none of which are clear-cut. Perhaps this is why beliefs in witchcraft are more prevalent in Sukumaland than among the Maasai, for in spite of their many modes of organizing people and many social positions power is negotiable and open. From an outside view one would deny the actual existence of witches among the Sukuma. Those who are revealed as witches are unfortunate victims of a belief structure which demands scapegoats. But the belief itself casts into sharp focus the realities of Sukuma social existence, especially within their capsules of safety, and by identifying them with the horribly spectacular nightmare witch and her vengeful epiphany, demonstrates to the Sukuma just how dangerous real action can be within the "comfort zones" of family and community.

The danger of the witch as the enemy within is that she constantly threatens to rip asunder the delicate facade of social relationships and formalities under which Sukuma communities labor. As witchcraft becomes a focus for the detritus of social ambiguities and a temporary measure of regaining collective concord and security, it ultimately recreates discord and leaves more unresolved ambiguities and fears in its wake. This sort of focus on fear inadvertently has the same result as the focus upon fearlessness among the Maasai warrior, for it spills out over its ideological context contaminating everything it touches.

External Enemies

Territorial boundaries have physical and conceptual characteristics. The geographical limits of a culture are enhanced by notions that outside lie alien peoples marked by different language, dress, custom, and attitudes, whose values are not shared or internally compatible. Both Sukuma and Maasai have elaborated fears of outside peoples and encourage anxieties about their powers to harm internally, but they do so with different intensity and meet the threats in different ways. As we shall see, they have sound basis for their development of precautions and defense, but, of the two, the Maasai have greater cause.

Alienation of Land

Maasai are more concerned about non-pastoral peoples penetrating their territory than fear of other pastoralists with whom they have traditional, usually enemy-like relationships. Other pastoralists raid and loot, seek war and revenge, activities with which the Maasai are familiar. Agriculturalists, on the other hand, may have always been important to the Maasai because of their crops, and in spite of their protestations of being pure pastoralists, Maasai have to some extent valued agricultural produce. Earlier in this century some Maasai groups encouraged small settlements of farmers in their territory, but in more recent years there have been a multitude of uninvited guests, for Maasailand is virtually surrounded by land hungry agriculturalists who do not appreciate delicate equations of land to livestock and see only unoccupied territory where Maasai have established drought reserves of dry season pastures. Unfortunately, most government officials, coming from agricultural backgrounds, also view Maasailand as prime opportunity for farming.

A second more recent form of threat to Maasai land, over which they have little control, takes the form of rental of large tracts for commercial agricultural schemes from local government. While some

and recruitment of school children each year still involves a "round-up" composed of teachers, local officials and police. A father who refused to allow his child to go to school can be taken to court and fined. So Maasai women weep and threaten to curse their older children who on their own volition elect to further their education. Warriors ridicule their educated peers, and elders complain that the end of the Maasai Way is soon to come.

In Sukumaland the situation is not so dramatic. The educational process has been at work more intensively, and to some extent they have grown to accept it as a necessary evil. Individuals will voice similar attitudes about the dangers of education, especially for girls, as the Maasai, but they do not view it in terms of destruction of their way of life. They also have had greater opportunity to see how education will help a person advance in modern Tanzania, which they realize means advancement of the kin group as well.

Are these fears irrational, having their roots in a fundamental antagonism towards the institutions of modern society? I think not. To the Maasai, boarding schools proved to be effective devices for deculturating children from their way of life, making it almost impossible for them to return to a successful and satisfactory life at home. The structure of the modern educational system is also antithetical to e murano, which is the powerful enculturating institution of Maasai youth. Boys in school are virtually excluded from almost all activities of warriors and prevented from dressing and behaving like warriors. Similarly, education removes Sukuma youth from participation in local organizations such as the basumba batale and dance societies.

In addition to removing young people at the most crucial times for celebrating and identifying with the values necessary to make successful men and women in local terms, modern education also competes greatly with local economics. Neither Maasai nor Sukuma households can easily do without the labor of older children. In fact all children have some domestic responsibilities. Girls are especially important as the adjuncts of their mothers. Their presence at school prevents them from working at home for most of the day. Someone has to assume extra responsibilities which school children cannot accomplish, and all too often this is an already overworked mother, a father, or in the case of the Maasai a warrior. The extraction of a child for school leaves in both societies a gap, the filling of which requires readjustment of everyone's lives. Thus opposition to school has a much more deep seated and practical basis than the catchall term, conservatism, would suggest (Catherine Hatfield 1983).

The other part of this picture is their fear of what will replace that learning which children will not get at home. In Tanzania until rather recently, the formal educational process was geared, perhaps unintentionally, towards transposing children away from the confines of their communities and cultures, and in the process created new sets of problems for Maasai and Sukuma parents. Authority of elders, which we have seen is a sensitive issue in Maasailand and can prove difficult in Sukumaland, is virtually eroded away by new opportunities and new reference groups. "Boys and girls want to choose their own spouses," a Maasai elder complains, a trend which hits at the heart of traditional marriage. Maasai youths return home with skills in reading and writing but with little understanding and appreciation of the requirements of livestock care. They are considered lazy and uninterested in what really matters by others. Sukuma youth are in a somewhat better position, technically, for most schools do emphasize basic agricultural knowledge. Of course, on their return home, they are full of new ideas about productivity and can be highly critical of their family's farming methods. The bitter truth, which both Sukuma and Maasai know, is that an educated man or woman is not prepared technically or culturally to resume life as a member of a traditional community. Their sights are always on the horizon, on the places beyond the boundaries of territory and values.

In responding to these external threats, the Maasai appear to have developed as tight and impenetrable an ideological exoskeleton as they construct protective fences and gates around their homesteads. They emphasize visible signs of difference: elaborate skin skirts, dazzling arrays of necklaces, earrings and other decorations, complex hair styles, gravure, spears and swords for warriors, all of which call attention to their aloofness from and lack of concern for other ways of life.[11]

Maasai also take great pains to ensure that they display behavioral markers associated with the Maasai image. For example, normally digging in the earth is not a Maasai pastime. Under a national mandate to produce home gardens and engage in self-help projects such as building roads, clearing water points, etc., they are placed in a dilemma. Warriors, who in the past have dug trenches for water (Jacobs, personal communication), now indicate great reluctance to get involved in these kinds of schemes. My Maasai friends emphasized great physical repugnance at the thought of eating pork or fish and barely tolerated chicken. In the field Maasai girls deliberately recoiled at oranges and one old woman refused a cup of tea made with tinned milk because it might have come from an *nguruwe*, pig in kiSwahili. These are small examples of the edifice of defense which the Maasai have taken from traditional custom and elaborated in the face of exterior threat. But perhaps the greatest part of it comes from the ever-present insistence on every possible occasion that the Maasai way is superior to all others. This approach to the world is not a new one. A Maasai child is taught to believe that of all the ways of life which God has invented, the very best was given to them. We can appreciate how important such a belief is to maintain courage and enthusiasm under the harsh conditions of Maasai life. The consistency with which it informs all other endeavors in Maasai daily affairs composes a powerful rationale for adhering to the Maasai Way with pride and content. The other side of this orientation is that it necessarily must denigrate the ways of life of others, *Il Meek*, who have great investment in their own lifeways, but who are less vocal about it. Maasai marks of superiority of course only appear to isolate them from external threat. In fact they operate to do the opposite: attract the attention and dismay of agents of development who dub the Maasai Way "primitive," an embarrasment to a developing nation, and who take every opportunity to destroy it. Sadly enough the Maasai exoskeleton is as dazzling, rigid, and fragile as glass.

In contrast the Sukuma appear to conceive their protective body as an endoskeleton, somewhat constructed on the lines of their homesteads. They have token fences and gates which are often left open. Just as their protection from evil lies in the use of spiritual substances, so are their responses to external threats and dangers less visible and more subtle. They also have far less to fear from external forces than the Maasai. The simple fact of scale, that the Sukuma number perhaps twenty times more than the Maasai, has a great deal to do with their relaxed defenses. Moreover, the forces of modernization are much more softened in Sukumaland as they derive from somewhat similar institutions two of which are a system of representative government and hierarchical authority and a subsistence base in agriculture. Development is not focused on the destruction of the fundamental structure of their lives, but when Sukuma perceive it to be so, their response is quiet and effective sabotage. The Maasai realize that their case is different and the threats to the integrity of their existence are very real ones indeed.

In this sector of the geography of fear, we find less satisfaction with Sukuma and Maasai defenses and precautions. Building fences and gates against the dangers of the night, avoiding places and occasions of danger, providing supernatural protection against supernatural power—all are effective and appropriate responses to dangers from without. However, in response to external threats from development, Maasai brittle visibility and protestations of their superior way of life, while serving to keep those inside temporarily undefiled, does not ultimately keep the enemy at bay. Similarly with the Sukuma, whose more mild external threats from development incite more subtle but nonetheless effective mechanisms of defense such as selecting custodians of the boundaries who have little power to facilitate two-way communication.

Perhaps such a stance is itself a developmental issue for the Maasai, for in protecting their boundaries and identities against these external threats, they are employing traditional responses which better serve against traditional enemies, where the reputation of fearlessness and visibile bravado of the warrior is a powerful force for caution. But in the context of development, such behavior in calling attention to itself serves as justification for more intensified efforts at invasion.

The Maasai have in their elders listening and responding groups who often appear willing to compromise creatively and effectively. (Tignor 1972 describes the often tragic consequences of the cooptation of Maasai elders by the colonial government of Kenya.) The Sukuma, who should be experts at finding alternatives to undesirable edicts and plans, unfortunately also fall back on a pattern of formal leadership which may possess the skills of negotiation but lacks the social power to persuade internally. Both defenses in this arena are ineffective and possibly ultimately disastrous, for the important set of skills which both must learn in coping with this form of threat is how to coopt the enemy and in so doing bend it to one's needs, but at the moment the threat seems too overpowering to permit taking such innovative risks.

Conclusions

In terms of conceptual armament, what has this exercise revealed? We obviously need to be more sensitized to the phenomena of the emotions from a cultural perspective and explore creative means of investigating them. A first step requires better understanding of how emotions are patterned in our own society. Bailey's work (1983) is a useful beginning in that he demonstrates how individuals use different emotions consciously to achieve personal ends in British and American society. We are aware that age, sex, status, and geography determine how and when and where individuals express emotions, that their repertoires are not left up to the devices of personality and chance. Anyone who has ventured into the psychological literature on emotions is aware of how difficult it is to define anything. Rather than being a deterrent to continued efforts, it should be a stimulus to look for different directions, which, of course is what sociophobics is about. For the culturally sensitive, such a search begins with trying to understand how a people define different emotions and how they employ them. We have come up against such an example in discussing the "fear" that is the basis of respect and authority among the Maasai and Sukuma and the "fear" that comes from threats of physical abuse or attacks by witches. It is necessary that these different refractions of fear be clarified in order to understand how they work and to what they are related. I have not been very successful in this analysis in meeting that requirement. Perhaps it requires more field research.

I felt comfortable in using my interpretation of Douglas' model of precautions and markers to identify a society's concern with points of threat and danger and from them infer beliefs about circumstances of danger. But, as the analysis of marriage indicated, there exist situations which are threatening to a segment of society but which are not given traditional markers. One needs to be sensitive to potential circumstances of fear which will not be clearly marked, and in doing so not be afraid to trample over sacred emic/etic distinctions for the purpose of arriving at a better understanding. I did feel somewhat ill at ease in touting arranged marriages and brideprice as markers of danger and precautions against the threats which are inherent in some aspects of marriage. I don't think that Douglas had so broad an interpretation in mind when she developed her model. I would want to do some more careful thinking about what constitutes cultural identifiers of threat.

Integral to the framework I have adopted has been the correlation of fear with threat and danger. In the introduction, I provided some implicit justification for this through an appeal to the authority of writers on the subject of emotions. Focusing on fear as a subjective state in an individual creates rather serious problems for research, which is probably why Arnold emphasized the directional aspects of emotions rather than their static condition. In this way, they become objectified and observable through situations and actions. I have held to this concept primarily because it served my own vested interests in analysis and fit a cultural approach better. In so doing, I have tended to ignore a really fascinating area of study which is the complement to the kind of structural approach I have taken: how do individuals respond to the patterning of emotions which their traditions require of them? (A similar criticism of Douglas' approach can be found in De Vos, 1974). I have diffidently approached this subject with respect to Maasai warriors and the expectations of fearlessness which form the foundations of their positions, but it remains an incomplete and important part of a study of this kind.

Concerning the two societies, it is surprising how many commonalities the Maasai and Sukuma share despite their very different subsistence bases, lifestyles, and self-proclaimed identities. Anthropologists may have been too heavily conditioned to see major differences between pastoral and agricultural societies to the neglect of identifying commonalities. After all, in East Africa, both the Maasai and Sukuma, although having different histories, do share in a common fund of cultural traditions, and, in spite of strong boundary maintaining devices in both, they are neighbors. As would be expected, we found common approaches to fear and fearlessness in these societies, although structured differently and with different impact. We also found some radically different approaches to threat, danger, and fear, most of which were also related to different institutions and values. I hope that this part of the analysis gives greater credence to my initial assertion that indeed cultures pattern emotions, just as they do any other aspect of the person and his/her relationships and operations as social beings.

We have also found that patterning of fear in one sector carries many implications for other sectors. That fear states are relatively unacknowledged in marriage tends to create special difficulties for women caught in situations where expected behavior and reality don't correspond. Conditioning warriors against fear by causing them to deliberately transgress boundaries where expression of fear is considered appropriate, not only fosters difficulties for warriors themselves in other areas of life, but also creates problems for the society that must maintain control over them. In being encouraged to destroy distinctions between the tamed and the wild, danger and safety, warriors appear to be encouraged to objectify their own culture with the consequence that other taboos, such as surround respect and authority, are also liable to reinterpretation. The association of aggression with fearlessness—and the two are not genetically allied—exacerbates the situation, especially given ambiguities inherent in the Maasai warrior position. As we have seen, the Sukuma are less prone to this threat.

Witchcraft carries its own spillovers in a society in which it is a dominant means for explaining and coping with internal discord and conflict. The belief provides a focus for fear symbolizing evils resulting from human interests and interaction. It also provides markers to indicate where danger lies and mechanisms to avert or remove its threat; however, the mechanisms so invented do not touch upon the "real" sources of discord which give rise to the belief initially, so consequently become ineffective in providing palliatives for fears so engendered within the social body. Moreover, witchcraft leaves no social relationships free from its infection, save that perhaps of parent/child.

External fears, real or perceived, have similar tendencies to contaminate. Both Sukuma and Maasai employ internally powerful forms of warning and escape to confront external threats. These may work when the threat is from another ethnic group, but is much less viable when the enemy without consists of agents and ideologies associated with development, supported by a national system. Traditional mechanisms of defense in these societies work to stifle potential means of resolving issues in an atmosphere of open communication, and, in the case of the Maasai, only brings into being counter-responses (which according to this analysis would also be fear-induced) by external agents against perceived dangers to their own programs. In these instances, the mechanisms which these societies have devised to avert the threats to autonomy and identity become ineffective and ultimately incite greater situations of danger.

All the foci of fear we have explored in this essay appear to have had direct objective referents in real relationships, situations, and environmental hazards, with the exception of witchcraft, where sources of threat are real enough but restructured and hidden in the composite character of a human evil-doer. Do all culturally patterned foci of fear have objective bases? Here we have an exciting area for investigation which carries sociophobics beyond any one discipline and invites involvement in a wider range of conceptual frameworks. My feeling is that cultures can impose as irrational a set of fears on their members as ones having bases in objective reality, but a lot depends on whose perspective we are utilizing. Males in Sukumaland may consider female fears associated with marriage as irrational, but we have seen that in some instances there is real cause fo fear. Warriors are encouraged to deny fear where the rest of society insists fear inheres. The ethnographer considers witches symbolic representations of social evils, but the Sukuma identify real persons in their communities as evil-doers and mark them with danger. Perhaps we can root culturally patterned fears in ecological adjustments. There are already such examples in the literature (avoidance of areas of sleeping sickness causing tsetse fly which Hausa define as residences of dangerous spirits, Niehoff 1966: Ch 7; *ples masalai* among the Fore of Papua, New Guinea, Lindenbaum 1979). We might even find such environmentally protective functions in the geography of fear discussed for the Maasai and Sukuma. But, as valuable as such an exercise would be, I think we will still discover that cultures do create areas of danger and threat where from an objective view none exist, ignore or court dangers which are real and not just perceived, and develop inadequate means of coping with threats concurrent with patterning fear around "real" referents. At the onset of this rather challenging and exciting adventure, it is encouraging to know that others have ventured perhaps inadvertently on the same journey and that contemporary explorers need only discover contexts whereby their experiences become useful. I can only encourage those who take it up to be somewhat like the Maasai warrior and his Sukuma dance society counterpart, who take the risk of venturing beyond socially defined boundaries and into the "wild" and unknown. The kind of intellectual contamination which such forays can produce may prove ultimately of immense theoretical and methodological worth, which the threats to one's conceptual safety and disciplinary comfort are indeed small prices to pay.

Notes

1. This essay is a revised and expanded version of a paper given at the first symposium on Sociophobics at Ball State University in 1981. I owe a great debt to the participants of that symposum for their comments and their contributions. Much, if not most, of my thinking about the subject has come from their stimulus. I am also very much in debt to Ndugu Rueben Ole Kuney, M.A., Monduli, Tanzania and Reverend Franz Mol, MHM, Narok, Kenya, who graciously responded to my appeal for help in better understanding how fear is culturally defined among the Maasai. In this connection I am also grateful to Ndugu Marko Ole Paayo, Olduvai, Tanzania, for similar help. Their patience in answering what to them must have seemed like both obvious and naive questions is an indication of their good will, trust, and patience. I must admit, however, that the interpretations given in this paper are mine, so as to absolve them of any misconceptions about a people whom they know so well.

2. Maasai women have another recourse only resorted to in extraordinary circumstances which require that feminine outrage be expressed collectively, supported by divine sanction, against a male.

3. Llewelyn-Davies writes that such a man is called *ol kirikito* among the Kenya Maasai. He is considered to be a worthless person by his community, yet a person of danger because of his self-inflicted poverty and envy of others. He has destroyed the foundations upon which respect and male authority are built. On the other hand, given the uncertainties inherent in the Maasai environment, it is always possible for a "good" man to lose everything almost overnight through a sudden disaster. He and his dependents are welcomed into the sympathetic and generous bosom of kin, affines, and peers and is usually given the livestock needed to start over.

Fear of economic disaster must be a powerful incentive to maintain the consistent care in planning and vigilance surrounding livestock keeping in Maasailand, and a great stimulus for the Maasai to so readily adopt modern disease control measures. At the same time this fear arouses great reluctance to adhere to management schemes based on livestock quotas, for one of their major precautions against economic failure is to keep many more animals than are needed at any one time for a family as insurance against loss.

The Sukuma precaution in the area of livestock keeping is different. They tend to divide livestock into smaller groups and farm them out in diverse areas. In this manner, a disease or some other problem would only affect one section of the herd. Maasai do not customarily use this practice. I suspect that a livestock owner wants to have greater control over his herd than scattering it would permit. The only reason is that, unlike the Sukuma, for whom livestock are in some ways luxuries, adjunctive to subsistence, the products of Maasai animals are the basis of subsistence and thus would be needed where the family resides.

4. Both societies are most concerned that a household be characterized by domestic concord. Maasai women of one household perform a great many of their daily tasks together: gathering firewood, trekking for water, etc. They have good reason to do so in addition to the congeniality that can alleviate collective

drudgery. In Maasailand, there is always safety in numbers, not so much against other people but against predators. Within the home, women also do not appear to be stingy about sharing resources with one another.

Sukuma wives tend to operate under a more formal set of domestic obligations which require collective labor, especially in the household's common fields. This more consistent involvement in promoting the common good may have its darker side in fostering discord resulting from measuring individual responsibilities and rewards against perofmrnace. Where the Maasai appear to trust in their ideal of males' adherence to a model of proper use of authority, the Sukuma appear to trust formally in their ideal notions of cooperation. Both ideals of course get greatly transmuted in reality. Although I have no hard data to back me up, I would opine that co-wife conflict is much more covert, intense, and devastating among the Sukuma than among the Maasai where domestic responsibilities are more clearly defined and individualized.

5. From a western perspective it seems patently unfair to place the burden of infertility only on females, as the Maasi and Sukuma do; however, they are certainly aware that males can be infertile as well as impotent. The problem is that, given the relative freedom in choosing sex partners who are not spouses, especially among the Maasai, women who do not bear children are either very unlucky in their choices of sexual partners or else absolutely faithful to an infertile spouse (which certainly is possible). Otherwise they would be infertile.

6. Schuchat and Walder's paper, prepared for the second Sociophobics symposium in Vancouver, 1984, presents some interesting parallels between the practice of Maasai warriors and Sukuma dance society members and therapeutic measures used to help Americans resolve various phobias. Both warriors and dance society members deliberately break down the barriers of fear by venturing into areas considered dangerous. In the therapeutic process which Schuchat and Walder describe, phobics are encouraged to utilize an in vivo approach to their fears which involves among other things desensitization to the situation feared, rehearsal of appropriate actions to be taken in the situation, and finally cognitive restructuring. Maasai courting times and places of danger and Sukuma daring to handle creatures defined as dangerous are in a sense overcoming "phobias" dictated by their cultural traditions. Of course, in their cases, objects, places, and times defined as dangerous objectively are. An interesting area for further investigation is how different cultures structure such therapies. The one described by Schuchat and Walder, with its emphasis on goal setting, education, Z"hot lines," etc. are very much in keeping with an American process of understanding how control is achieved. What can we learn from the ways by which other cultures encourage their members to overcome fears?

7. Under some circumstances membership in a dance society creates problems similar to that of warriors in dealing with their communities and families. In Sukumaland, domestic difficulties begin to arise when a youth begins to get so involved in a dance society's activities that he begins to neglect other responsibilities at home. With its powerful surrogate father and kinship orientation, the mbina has great potential of encouraging conflicts in father/son relationships. Most Sukuma fathers do not encourage their sons to become dance society

members. They positively discourage daughters from participation, fearing that they will learn "bad habits" as a result of their participation.

8. Bailey (1983) provides us with a parallel to the training of warriors in the conditioning process of soldiers in the British army. He distinguishes between two kinds of selves which this kind of training fosters. The first, the civic self, involves deliberate suppression of one's individuality and personal display of emotion, for "efficient warfare requires the elimination of excessive fear and excessive impetuousity and is better conducted by concerted action than by individual initiative" (p. 52). This form of self is contrasted to the tactical self in which there is a similar suppression of personal emotion in order that a person not become victimized by "losing his cool" in situations of challenge. Both selves absolutely require complete control of emotions, but for different reasons. Where the former is an imposition to maintain and protect the social body, the latter becomes a device in a person's quest for gain or power. This distinction correlates nicely with the two goals of e murano, to devote oneself completely to service to the community, but at the same time to serve one's age set—and oneself.

9. There is a consistency with which the Sukuma deal with supernatural powers through persons. Just as revealed witches are believed to act with cause or reason, normally some breach of ideal social behavior against them, so also do ancestors appear to be relatively thin skinned. They are viewed as frequently demanding that their descendents make restitution for improper acts, becoming distant monitors of behavior with the powers to intervene in human affairs. In spite of this belief, the Sukuma take as many risks in incurring ancestral wrath as they do in courting revenge of witches.

10. Obtaining legal title to land was a great incentive for many Maasai to enthusiastically promote the organization of ranching associations, but few titles were forthcoming, for application as an association required completion of a complex set of documents, one of the most important of which was a proposed range management plan which included an agreement to adhere to stock quotas. Another reason was political. In some areas of Maasailand, non-Maasai, fearing that such a title would mean their exlusion from water supplies, were able to convince local officials to block the process, at least temporarily.

11. Carrying these visible symbols of Maasainess into the public, has for some time created real problems for all Maasai. Various administrative powers in Maasailand have gone to great lengths to discourage wearing traditional attire in dispensaries, cattle markets, hospitals, shops, and even in using public transport. They view the Maasai image as an insult to the country's efforts at modernization. Before I arrived in Maasailand in 1973, warriors were forbidden to use red ochre and the sources of the materials were closed. At one point warriors *ol taika*, carefully braided and tended pigtails which are sources of great pride and markers of entry into senior warriorhood, were snipped off in raids by police and sometimes soldiers at cattle markets. In frustrated and impotent rage, many warriors went into empushuna. One edict which naively got brief promotion

was to the effect that Maasai women were to abandon their skin skirts and capes and replace them with "modern" dresses. This incited a riot of fury from women who cursed their local elders who had agreed to the edict and were only persuaded with some difficulty not to march to the capital to bear their outrage to the president.

6
The Production and Management of Fear in Urban Contexts

DeWight R. Middleton

Our emotions are intimate and ever-present ingredients in the raw material of our daily lives. Our emotional substance, like most of the raw material that we carry with us into this world, is toned and shaped by the cultural environment in which we mature. In the context of particular shaping and tempering processes, we learn a style of emotional expression that we share with other members of our culture and that defines for us the appropriate circumstances under which we will display grief, joy, anger, or fear, as well as the intensity with which we will express these feelings. Much like sexual behavior, members of society share a collective interest in managing individual emotional expression because unexpected and inappropriate displays of strong feelings are potentially disruptive—they tear at the social fabric. Once subordinated to cultural direction, on the other hand, emotions are turned effectively to the cause of social cohesion. But studying this process is difficult. In the excursions of social scientists into the mazeway of human behavior, the cultural regulation of individual emotional expression has proved to be an elusive and formless theme, a shadowy subject that shows itself to the interested eye only fleetingly. Rarely—as this collection of essays makes abundantly clear—have the emotions occupied the center of attention. In an attempt to remedy that somewhat, this paper explores the cultural production and management of fear in urban contexts. Because of the inchoate state of our subject, it will be necessary to give careful attention to the general perspective taken here before focusing directly on urban contexts.

Traditional Problems
in the Epistemology of Emotions

Izard (1977:496) observes that "the term emotion is a chronic source of controversy and misunderstanding in science, art, and literature, as well as in everyday life." This confusion is due principally to the "complexity, flexibility, and relative invisibility" of emotions—properties that plague their epistemological status. The research literature shows clearly that psychologists themselves have found it easier and more productive to focus on cognitive and perceptual behavior rather than on the mercurial stuff of emotions. To explicate the view of a social science of the emotions, we must examine at least cursorily the problems of definition and observability noted by Mandler. We must also explore some of the basic reasons behind the history of the indifference of social science to emotional phenomena.

Inquiry into the nature of emotional phenomena is a task undertaken traditionally by philosophers, psychologists, and physiologists. From Aristotle's priority of the mind to Cartesian dualism and Gilbert Ryle's critique thereof, Western philosophers have argued the enigma of mind-body relationships at length. Basically, argument centered on questions of the degree to which mind and body are independent, whether one entity is more determinative in its influence than the other, and a host of derived questions that need not concern us here. Emotions were assumed to be located in the realm of the body, and ideas in the realm of the mind. Emotions and ideas were considered given—properties of the species—and thus their origins were not questioned. These philosophical issues guided early psychologists in their initial explorations of the emotional landscape by the fundamental way in which they, collectively, framed their argument.

In an early and widely influential work, William James (1884) reversed the view of Aristotle and those who followed him by awarding emotions priority over the mind, and thus, with the aid of a Danish physiologist named Lange, induced later psychologists to devote their efforts to describing the physiology of emotional states in the belief that in doing so they were describing the emotions. Walter Cannon (1927) directed a devastating criticism at the James-Lange position by noting, among other things, that emotional behavior need not be accompanied by visceral arousal and that, as a matter of experimental fact, there is no correlation between different arousal states; only a single, global state of arousal exists.

Although psychologists have become increasingly uncomfortable with the obvious over-simplification of the traditional view, a more attractive alternative model has only recently surfaced in the form of cognitive priority. Commenting on experiments involving injections of adrenalin, Mandler (1975:100) observes that we should not be surprised to discover that adrenalin injections do not produce qualitatively different emotional states unless they are accompanied by the cognitive interpretations that serve to give the emotion a particular quality, or identity. In other words, it is the mind (more accurately cognitive processes) that imparts meaning to general states of visceral arousal. The implication of this view of the psychologist is that he must develop an explanatory model of the emotions that includes both individual disposition and environmental situations—a model that promises to be more appropriate to the actual complexity of emotional states.

As Ryle (1967[1949]:424) points out, Cartesian thought distinguishes that which is of the body, "the outer," from that which is of the mind, or "the inner." As long as emotions are defined as visceral phenomena, they lie in realm of the outer, but when factors of cognition are introduced, the emotions recede to the domain of cognition and appear, because of their disembodiment, to become inaccessible to direct observation. Today, we possess abundant evidence for the existence of a complex relationship between mind and body. This fact is dramatically demonstrated in the current use of biomedical feedback techniques to control certain medical conditions. What is less certain is the precise nature and mechanics of such mind-body transactions.[2] Given the greater role of cognition, the question naturally arises as to how we can observe the quality of "internal" emotional transactions except through relatively "unreliable" reports based on individual introspection. This condition may pose a serious epistemological problem for the psychologist, but not for the social scientist, because as social creatures humans communicate feelings as well as ideas and in the act of communication, inaccessible emotions are objectified.

It is precisely because humans must communicate (or express) emotions, that I take exception to Mandler's (1975:86) suggestion that folk beliefs about the reality of emotions are of little scientific value, although I appreciate his caveat that common language categories are vague and mislead people to believe that underlying conditions are invariant and real in some ontological sense. But if, as Mandler himself suggests, cognitive variables identify undifferentiated arousal states, what can the independent variable be but different situations, beliefs, and languages? The effects of these variables on emotional potential is exactly what I mean by the production and management of emotions.

Further, evidence is accumulating in favor of the influence of a specific cognitive organization and value system on the structure and interpretation of emotions. The Ifaluk of the Western Pacific, for example, define and sort words for different emotions based on the situation in which an emotion commonly occurs rather than on internal physiological states as is common in Western cognitive organization (Lutz 1982). I accept also the argument by Lutz (1982:125-126) that verbal reports should not be dismissed as unreliable in the tradition of "scientific" social observation, but considered as "cultural conventions for communicating personal experience to others or concealing it." The meaning of emotion words guides individual interpretation of context and of the individual's place in that context.

As Darwin (1872) noted long ago, the most primitive way in which we express emotions is through facial display. Izard's own strategy is to emphasize facial expression as a window opening on the region of the emotions, and as the most reliable transcultural method of "defining and assessing emotion constructs" (1977:498; see also Izard 1971). He cautions, however, that one must allow for degrees of voluntary and involuntary expression. It does happen, of course, that we consciously manipulate emotional expression in certain situations in order to mask the inner state from interpersonal perception. We also know that such attempts to conceal are not always successful because of the strength of the emotion, poor control, or a highly perceptive observer. Such interplay, of course, underscores the flexibility and richness of human emotions.

The works of Izard, Ekman (1974), and others produce substantial evidence that with respect to basic emotions such as happiness and sadness, anger, fear, surprise, and disgust, facial display is constant across cultures and thus constitutes a basic panhuman form of non-verbal communication. The conditions under which these emotions are evoked, however, are learned and therefore cross-cultural variables. Furthermore, it may be that these questions of definition and observability have been overstated because of the mistaken notion that what is emotional is individual and subjective, rather than social and objectified. While these influences explain some of the reason for the avoidance of emotions in the social sciences, we must look in addition at other influences.

Fear of committing the fallacy of reductionism has influenced profoundly the roster of acceptable social research problems. Durkheim (1897) was the most persuasive thinker in this regard. He explained the incidence of suicide by reference to social facts, not psychological processes. The cause of suicide, he argued, is to be discovered in various forms of social cohesion, not in the dynamics of individual psychological conflicts, which are held constant. Attempting to explain the larger social fact by reference to the smaller individual unit is to engage in unacceptable reductionist argument. In this view, allegedly subjective states are left to the psychologists, thus placing them outside the normal scope of social science. I disagree. It would appear that emotions, like the causes of suicide, are both individual and social, and the latter dimension is appropriate for social science investigation.

A second reason for the indifference of social science to emotional phenomena is rooted in its zealous attempt to emulate the spectacular successes of the "hard" sciences. Driven by this enthusiasm and by a positivist confidence in "objective" measurement, the social sciences struck boldly and naively into an uncharted universe of reliability and replication criteria, statistical matrices, and the hallowed "hypothetico-deductive" method. Such an approach fixes on external, easily countable, and immediately observable social phenomena, but eschews the allegedly subjective and shadowy domain of the emotions. Similarly, behavioral psychologists have been exceedingly uncomfortable with the topic of emotions—a mentalistic term in their positivist minds (Mandler 1975:10).

This intellectual heritage and these mistaken ideas about the nature of human emotions are among the most important reasons in social science for neglecting the production and management of emotions.

Culture and the Experience of Emotion

One of the salient facts of human life, and the critical missing element in traditional models of the emotions, is that emotions are culturally learned and socially constructed. Humans are complex social creatures whose daily interaction hinges in large part on their communication of culturally shaped feelings. The content and malleability of emotions are characteristics embedded in individual and cultural experience. This premise was clearly stated by Hallowell (1974[1938]:251) some forty-five years ago:

> Since culture includes the content of socially transmitted experience to which each new individual born into a society is exposed, it provides the primary frame of reference to which all varieties of learned behavior may be related. With respect to emotions culture defines (a) the situations that will arouse certain emotional responses and not others; (b) the degree to which the response is supported by custom or inhibitions demanded; (c) the particular forms which emotional expression may take. It is to these norms that the individual will learn to accommodate his behavior and in terms of which his affective experience will function.

In the particular case of fear, culture structures dangers and responses of fear as well as institutionalized "alleviation of culturally constituted fears" (Hallowell 1974:251-252).

In spite of Hallowell's cogent observation, anthropologists have subsequently given little explicit attention to the subject, except in isolated cases, for example, in the work of LaBarre (1948), H. Geertz (1959), and Robarchek (1979). Izard (1977:503-506) points out, however, that many studies of the culture and personality genre implicitly assign emotional motivation (shame-guilt, fear-anxiety) an explanatory role.[2]

Some of the reasons for this indifference were noted earlier. But additional factors such as anthropological preoccupation with the role of cognition in human evolution and cultural adaptations, and the influence of linguistics on some early problems of culture and personality should be mentioned too.

The emotional style, or ethos, of a culture coordinates the emotional expression of its members. But delineating the ethos of a culture and specifying the processes by which individual expression is embraced and organized will not explain all variations from the norm because of differences in individual life histories (Hallowell 1977:250-251; Robarchek 1979:563). These variations are to be expected, but they do not diminish the role of culture. The fallacy in the assumption by some early theoreticians of an extreme goodness of fit between individual personality organization and cultural configuration is clear (Bock 1980:32-33). Wallace's (1970:22-23) subsequent substitution of the concept of the "organization of diversity" for "replication of uniformity" more accurately mirrors the actual case. Individuals will usually try to adjust their emotional behavior to what is valued. Although it may sometimes be the case, we should not imagine a thin cloak of observance thrown loosely over wildly divergent emotions and motivations. Individuals do, in fact, internalize culturally defined dangers and fears in addition to those that are idiosyncratic, and, even in the latter case, they often attempt to rationalize their phobias in some more relevant and acceptable manner (Hallowell 1974:261).

Contexts of Fear

The stance I take here is that any emotion an individual feels is one that he must express eventually to others, and in that act of expression the emotion becomes objectified as a social fact. For social animals such as ourselves, the proposition that emotions can be held but not expressed generally makes little sense, except as culturally learned masking behavior. Even such an internally focused view as psychoanalysis is based on indirect, or deflected, expression of feelings "imprisoned" in the subconscious. Whether emotions are expressed directly or indirectly they are culturally mediated and contextually sensitive. Our job is to learn the collective language of emotional expression in its various transformations as Freud learned to decipher expressions of intrapsychic conflict, or, indeed as we all learn in our infancy to read the facial expression of our parents.

I assume further that the feelings we label fear are in the neonate a general, undifferentiated emotional state—a potentiality in Scruton's (see this volume) terms—that becomes subjectively differentiated during the process of socialization as a result of learned cognitive processes which identify and define particular situations as dangerous (Robarchek 1979:557). The general potential to fear is channeled, focused, and attached by particular social and cultural expriences. I see no compelling reason in this initial inquiry to define fear in any precise or operational manner, but I proceed rather on the assumption that we, the species, know fear intimately, and at a primitive level regardless of the name we give it.[3] The degree to which fears expressed at the cultural level of analysis are isomorphous with those held individually is probably great, but certainly not total. We have no evidence that warrants expectation of complete congruence, and plenty to the contrary. We know that culture sharing is incomplete along dimensions of age and sex even in very simply organized societies, and so we should anticipate significantly wide intracultural variation in urban contexts.

Anthropologists routinely employ contextual interpretation of cultural practices and beliefs as they are discovered in specific social, historical, and natural settings. The concept of cultural adaptation, for example, has figured heavily in studies of cultural evolution; it directs attention to critical features of the environment to which a group must adapt in order to survive. The role of cultural context in shaping the emotions has recently been described by Robarchek (1977:774):

> Culture, then, while not the only source, is a major source for the attribution of *meaning* to situations inducing arousal. This attribution of meaning is central to the process of evaluation and interpretation that determines which specific emotion is experienced. Thus, cultural beliefs define certain situations as threatening and the appropriate emotion as fear. Other situations may be defined as thwarting and the appropriate emotion defined as anger.

Regulating time, place, and degree of emotional response to particular situations is a critical element of the cultural task of mustering and channeling individual motivation and commitment in adaptive processes.[4] To the degree that such regulatory practices produce a consistent unity of expression, we may speak of emotional style. Emotional style is also known as ethos. The term "ethos" denotes one particular kind of "object" to which value is apt to be commonly attached by members of a society. That "object" is style of emotional quality of socially patterned behvior (Wallace 1970:145). Thus style, or ethos, is achieved by centering emotional expressions on valued attitudes and symbols. The process of molding emotional expression is most easily observed in smaller, tradition-oriented communities with greater uniformity of behavior, but in large urban settings I would anticipate discovering a number of smaller communities exhibiting somewhat different emotional styles. The more heterogeneous the urban context, the more likely it will be that such communities will exist. The presence of ethnic groups is an obvious example. In the remainder of this study, I will focus on the particular emotion of fear as it is produced and managed in urban contexts.

The Rise of Urban Life
and the Transformation of Fear

The specific expression of fear will vary in content and intensity according to sociocultural context. Thus, the rise of urban society presents to people new challenges and opportunities, new problems and fears. This is not an entirely novel idea, for references to the shifting fears and dangers generated in different places and epochs are common and have received sporadic recognition. In his remarkably detailed but conceptually weak compilation of fears, Tuan (1979) notes that Medieval, Renaissance, and American Colonial citizens feared falling and burning buildings (1979:149, 153-54), getting lost in an urban maze (1979:150), and being run over by hoof or wheel (1979:150); they feared disease, violence, and crime, different social groups and classes, and public disorder and rebellion. These fears are contrasted to those of the countryside where residents feared bandits, famine, harshness of nature, wild pigs and wolves, and becoming a farm laborer or migrant worker (1979:130-144). In rough summation, it is clear that the roster of salient fears in early cities was shaped by problems in designing the built environment on a new scale, and by perturbations in relationships among distinct social groups who nonetheless shared space. Tuan's treatment of rural and urban differences in the landscape of fear is essentially a counting and sorting exercise covering an enormous range of time and territory, but it does suggest that more systematic exploration of this theme would be worthwhile.

The hallmark of urban society is the organization of social life on a vastly different scale. In his classic examination of the social consequences of size, density, and heterogeneity of urban life, Wirth (1964[1938]) pays little attention to emotional style and adjustment; he focuses instead on aspects of cognition and social organization. He describes the sophisticated, rational urbanite who is free of the personal and emotional controls of intimate groups (1964:71-72). He emphasizes the qualities of utility and efficiency, and recognizes the priority of the clock and the traffic signal. Indeed, it is the lack of emotional involvement among urbanites that Wirth stresses. Wirth's ideas have received voluminous criticism and revision through the decades, but little of it has been addressed to his distorted image of the emotionless urbanite. Even

Milgram's (1970) famous response to the notion of "psychic overload" stressed social organization and cognitive processes. Clearly, much of Wirth's work does deal indirectly with the emotional dimension of urban life, but in this he is only exemplary of the social science tradition against which I argue.

In her recent study of urban danger, Merry (1981:165) attempts to delineate contrasting urban and rural profiles of fear:

> The resident of a small-scale society is afraid of accidents, wasting disease and death; the urbanite particularly fears violent attacks and neighborhood change. The causes of misfortune are also perceived differently. A person in a small-scale society believes that many misfortunes are caused by the action of supenatural forces propelled by another's ill will: the urbanite sees his misfortune as the undeserved consequences of random hostile acts as committed by others. Yet in both kinds of society those who suffer misfortune do not know exactly whom to blame, nor is there any obvious connection between perpetrator and misfortune.

This general characterization of urban-rural differences with respect to danger is suggestive, but needs to be anchored in specific, detailed studies—as Merry, in fact, proceeds to do. Many more are needed.

In the present context, however, a more relevant and stimulating proposition is contained in Merry's assertion that danger, and by extension fear, emerges from the organization of social relationships which differs in fundamental ways in rural and urban societies. She also observes (1981:196) that:

> The ability of a small-scale society to maintain social order depends on the extent to which its members are incorporated into networks of ongoing relationships that they wish to preserve and on the degree to which rules, norms, and customs of behavior are shared. Urban settings characterized by transiency and heterogeneity lack these social characteristics, and consequently have diminished informal control.

Merry suggests further that danger becomes a serious public issue in large cities with diverse populations "only" under conditions "of rapid growth, social change, and deepening class cleavages" (1981:214). The supposition that danger and fear arise from problems in social relationships is a familiar one to anthropologists who are accustomed to predicting the pattern of witchcraft accusations as a function of fissures at the weakest points of social organization. The link between emotions and social organization is to be seen not only in the fears or joys produced by the state of social relationships, but also in the ways in which, as Siegel (1955) suggests, emotions and emotional style serve organizational purposes.

The urban revolution provoked a dramatic shift in the character of ancient human adaptations to confront the new challenges of life amidst social and cultural complexity, in the context of a built environment, organized on a scale previously unimagined. Such adaptive shifts no doubt entailed shifts in emotional stimuli and responses to a degree as yet undiscovered.

The immediate task, however, is to muster specific examples of the production and management of fear in urban contexts. Toward this end, the remaining sections of this paper are organized along traditional lines of urban inquiry: sociocultural diversity using the example of ethnicity; levels of organization with particular reference to the domains of home, neighborhood, and public space; and architecture, and space utilization.[5] Structuring inquiry along these familiar lines should provide a better sense of the research potential inherent in the topic.

Sociocultural Diversity: Ethnicity

Given the intensity of emotions that is so easily sparked in ethnic groups, it is remarkable to discover that any systematic appreciation of the role of emotional shaping in ethnic groups is absent in the literature of social science. Indeed, older studies of prejudice and frustration-aggression came closer to the mark, although ultimately missing it. More recent theoretical perspectives such as Barth's emphasis on boundary maintenance, Cohen's stress on symbolism, and various continuing views of ethnic groups as political and economic interest groups rather than passive repositories of transported traditions, still provide no integral role for emotional sharing and communication in their conceptual designs. In his introduction to a number of articles collected under the label, "The New Ethnicity," Bennett (1975:7) describes "the new ethnicity: the organizing of a group for bargaining purposes that proclaims its rights to resources by its badges, that is, its outward display of cultural symbols and its (hopefully) inner sense of cognitive and emotional unity." Consistent with my argument, the ensuing articles do not address themselves to the subject of "inner" emotional unity, nor to the cultural direction of emotional expression; some do probe issues of cognition. Again, assigning emotions an "inner" quality is to dismiss them from further study.

The subject of ethnic symbols offers us further opportunity to clarify our approach to emotions. Note Cohen's (1974:x) view of symbols: "Symbols are thus essentially objective, not subjective forms. They may be originally the spontaneous creation of specific individuals going through subjective experiences, but they attain an objective existence when they are accepted by others in the course of social interaction within a collectivity." His argument parallels my position: Emotions clearly are held by individuals but they are objectified and enter the domain of social science when they are shared and communicated within a collectivity. Cohen (1974:xi), however, is also quite explicit on the emotional impact of ethnic symbols: "Unlike signs, symbols are not purely cognitive constructs, but are always emotive and connotative. . . . In situations where ethnicity is a relevant issue, labels such as 'Jews,' 'Negroes,' or 'Catholics,' (as the case may be) are not neutral intellectual concepts but symbols that agitate strong feelings and emotions." Because Cohen is most interested in what people do rather than in their motives, intellectual or emotional, he gives no further consideration to the emotional element, and here I depart from his viewpoint. Cohen observes that individuals can commit public acts for different reasons. It is clear, of course, that public adherence to norms often blankets a variety of individual motives, emotions, and intensities of commitment, but this point can be over-emphasized. Systematic departures from stated norms are among the well documented facts of social life. Ethnic group members can commit themselves and adjust their behavior around important group symbols out of dispassionate self-interest as well as emotional attachment.[6]

Emotional style is among the common distinguishing features of ethnicity. A cohesive, functioning ethnic group charges key values and symbols with emotional content as an adaptive strategy for survival or for competitive edge. Members of other groups perceive and react to emotional style as well as to language and costume. In the early decades of this century, for example, the Latin community in Tampa, Florida was separated from the Anglo population not only by residence, language, and wealth, but also by emotional style (Middleton 1981). Anglos considered Latins fiery, irresponsible, and generally ruled by emotions, while Latins thought anglos cold, calculating, and lacking in emotional involvement with life. Within the Latin community lived Cubans, Afro-Cubans, Spaniards, and Italians who, although they suffered internal conflicts among themselves, were unified in part by their common Mediterranean emotional style. Because the cultural differences among them were small compared to the perceived gulf between them and the Anglo population, the various Latin groups more easily and accurately understood the meaning of one another's emotional expression. Successful entrepreneurs who operated across Anglo-Latin boundaries no doubt had to decipher emotional expression as well as language.

The role of fear and misinterpretation in ethnic conflicts is an all too frequent theme in the study of ethnic conflicts, and they are exacerbated by competition over scarce resources as was the case in Tampa. Merry notes in her study of crime in a multiethnic neighborhood, that ethnic groups may scapegoat others out of fear. In this case, "crime serves as an idiom for expressing and legitimating the fear of the strange and the unknown" (1981:14). The crime issue "justifies and reinforces hostility that stems from class conflict and racial and ethnic differences" (1981:15).

Many observers have described urban situations where close contact between groups is regarded as dangerous and to be avoided at the risk of pollution and negative sanction. In two frequently cited examples, Cohen (1969:53-54) records Hausa fears of contact with Yoruba women, and Mayer (1961) reports the fear that Red Xhosa men hold of the temptations of School women in East London. Fearful avoidance of alternative life styles is not limited to ethnicity as pointed out by Rainwater (1966:28) and Hannerz (1969:65-69). In heterogeneous urban places widely considered to be dangerous, behavior that is not understood in the sense of being predictable may readily evoke fear. One result of this condition is that many individuals tend to avoid strangers and other ethnics, and to withdraw into their own narrowly circumscribed world (Merry 1981:230-241). The greater the cultural difference, the less social interaction; thus the greater ease of communication between blacks and whites than between either of them and the Chinese (Merry 1981:238-239).

As Scruton comments in his introductory essay, the expression of fear is learned communication. We send messages about our own feeling which we expect usually to be received with empathy because they are shared feelings. When we express our fear of another ethnic group we convey a double loaded message of external difference on the one hand, and of internal solidarity on the other.

Urban Migrants and Changing Fears

Migrants to the city experience a change in cultural context, and a shift in emotional climate. The degree and nature of change depends of course on the interaction of a number of well documented variables such as push/pull motivations, educational level, age, sex, and social class. Of additional potential importance are the presence or absence of supportive kinsmen or fellow villagers, degree of cultural difference, and character of the city itself. Although migration does not necessarily require very great changes, depending on the degree of cultural difference, the evidence generally warrants the expectation that migrant adaptations will involve significant adjustments in interpersonal and intrapersonal emotion communication.

Migrants often find themselves in multiethnic areas where intense economic and political competition produce feelings of fear and hatred. Merry (1981) shows how the general threat of violence in a multiethnic neighborhood generates scapegoating behavior toward other ethnic groups. Such fear serves to strengthen internal solidarity and clearly demarcate ethnic boundaries. Douglas and Wildavsky (1982:2) observe that fear of risk, and the confidence people have in facing it, "has something to do with knowledge and something to do with the kind of people we are." In other words, fears have something to do with who we are, what we know, and how we feel about that identity and knowledge. Identity, knowledge, and emotions are key dimensions of self and group that undergo modification in form and intensity in a different cultural context.

Migrant adaptations to cities furnish a natural laboratory for the study of changing profiles of fear. They offer us an opportunity to observe processes by which urban groups produce, rank, and communicate fear.

Levels of Urban Analysis

Because of the sheer number of individuals that come to share a common space, the achievement of urban life necessitated the organization of human relationships on a vast new scale. As cities grew and their populations surged, the social distance between private world and public domain widened dramatically and the gap between them was filled with neighborhoods and various associations. These groups and associations served to buttress the individual against the full impact of the city, and to mediate his interaction with various elements of it. In this section, I attempt to elucidate patterns of fear in cities on three familiar levels of analysis, the household, the neighborhood, and public places.

Households

The residence in which people sleep, eat, and relax is usually considered to be their first line of defense against the dangers and threats of the urban environment. Household membership is notoriously flexible cross-culturally and most social investigators have learned to be cautious about making facile assumptions regarding the social unit contained therein. Thus households in a particular context may harbor widely divergent combinations of kin and non-kin members (see Eames and Goode 1977:153-157). Two general factors affect household living arrangement. One well documented influence is that of larger economic forces that often deliver devastating blows to the integrity of the household unit and provoke a reorganization of domestic relationships—a reminder that the household is only a refuge, not a fortress. The other important factor is the degree of mutual support expressed in terms of a continuing exchange of goods, services, and understandings (Marshall 1977). The ties of "blood" relationships do not ensure effective exchange any more than other types of relationships preclude such transactions. It is important here to note that exchanges include emotional support and empathy as well as material goods and services (see Liebow 1967 and Stack 1974). Counting on others in the household to furnish emotional and economic support contributes to our sense of security as much as hard walls and locked doors contribute to our physical protection. .

The house in America has considerable symbolic value as well as its obvious sheltering function as Rainwater (1966:291) notes in his study of the infamous Pruitt-Igo federal housing project in St. Louis:

> Housing as an element of material culture has as its prime purpose the provision of shelter which is protection from potentially damaging or unpleasant trauma or other stimuli. The most primitive level of evaluation of housing, therefore, has to do with the question of how adequately it shelters the individuals who abide in it from threats in their environment. Because the house is a refuge from noxious elements in the outside world, it serves people as a locale where they can regroup their energies for interaction with that outside world: There is in our culture a long history of the development of the house as a place of safety from both nonhuman and human threats, a history which culminates in guaranteeing the house, a man's castle, against unreasonable search and seizure. The house becomes the place of maximum exercise of individual autonomy, minimal conformity to the formal and complex rules of public demeanor. The house acquires a sacred character from its complex intertwining with the self and from the symbolic character it has as a representation of the family. This is a concise characterization of the house as a bulwark against various sources of urban danger. Thus the common technique among fearful residents of today's troubled cities of retreating to their homes where they remain behind locked doors. The security of the home despite its closed doors festooned with locks is certainly not complete. The home often is not very effective against the dangers of commercial exploitation, the "symbolic violence" of caretakers (or research teams), nor from the verbal assaults of neighbors (Rainwater 1969:292).

Houses and apartments are parts of larger structures and areas which tend to enhance or mitigate against security. The Pruitt-Igo Project was, from a human relations standpoint, poorly designed (Rainwater 1969, 1970; Yancey 1971). The poor design of structures contributes to the production of new fears because it sets up conditions—dark halls, cul-de-sacs, separation of play areas from domestic work areas and from public surveillance—that are exploited by deviant residents and strangers for violent purposes.

The household is the first line of defense against outside danger, but few individuals, even in neighborhoods with high crime rates, depend solely on this basic unit for complete support and protection.

Neighborhoods

The idea of neighborhood recognizes a sense of shared spatial identity based on common residence. Neighborhoods frequently, but not necessarily, are characterized by heavy emotional investment on the part of neighbors. The unity and distinctiveness of ethnic neighborhoods come immediately to mind as examples of emotional commitment. Neighborhoods are sometimes defined clearly and defended vigorously as Suttles (1968) reports in his study of the Addams area in Chicago, or as exemplified in the Latin community in Tampa, or loosely demarcated and undefended as observed in a neighborhood of Marita, Ecuador (Middleton 1974). Even in amorphous areas of ambiguous identity, residents cognize an immediate territory in the vicinity of their home where familiar but socially distant neighbors behave in more or less predictable ways. Routine behavior offers no surprises. It is not necessary for neighbors to know each other intimately to feel secure, because danger is perceived in the appearance of strangers whose behavior by definition, is unpredictable. As Merry (1981:14) suggests, there is an important difference between "real" risk and perceived risk. Neighbors in an area with a high crime rate may not express the greatest fear of crime; they have developed coping strategies that make them feel more secure in familiar surroundings. Part of their efforts to cope involve cognitive ordering of their environment, but part also includes behavioral strategies. In some dangerous places, for example, to know just one gang member or street corner regular is sufficient to secure a wary neighbor's safe passage through the area (Hannerz 1969:69).

The neighborhood is an intermediate order of urban activity of variable importance depending on local urban structure and dynamics. Ethnic neighborhoods are, again, particularly relevant examples of important arenas of activity. Ethnic lifeways supported by neighborhood stores, churches, factories, and clubs are likely to be especially vital and cohesive. Such high degrees of "institutional completeness" (Breton 1964), as in the early years of Tampa's Latin community, provide a firm and critical social foundation for a cohesive neighborhood. When this institutional structure begins to disintegrate, however, so does the strength of social relationships. As the support structure deteriorates, for example, the appearance of increasing numbers of transients and strangers whose behavior is not understood and who appear to operate outside the bounds of traditional norms and expectations produces new fears.

The well known strategy of "block busting" employed by urban real estate speculators seizes on these developing fears and feeds them, hoping to induce people to sell quickly and cheaply. The more neighbors sell and move out of the area, the more others fear becoming stranded—a vulnerable island in a sea of strange faces and behaviors. Mobile friends and neighbors tend to put social distance as well as spatial distance between them and their former neighbors. On the other hand, those who are caught up in urban relocation projects find that a new location entails fundamentally altered social networks and subsequently they may experience a new vulnerability. Under such stress, they may feel an intense desire to return to the old neighborhood regardless of its changing character (Fried 1963).

Those residents of lower class and ethnic neighborhoods who travel to the government and business center of the city to conduct necessary business find themselves engaging in transactions characterized by social class differences in power and authority. The unfamiliarity of the place and of the faces contrasts with those of the neighborhood and produces fear. Such fearful interactions are not usually made easier by the bureaucrats and clerks who readily capitalize on the discomfort of their visitors.[7]

Public Places: Appearances, Locations, and Dangers

Transient encounters among strangers are among the unavoidable elements of everyday urban life. Such "traffic relationships" (Hannerz 1981) are generally routine and safe because they are governed largely by internalized rules of public demeanor, and because behavior toward strangers is cued by "appearances and locations" (Lofland 1973:22). Behavior in the public arena is cued by categorical and easily observable characteristics such as age, sex, race, and dress. These social flags aid in establishing the primary identity of strangers as members of a group or category rather than marking their individuality. Moreover, we make these identifications in context so that, for example, the flag we interpret as non-threatening in one location might in another be seen as a flag of danger. Lofland (1973:28) suggests that the preindustrial city was characterized by mixed public space use and overt heterogeneity of populace, while the modern city features specialized space use and masked heterogeneity; the preindustrial city is dominated by "appearential ordering," and the modern city by "spatial ordering" (1973:28). Both ordering mechanisms are present to a degree in both types of cities.

These "solutions" to problems of ordering relationships among strangers in public places do not eliminate sources of urban danger, but they are effective in varying degrees. Lofland (1973:79-87) suggests that "appearential" cues are becoming less reliable in the modern city because there are fewer uniforms, hence the ascendancy of specialized space as the predominant cue. A reduction in reliability of basic cues should result generally in a heightened sense of danger and feelings of fear, and the design of buildings and spaces may either heighten or reduce perception of danger and fear.

In close encounters with strangers in public places we perceive the social flags, read facial expressions, and interpret feeling states such as anger, fear, or disinterest. While making these interpretations we attempt to manage our own expression. Urbanites often adopt neutral body language, minimize expressivity in facial expression and avoid body and eye contact in an attempt to fashion a public shield (Lofland 1973:140-157). Outside the shelter of the home or the familiarity of the neighborhood, we manage more carefully our expressive behavior (Goffman 1971). We don a mask not just to ward off immediate threats and unwanted interaction, but as an everyday matter of adaptation to passing strangers. In his provocative study of bathers on a urban public beach, Edgerton (1979) describes a complex repertoire of cognitive and behavioral strategies, including some of those noted by Lofland, that strangers employ in maintaining public order and avoiding conflict in what are often crowded and stimulating circumstances. An urbanite who matures in the city learns to read and to manage as a matter of habit and survival, while a rural migrant will have to learn upon his arrival.

The traffic of strangers in public places generally follows customary practices and we scan the flow routinely without necessarily experiencing fear. But in the cities of today, potential danger seems ever present. It seems plausible to suggest that in many cities both appearances and locations have become increasingly unreliable cues of danger and security.

The Built Environment

Urban structures and spatial organization are symbolic representations of the structure of constituent social relationships. The Pruitt-Igo low-income housing project stands as a symbol of power relationships—designed by those in power for those without power. Spaces and structures also communicate value. The Pruitt-Igo project replaced horizontal slums with vertical slums. Human behavior is influenced by the environment that humans build. Fundamental deficiencies in the design of the Pruitt-Igo projects encouraged violence and stimulated the arousal of negative emotions.

The nature of human interaction in the context of designed structures has been extensively explored by various scholars, Lynch (1960) and Newman (1973) being but two familiar examples, and now land use patterns are being subjected to the same scrutiny. Lofland suggests that modern cities rely on specialized land use as a primary behavior cue; a cue which is a symbolic expression of value and power. Perin (1977:3) states the case in cogent fashion: "Land-use planning, zoning, and development practices are a shorthand of the unstated rules governing what are widely regarded as correct social categories and relationships— that is, not only how land uses should be arranged, but how land users, as social categories, are to be related to one another." Perin then proceeds to decipher the social meaning of spatial arrangements by use of methods derived from semiotics. The fact that various policies and regulations stimulate anger and fear is well recognized, but the emotional aspect has received little explicit attention.

Discussion

A city is more than just a random collection of buildings and people; it is a dynamic field in which emotional phenomena of different orders are linked in a complex system of transactions. A city exhibits an ethos that blankets the diverse emotional communities which endure within it, and that is linked to an identity forged by citizens out of the raw material supplied by the natural setting, historical background, and human motivations. In responding to different challenges, citizens will necessarily fashion different identities with corresponding differences in ethos. The degree to which urban ethos is similar or different cross-culturally remains to be determined, but it may be expected that the usual combination of underlying similarity and particular variation in time and place will prevail.

In his examination of urban ethos in the South, Brownell (1975) suggests that urban boosterism is a critical ingredient in identity building because it musters support for, and justifies, social control and municipal development policies in the absence of institutional changes. The process of creating an urban ethos includes the use of metaphor, imagery, and symbol to communicate value and to arouse in citizens an emotional commitment to causes and plans. This may not be a wholly conscious and coordinated process, but the emergent ethos, regardless of the relative proportions of planned and unplanned activity, will reflect the structure of urban "power relations" (Cohen 1979:89). The focus of Brownell is on the arousal of pride and commitment in practices of boosterism; what we need to know more about is the role of fear in such practices. Because each city is a different context, the role may vary considerably.

Although this inquiry has been at best preliminary, it seems unassailable to conclude that a systematic examination of fear in urban contexts should furnish us with a substantial and more complete appreciation of the complex nature of human life organized on a large scale and contained in a built environment. Given what has been said about the question of cultural shaping of emotional potential, the more general project might proceed via the following research topics, which though by no means exhaustive, do nonetheless apply to a variety of cultural contexts: (1) examining the role of fear as technique and content in basic processes of socialization (including schooling), and culture transmission; (2) delineating the media and symbols by which fear is expressed and communicated, and specifying rules of interpretation; (3) measuring the effects of such obvious variables as age, sex, class, and ethnicity, and others to be discovered, on the content and intensity of fears; (4) inspecting the nature and effectiveness of strategies of fear production and management as part of conscious attempts to muster commitment to groups and causes, or to create divisiveness; (5) investigating changing intensities and profiles of fear, and their alleviation in the context of social and cultural change; and (6) probing the relationships between fear and risk taking in creativity, innovation, and entrepreneurship, among other considerations.

Finally, let me state unequivocally that given the criticism of traditional "scientific" and "objective" social science and its indifference to emotional expression, the methods employed to answer these questions must contain a healthy admixture of more reflexive and interpretive attitudes—perhaps such as those espoused by hermeneutics and phenomenology where the roles of the observer and the observed in ordinary reality and analysis must be taken into account. Directing attention to the conditions under which fear arises from both the actor's and a wider anthropological viewpoint might restore some lost dignity to those we study and thus to ourselves, because we would be less ready to sacrifice our fellow humans on the altar of sacrosanct theories. Failure to build the emotional substance we bring with us into this world and into our intellectual analysis of the human condition is to deprive ourselves of a vital piece of humanity.

Notes

I am indebted to David Scruton for stimulating my interest in the subject of culture and emotion. I also wish to thank Ivan Brady for several productive discussions of the general importance of the subject to a reflexive and interpretive anthropology. Charles Bishop and Estelle Smith offered emotional support and some pointed questions. No one is, of course, responsible for what I have written here but myself.

1. Although I proceed on the assumption that a satisfactory definition of fear, or emotion, is not dependent on the detection (of the observer) of changing visceral states, we clearly stand on the threshhold of rapid advance in precise measurement and better understanding of body-mind mechanics. However, I would not anticipate such refinement in knowledge to alter my present stance.

2. In the literature of psychology, fear is often taken to be a response to specific stimuli, while anxiety is considered to be an unfocused state. This entire question needs a hard-nosed reexamination.

3. Definitions of fear often take as a critical event in the individual's response to the triggering stimulus the perception of his own state of arousal.

4. The role of emotions in an individual's adaptation to his own culture, and in a culture's adaptation to its environment needs systematic scrutiny. The ethnographies of Turnbull on the Pygmies of the Congo and on the Mountain Ik seem particularly rich in this regard. The adaptive problems and emotional styles of the two groups are strikingly different.

5. Several other topics could just as well be considered except for the lack of space. The roles of formal schooling and bureaucratic organization are two examples (see, for example, Wallace 1970:117-120 on the latter).

6. Studies of entrepreneurship, risk taking, innovation, striving and coping are heavily cognitive in orientation, and would probably benefit from reexamination along the dimension of emotions.

7. Again, studies of emotions take them as organization "problems" in motivation, communication and efficiency. Developing concerns regarding "burnout" and the problems of women in organizations may force a look at emotional concomitants. But the "social problem" cast of these developing concerns may prevent their being linked up with general theoretical issues such as those herein proposed.

7

Ethnographic Fieldwork
and the Worlds of the Phobic

Molly G. Schuchat
and Marcella G. Walder

Introduction

We propose to show that what are generally regarded as aberrant psychological conditions, phobias, the study and treatment of which have traditionally been in the hands of psychologists, can be looked at from a different set of principles. The thesis of this book is that fearing is a cultural experience, and while phobic anxieties may be extremely intense and seemingly unreasonable, there is no reason to regard them as a different order of experience from "ordinary" or "normal" fearing.

If fear acts are essentially cultural experiences, and the reactions to them essentially culturally sanctioned behaviors, what happens with respect to these when individuals and families move in and out of clan, class, community, or country? Such movements are increasingly common experiences in the modern world, on both voluntary and involuntary bases, as people leave their home cultures for others as immigrants, sojourners, and tourists. Paradoxically, agoraphobia, the most common phobia among Americans, involves paralyzing panic attacks at the very thought of leaving the house.

In this paper we are suggesting that anthropological field workers have certain significant behavioral features in common with people who are phobic. By comparing and analyzing these common features it should be possible to clarify some aspects of the nature of phobias and fieldwork. We are not saying the ethnographer is a phobic. We are using ethnographers as the means to an end. By attending to field work and culture shock, common features of our professional life, aspects of the lives of others in our native culture may be illuminated.

Basis of Comparison

All humans live in a world in which reality is experienced through symbols. The archetype of symbolic experience is provided by language. It is Scruton's contention, in another essay in this volume, that fearing is, in fact, a technique of communication, analogous to language. It is through culturally mediated symbols that culturally significant meanings are transmitted from sender to other, including self.

The universe each human occupies is an organization of symbols, with which we are at least workably comfortable, since we are familiar with them. Although no two symbolic universes can be identical, involving as they do uniquely individual life experiences, still, since the symbols are cultural instruments, social participation in the "same" symbol system provides a high degree of commonality of reality experience.

But the ethnographer and the phobic, both participants in the "same" symbolic structure/system, have in common with each other certain unsettling experiences that take each of them out of that symbolic universe. We propose to examine these departures to discover if they share qualities that will enable us to extrapolate from the situation of the ethnographer to that of the phobic.

The ethnographer and others entering a new culture frequently experience what has come to be called "culture shock." We propose to compare this with phobic behavior, wherein individuals go to enormous lengths to avoid a narrow or wide range of creatures, spaces, artifacts, activities, and relationships, because prior encounters have elicited intolerable physical discomfort.

In this way we will also see more clearly the perverse intrusion of an individual's culture into the larger, intercultural world. We hope that this may offer fresh insights into phobias and their treatment. It should also help to clarify problems in field work and ethnography. Perhaps it will lead to more solutions of the general problems of encounters between the private and the public cultures. And that should offer us greater satisfaction in bridging the chasms that gape in our increasingly atomized worlds.

The Ethnographer, Field Work, and Culture Shock

The core of anthropology is field work, which Leach (1971:3) calls an extremely traumatic kind of experience, where "the personal involvement of the anthropologist in his work is reflected in what he produces." What he produces, of course, is ethnography.

Ethnography is concerned with perspectives growing out of an interest in the interpretation of reality as seen by the group members. Agar (1980:195) describes the process as dialectic rather than linear, "best modeled by a pattern that is gradually discovered and interrelated with other patterns." Marcus and Cushman (1982:27) define it as an account resulting from having done fieldwork, "a relatively undisciplined activity, the folklore of which has given identity to an academic discipline. . . . Doing fieldwork is quite different from representing it with an ethnography."

Fieldwork involves direct, prolonged contact with group members, doing the work oneself, learning from informants, and seeking patterns. So to do it one delimits a field (a culture, geographic area, a cultural process, or product) and enters it, establishing contacts and, one hopes, rapport, learning the situation, observing events, individual behavior, and group interactions, taking endless notes with pencil, camera, recorder, collecting cultural material printed, sculpted, sewn, and cooked, and using oneself, trained as an instrument of observation and analysis. One acquires key informants, individuals to whom the ethnographer returns again and again over the course of field trips—experts who understand their society as participants although they may not previously have articulated this knowledge to themselves, let alone to others.

With these key informants the ethnographer repeatedly checks her own comprehensions and analyses. Other persons are interviewed, in a manner emphasizing the meaningfulness of insights gained from individual cases rather than analysis based on quantification. Data can be distorted through the inexperience of the observer and by physical and cultural limitations of the perceptions of events. Williams (1967:27) warns that interview data can be distorted through mechanisms for defense of the ego in operation in every human group and due to randomly distributed differences of capacities for learning and insight in a society. Human beings in every culture rationalize, project, and sublimate their desires, wishes, and fears.

Freilich (1977:3-37) points out that fieldwork in anthropology is both science and mystery, or rite of passage. Looking at it as science includes a knowledge of the language, a reading knowledge of the previous work in the area, as well as participation and interviews. Reliability checks are a part of this, as well as techniques for gathering, storing, retrieving, and analyzing material. There are time constraints on the field period, so an efficient use of time as well as concern for the reciprocities involved, are very necessary. This, of course, is also learned in doing the fieldwork. We suggest that it means you cannot say goodbye until you know how it is done.

The fieldworker has a role, ranging from going native to privileged stranger, but usually located somewhere in between. The less privileged a stranger, the greater the culture shock. Life in the field involves learning how to survive physically in the setting, whether it is an unfamiliar neighborhood of a well known city or a previously unmapped bit of jungle. It involves learning how to survive psychologically, as well, replacing old cultural rules with the integration of the aspect of physical survival, psychological comfort, pragmatic everyday rules, and the solution or acceptance of moral dilemmas presented by the juxtaposition of two divergent and perhaps completely unrelated systems. This all occurs, suggests Freilich, as the ethnographer is isolated from her culture of orientation, away from family or other familiars.

However, this may be as much an artifact of the American myth of independence as of fact in today's anthropology—or even much of yesterday's. Husbands, wives, children, significant others, and colleagues are hardly infrequent in the field, any more than imported cooks, scribes, interpreters, photographers, and visiting professors.

Williams (1967:27) explains how initial research activities may bring the new fieldworker problems of extra hospitality and the good humor of the community, with jokes at the field worker's expense, until she learns the local ropes. But as the forms for gift acceptance are learned, the greetings, the significance of the ways questions are asked, these data will provide a means for understanding behavior ranging from indications of direction through lifestyles of affirmation and negation, to postures typically indicating relaxation, acceptance, resentment, or hostility. Commenting on his own fieldwork among the Dusun, Williams reports that as a group they "consistently misled him concerning property, avoided talking about aggression while being highly aggressive, openly boasted of sexual conquests while actually being conservative in sex activities but gave precise, accurate, and consistently truthful answers to most difficult questions of religious behavior."

Leibow (1967:249) describing a field experience in retrospect, writes about perceptions of rapport between a white ethnographer and his street corner black male informants in urban America. His principal informant, Talley, confesses that he had lied to him for quite a while, but could no longer bear to have their friendship so shakily based. Liebow then goes on to say that when the word "nigger" was being used easily and conversationally or when, standing on the corner with several men, one would have a few words with a white passerby and call him a "white mother-fucker, I used to play with the idea that maybe I wasn't as much of an outsider as I thought. Other events, and later readings of the field materials, have disabused me of this particular touch of vanity."

Based on his field work in Zinacantan, Cancian (1967:1073) postulated more generally that "when an informant makes an error that results from lack of precise information, he is most likely to approximate the truth in terms that are meaningful to him."

In locating proper informants for a study of Hungarian refugees from the 1956 revolt against the Russian occupation, I cast a net among my American acquaintances, asking them to direct me to their refugee friends. The 1956 immigrants were called Freedom Fighters by themselves and by receptive Americans and, of course, the press. But I was making inquiries in 1967-8, eleven years later. Most of the folk to whom I was referred proved to be immigrants from previous waves of migration. However, the general American attitude was that all noble Hungarians (their friends) had to have been Freedom Fighters, which fact of our native prestige system I continually found useful to keep in mind both while seeking informants and understanding their experiences in the United States. We have to learn the fieldwork culture and also understand our own sufficiently well to be able to check, recheck, and capture these nuances.

Field workers must always be objective observers enough to inhibit their suspension of disbelief and yet participants enough to understand, if not share, behaviors—and emotions—that reinforce the values of the culture.

No matter how alone many of us feel we are in the field, Laura Bohannan (1964:174) summed up the initial stage in her novel of African fieldwork, describing the strain of being always on guard surrounded by curious people in another culture:

> But about all else, it was only in the privacy of my own hut that I could be my real self. Publicly I lived in the midst of a noisy and alien life. If I wanted conversation in my language, I had to hold it with myself . . . I could escape my cultural isolation only by being alone for a while every day with my books and my thoughts. It was the one means of hanging on to myself, of regaining my balance, of keeping my purpose in being out here before me, and of retaining my own values.

Direct exposure to an alien society produces feelings of disorientation and helplessness due to what is called culture shock. Oberg (1960:177) called it an "occupational disease" suffered by people who are introduced suddenly to a culture that is very different from their own. It is "precipitated by the anxiety that results from losing all our familiar signs and symbols of social intercourse, such as customs, gestures, facial expressions, or words." He first circulated this definition in the form of a memo widely used in overseas training programs in the late 1950s, when economic assistance was in its heyday and educational and cultural exchange in their ascendancy.

Anthropologists were hired to advise on how to cope with the phenomenon, drawing on their own background in culture crossing. Together with mercenaries and missionaries, they are the prototypical soujourners in other cultures, but their goal is neither conversion nor containment, but rather understanding. In the training situation, they were applying their understandings to preparing visitors for short term adjustment to new cultures where permanent settlement or understanding was not the purpose of residence amidst the alien corn.

Careful planning and sufficient money can insulate a traveler from the inconveniences of a strange environment. It is possible to go around the world sufficiently wrapped in a cultural bubble so there is no direct experience that is different from what one leaves at home. When you are with members of a group who share your culture you do not have to think about it, for you all know what to expect of one another, and the differences are only seen through the bubble, not heard, smelled, or felt. By living in an ethnic enclave, holding aloof from the alien society, many others besides such insulated travelers have built a stationary bubble within which they are able to survive and perpetuate themselves, even for many generations.

However, once removed from such insulation, culture shock can well set in. Bock (1970:x) in a reader published in the early 1970s, states that although it is largely an emotional matter, it also implies the attempt to understand an alternate way of life, by choice or out of necessity. He says that immigrants, refugees, and all kinds of travelers have been subject to it, in varying degrees. They want to, or must, merge. Although the shock may be great, so are the opportunities.

Psychologists have also attended to the subject. Church (1982:540) in his review of the literature, found that researchers viewed culture shock as a

> normal process of adaptation to cultural stress involving such symptoms as anxiety, helplessness, irritability, and a longing for a more predictable and gratifying environment . . . manifest in such behavior as excessive preoccupation with the drinking water, the food, and minor pains, excessive fears of being cheated or robbed, fits of anger toward or avoidance of local people, and a longing to be with fellow nationals.

Some researchers postulated stages of adjustment in the form of a U curve with an initial delight with the new world followed by aspects of hatred that revert to a much higher level of comfort and acceptance.

But further research (Church 1982:542) has indicated that such stages occur in only 20 percent of foreign students in many host countries.

Cleveland, Mangone, and Adams (Church 1982:545) described many of the cultural differences to which Peace Corps volunteers, missionaries, technical assistance personnel, and businessmen had to adjust overseas. They found that about one fourth of missionaries did not complete their assignments. Another study reported that a third of families of Americans working overseas returned before the worker's assignment was completed.

Williams (1967:15-16) and Bock (1970:ix) both warn of the tendency to confuse "Life Shock" with culture shock. The former is encountered in any society as one faces the processes of life, birth, and death. Life shock can be reduced greatly with some study and preparation before any extended fieldwork in another culture. Williams suggests that a visit to a hospital emergency room offers a range of encounters with illness and death from which most Americans are shielded in the normal course of their daily lives.

But being aware of these processes cannot prepare individuals for the culture shock which results from living closely with people whose cultural categorizations of experience will be totally alien in a great many ways. Culture shock is an experience that can only be dealt with in the field on the basis of the situation and the individual's perceptions of both her own and the local cultures.

Phobias and Their Treatment

The phobic response is essentially psychophysiological. It is a fear response. It is manifest in some of the following characteristic symptoms: dizziness, rapid heart rate, feelings of faintness or weakness, perspiration, diarrhea, nausea, increased urination, flushed face, weak knees, palpitations, breathlessness (hyperventilation), and dry mouth.

The phobic person experiences these symptoms as anticipations of disaster, catastrophy, and doom, frequently described as "what if I lose control, faint, have a heart attack, or die?" This increase in the amount and intensity of worrisome and fearsome thoughts accelerates the physiological responses to a level known simply as a panic attack.

Although phobic fears and behaviors are available to people of all ages, they tend to take hold in the late teens or in adulthood as a precipitating anxiety attack in the face of a fearsome event. The reason may not be apparent, but the symptoms are severe panic in circumstances that do not in reality warrant the emotional reactions evoked. The most common phobias are fear of being in crowded places, open spaces, in transit, being observed, and speaking with others.

They may be categorized as associated with:

Objects (cats, feathers, snakes)

Space and Place (public squares, streets, rooms, elevators, airplanes, bridges, heights)

Functions (defecating, walking, blushing, eating, public speaking, meeting people)

Activities (driving, flying, walking distances, entering social gatherings)

Complications may ensue because of secondary reactions such as loss of self esteem and depression. There are different viewpoints about phobic personality and individuals described as obsessive, hysterical, passive, or dependent. All can experience phobias (Mavissakalian and Barlow 1981:2).

A phobic neurosis is a condition characterized by intense fear which the person consciously recognizes as of no real danger. Such irrational fears have been with us throughout western history. The word, itself, comes from the Greek word *phobias*, which means fear, terror, panic, or flight. In the fourth century B.C. Hyppocrates wrote about a man phobic about flute playing and another phobic about heights and bridges. In the sixteenth century A.D., one of the characters in Shakespeare's *Merchant of Venice* observed that some people are upset if they see a cat. In the same period, Queen Elizabeth feared roses. (But how irrational was that when the family dynasty had been long engaged in "the war of the roses"?)

Almost two hundred years ago a judge excused a man from jury duty because of his fear of being with crowds of people. And in our own twentieth century, during parts of his life, Sigmund Freud himself was afraid of traveling (Freedman 1975:367).

Freudian theory proposed that phobias are the results of repression and the displacement of the internal conflict to an object or situation in the outside world. When the conflict was discovered through psychoanalysis and then worked through, the anxiety/phobia would disappear.

Later clinicians followed Freud with a variety of treatments, including analytically oriented psychotherapy, paradoxical intention, relaxation training, autogenic training, and hypnosis. But the general conclusion seems to have been that treatments in which the patient takes a passive role do not appear to be helpful. There is a surprising amount of agreement that it is essential, at some stage of treatment, for the phobic person to practice returning to the avoided situation (Matthews, et al, 1981:69).

The development of social learning theory formed the foundation for the next steps in research and treatment. In the last twenty years the literature seems to agree that some combination of techniques are important for an adequate phobia remediation program. These include 1) behavioral aspects, such as modeling, behavior rehearsal, role playing, graded invivo exposure, reinforced practice, 2) imagery-based exposure methods referred to as systematic desensitization and imaginal flooding, 3) cognitive strategies, such as Mechenbaum's self-instruction or self-statement training, stress inoculation training, rational-emotive therapy, and systematic rational restructuring, and 4) physiological control methods, such as relaxation training and deep breathing.

The unifying thrust is that there must be a systematic program of ways to think about the signs and symbols of the world—systematic programs that present ways of logical thinking about the phobic situations, ways of practicing and approaching them in the real world and ways of dealing with the emotional arousal.

Slowly, as phobia treatment programs became more effective, more people found their way to them. During this time the media increasingly focused on health problems. A major break-through in educating the public took place when the Phil Donahue television show featured a program on phobias. All over the country people became aware that they were not really crazy, they had phobias! And phobics began to come out of their closets.

So what is the state of the art in 1985? Behavioral programs are effective, chemical components continue to be investigated, questions are still unanswered as to how much of this technique coupled with that technique is the very best combination, but enough is known to help people with phobias get relief from their incapacitating fears. There is uncertainty whether the combinations are additive or interactive.

Programs vary as to whether they meet the needs of individuals with simple phobias or complex phobias. The latter tend to have other problems besides their phobias. Therefore, a treatment program that is too narrow and does not attend to the person's emotional well-being leaves the superficially desensitized individual vulnerable to backsliding because of unsolved intrapsychic or interpersonal problems (Chambless 1982).

Some programs are for individuals and others for groups. Informal observations suggest that group treatment supports an increase in the phobic person's social network, which means more support, and additional help for the invivo practice (Hand et al, 1974; Teasdale et al, 1977). Most important, however, is the sharing of a common understanding, a language to describe it, and a joint attack on the problem. Not being alone lessens the feeling of isolation and reinforces a sense of not being "crazy."

Exposure to the feared situation in a planned way can lead both to a reduction of fear and less avoidance of the stimulus, while the combination of exposure and other coping techniques has good results.

At the same time, if relational and/or internal problems complicate progress there will be no permanent relief until they are addressed. Research has also demonstrated that involvement of the phobic client's family in treatment results in significant positive changes subsequent to termination of regular therapeutic contact (Mathews et al, 1977).

Neurotic and phobic symptoms have been shown to be linked to the patterning of marital and family relationships (Mittleman 1956; Fry 1962), while Hofner (1977) has suggested that improvement in agoraphobic symptoms is related to inclusion of the phobic client's spouse in the treatment process. Therefore, a responsible program will involve family members as therapeutic helpers.

The next step is to educate the helper as well as the phobic person. Learning to relate to fear as a learned physiologic, cognitive, and behavioral response, and supplying techniques for dealing with the fear and panic responses probably will reduce the "fear of fear" feelings and therefore erroneous beliefs about panic and anxiety. The Appendix describes a specific Phobia Remediation Program that addresses many of the above issues.

Phobics and Fieldworkers

In reviewing the family background of participants in our programs for phobia remediation, we found a rather common theme of misunderstanding of the sociocultural cues of American life in their family cultures. The behavioral results of these cultural miscues—disorientation and helplessness—seem similar to the culture shock which ethnographic fieldworkers undergo.

The ethnographer knows he will be rewarded for facing his culture shock and will return to his native culture with knowledge, reputation, and material goods. The phobic person, suffering panic attacks in his own society, does not have a comparable understanding of the goal of overcoming the fear of not understanding the native culture. He only knows that the experience of acute anxiety and attacks of utter panic are so severe that he must avoid what others might think are inoffensive symbols.

This particular therapeutic population is predominantly white, middle class, and suburban. But not infrequently the clients, although domestic born, are the children of immigrants—to America, to cities, or to a nonethnic locale. That is, they grew up surrounded by different cultures or social or economic classes. Now, as adults, they are on their own in a more generalized American society.

Some were the children of Italian Catholics, others of middle European Jews. Several, from middle class Protestant backgrounds, had alcoholic fathers. Across these several ethnic and class differences there seemed to run a common thread as the now adult children described their past: the families constantly taught and reinforced the idea that they were different from the surrounding world. Some perceived the difference as a mark of inferiority and others as intense familio-centricity. But all felt they had to protect the child from the effects of this differentness. However, in dealing with the perception of difference, the guard was never to be let down and the family was never to be discussed with outsiders or outside the walls of the castle—home.

Elsewhere in this volume Middleton says "our emotions are intimate and ever-present ingredients in the raw stuff of our daily lives," that are "toned and shaped by the cultural environment in which we mature." He reminds us that the members of a culture have a collective interest in managing individual emotional expression in both intensity and circumstance because unexpected and inappropriate displays of strong feelings are potentially disruptive to the situational social fabric. Although he refers to cultural groups larger than the family, it seems to us that in the phobia background situations we are discussing, the family is the culture. Since the family leaders find the exterior environment hostile, they try to keep it at bay. Although the parents have to deal with this strange new world, anything from that environment brought into the family is potentially disruptive to this shrunken but fortified island.

Johnson (1984:117) compares ethnographic research and field work to rite-of-passage-like transitional experiences. He suggests that fieldworkers become as little children going through their initiation rites in, say, Hopi culture. But unlike these children, the field worker knows "that there is a discernible structure and sequence to the sometimes prolonged and often scary ethnographic experiences." It almost seems that the phobic people we have been writing about have not gone through the initiation rites necessary to becoming Americans. Or rather, that there was no adequate leadership to guide them through them so that they would learn correctly.

Now, in adult life, many of the participants exhibit what is known as Type A behavior, the "hurry-up" sickness that functions as a drive toward unattainably high standards. The perfectionism behind Type A may lead to obsessive-compulsive behavior, which, after all, is nothing more than a magical formula to ward off panic attacks. A number of the clients of Jewish background exhibit obsessive-compulsive behaviors and phobias particularly relating to food and cleanliness. This might be an outgrowth of some of the Jewish ritual behaviors and attitudes which were undergoing secularization in their transportation from the legalistic tradition of East European Jewish village life. The interpretation and analysis of behavior that was part of the secret, guarded versions of that ethnic value system in the participants' families provided a fertile breeding ground for phobic behavior.

Most immigrant parents do not transmit such feelings to their children. Many young adults who are thrust into a new culture do not fear what they are ignorant of; they plunge into it and learn by doing. But some immigrants do not arrive free and untrammeled and are laden with family responsibilities already, either for parents or children. They manage to cope, themselves, but in later years they cannot bear the idea of their children facing similar experiences. They only retain the price they have paid, not the possibilities of exhiliration and liberation that they may have experienced as well.

Almost all of the individuals whose therapy and backgrounds we reviewed have social components in their phobias. That is, the individuals process incoming information in faulty ways, with miscues concerning communication as well as miscues about expectations of what is acceptable behavior in social situations. The social cues act as a camera lens, recording surface action, but phobic people see through a glass darkly and are tuned into their own internal reports rather than those of the people around them. They seldom look at the surface, being so caught up in hidden meanings. Their perceptions in social intercourse are governed by their fears. In their social isolation booths, the only feedback is the echo amplified unbearably inside and not the reality outside. The echo becomes the reality.

Some of the research on phobias suggests that the patterning of neurotic and phobic symptoms together with family and marital relationships, often involve one member needing the neurotic symptoms of another family member in order to sustain stability for himself (Chambless and Goldstein 1982:82). Traditional male/female role complementarity in many cultures is based on a strict division of the world into outside/public (male) tasks and inside/private (female) tasks. This division of activity spheres then calls for males to go out each day to meet the dragons and slay them, which behavior is rewarded by the safety of the women and the home.

Some men married to women with phobias seem able to fulfill their role expectations only because their wives are even less able to go out than they are. However, current American directives—or the media interpretation of them—urge women, too, to leave the safe home and face down, if not slay, the dragons waiting out there. Perhaps traditional cultural patterns mask what we label agoraphobia, or, indeed, condone it. But the current demands that women leave the safety of home might then induce or reinforce panic attacks, rather than alleviate them. And of course, having the women compete rather than complement "manly" activity removes reinforcement for traditional public male activity.

Under these circumstances, the increased inward glimpse from the outside world via TV really intensifies the feelings of isolation of social isolates and of those with phobias. TV's frequently unreal and idealized presentation of American family life, home decoration, personal appearance, verbal and social glibness, surely reinforce the feelings that the phobic's family is not as good as the standard brand and further distances some individuals enmeshed in a family culture based on "us against the world."

The phobic undergoes treatment in order to improve his functioning in his own culture, or to allow him to function at all. He has to learn how to be a native, how to respond like the mainstream American. The ethnographer undertakes fieldwork—and undergoes culture shock—because he wants to understand natives in a different culture. The ethnographer does this because he wants to compare and contrast social realities. He wants to understand universal as well as particular aspects of sociocultural functioning.

As an example, the *Washington Post* ran a page one story stating that the Department of Energy was paying a phobia authority to study public fears about nuclear power and to educate those who had an irrational fear of it. An estimated forty to fifty percent of the public fear nuclear power (Kurtz 1984:A1). But the fact that few, if any, nuclear accidents have taken place does not make an aversion to nuclear power plants either a phobia or a nonphobia. For a psychiatrist to use science to label fears as phobias is political strategy, not psychological theory. It also points to subcultural differences in the assessment of risk factors related to the use of new technology.

There are basic differences between phobic persons learning to deal with their behaviors and fears and ethnographers undergoing culture shock. Bock (1970:xi) writes that the anthropologist values culture shock for "liberation and understanding that can come from such an experience . . . to discover the roots of his own ethnocentrism and so increase his self-knowledge." The phobic person retreats from any situation that focuses his fears.

Learning about another culture as an ethnographer is an explicit, systematic study of the society. That is the goal for which sociocultural and self-knowledge are to be gained. Therapy is undertaken to permit adequate functioning within one's culture and fieldwork to understand more of the universe of societies. Only secondarily, if at all, is the ethnographer interested in his own improved functioning in the birth society.

It does seem in order to point out that some anthropologists do better in other cultures than in their own. They seem to feel more comfortable asking strangers—even strangers with whom they develop rapport (by smiles, touches, gifts, money, medicine, excitement)—than asking fellow clansmen how to do the daily stuff of social interaction. Some of these anthropologists are outstanding field workers, possibly because as bona fide strangers they are both able to ask questions and feel comfortable with the role of outsider. A few of them are probably phobics back home, for whom rituals of avoidance are necessary in order to get through each day. After all, is not going to another culture the ultimate flight from home-bred panic attacks? And then there are a few who go native, coupling their facility in learning to understand the other culture with the panic at the thought of returning home.

Anthropologists may learn to understand their own culture better because living as outsiders they are continuously conscious that they must either explain their deviation from the norm of Americans, or they must force themselves to accept or act in accordance with stereotyped expectations of Americans (or British or Zulu, whatever the mother culture of the ethnographer). We become conscious of how we have been doing whatever it is as opposed, often, to the way we now have to learn to do it.

Such pressures, of course, are always operating on the immigrant as well as the sojourner. They are particularly stressful for the immigrant who comes reluctantly to the strange world, and most particularly if there is no ethnic enclave, with some of the comforts and familiarities of home still at hand and at ear. But immigrants do not have plans to return. The pressures of constantly trying to understand as well as to make one's way may become heavy enough to lead to phobic behavior— in the next generation. For they may possibly raise a child for a world it has been taught to be feared to know too well.

The fact of fieldwork results in cultural relativism. That does not mean a blind acceptance of a mishmash of cultural attributes from a grocery shelf of world-ranging traits. Rather the relativistic posture is one whereby a participant observer can see that categories in his own or another society are not superior virtues whose meaning is not understood outside of the one culture. This is an attitude of mind and an awareness of self that is far easier to achieve through the experience of living or working for a long period in another culture. It presupposes a willingness to be totally lost, i.e. experience culture shock, in order to find the new world. In that way, the nuances of all the symbolic systems, not just the language, are appreciated and to a great extent understood.

The mystique of fieldwork is that knowledge can only be gained through such direct experience. But of course, if that is the case, how could an anthropologist ever hope to make it accessible to students? Or to nonstudents, even, back in the home culture? And how could he discover, buttress, and modify theories about human behavior, experience, and meaning? By the same token, how could poets hope to share their insights if words cannot communicate them?

The therapist has to learn to understand his client in the context of helping that person to see the differences between perceptions of reality that are connected with the social world the phobic is attempting to enter or reenter, rather than those that close him out of it. He does not have to have suffered from phobias himself to do this.

Informants as well as investigators in an ethnographic inquiry also acquire new insights and appreciation of relationships not previously considered. The very act of being asked raises things to consciousness. The technique of interviewing in order for the interviewer to enlarge his own knowledge, rather than to assist the informant in problem solving also seems to have unintended self-enhancing effects.

The phobic, like the ethnographer, is compelled to participate in a symbolic universe of which certain elements are askew. The difference is that the symbolic universe in which the phobic is sometimes adrift is his "own." He knows, and others know, that he ought to be comfortable with the various cultural cues, but he is not. The withdrawal of the phobic is not just fear, per se, but the disorientation of the symbolic castaway.

He is experiencing culture shock, as is the ethnographer, but that culture shock is a singularly disrupting experience because he is different from the ethnographer in that he is an unwilling, and in fact unwitting, foreigner. He has several problems. His very awareness that he ought to respond comfortably to cultural cues as others do is one. The fear of a panic attack or other fear response is another, which is actually much more acute than the fear of a feared object itself.

The ethnographer knows that he can map this unknown world, and by learning its symbolic geography not only tell others about it, but learn to be home in it, himself. He casts himself eagerly, despite his culture shock, into the discovery of its system of cues and meanings.

Conclusion

The purpose of this chapter has been to examine the principle that fearing is a cultural experience by comparing and contrasting phobic fears within a culture to the culture shock fearing of the ethnographer in a strange culture. By comparing field work with the treatment of phobias we see, as well, that once the phobic is no longer considered "crazy" by himself and others, he can be taught to deal with his phobias and overcome them, just as the ethnographer deals with and overcomes culture shock. Like children come to erroneous conclusions or connections about the relationship of events, the phobic person also connects events which are believed emotionally, if not intellectually. So does the ethnographer experiencing culture shock.

The phobic person and the ethnographer do the same thing in working on fears or resolving culture shock. The phobic stays in the feared place using coping techniques and coping thoughts until he is more comfortable. The ethnographer redefines symbolic systems until he approximates the new culture's meanings, increasing his comfort in the process. Of course, in treating phobias the phobic person does likewise, in challenging the erroneous beliefs and connections and learning to redefine his own symbolic systems. Both the anthropologist and the phobic follow systematic processes, field work and behavior therapy, to reach their goals. Both solutions lead to the dissipation of similar fear responses, variously called phobia and culture shock.

8
Toward an Apprehension of Fear

David Parkin

Two Types of Fear: Raw and Respectful

If we regard our problem as being the cultural construction of fear, then we may legitimately start with a culture's semantic constructs. In English culture and language, for example, we find the word "fear" associated with a number of others which straddle the domains of religion and authority.

Thus, the nineteenth century use of "fear" could merge with its use of "respect" and "reverence" or "veneration," e.g. "Fear the Lord." This was appropriate for a Christian ethic then based on the sanctions of hellfire and brimstone. The implication was two-fold: 1) the mortal worshipper would recognize the supremacy of God and would hold Him in high regard, but 2) the God would, for His part, be expected to protect the worshipper who venerated and prayed to Him, or would at least make misfortunes and tragedies bearable and explainable.

This divine paternalism perhaps parallelled the secular paternalism of late feudalism in the seventeenth and early eighteenth centuries. As the feudal structure gave way by the nineteenth century to industrial society and its new forms of patronage and competition, this idea of a stern but paternalistic God became used more generally to reinforce authority. Throughout the shift from preindustrial to industrial society, then, the constant feature was that God should be held in high *regard*, i.e. *respected* through prayer and good deeds, and was to be *feared* if such obligations were not carried out. The concept of fear thus encompassed that of respect. It is here a legitimate instrument of authority, and is found in secular hierarchies as well. This is institutionally controlled fear.[1]

Authority depends on constant and not merely occasional veneration. This is revealed in the etymology of the term "respect" or "regard," through the use of the repetitive "re-," e.g. *"constantly* looking up to" or some such. Similarly, the verb "revere" derives from the Latin *(re)vereri* which contains both the prefix of repetition and actually means "to fear." A hierarchy of control is explicit in these connotations of fear.

But what about the opposite? This is uncontrolled fear which is not contained within a recognized hierarchy but appears, rather, as an immanent force unlocated in time and space and effective in a random, capricious, and rampant manner. This is the fear instilled in mortals by ghosts or spirits which must be eliminated or tamed through exorcism. This attribute of fear is shared by such other concepts in English as fright, terror, dread and horror, each differing from the other in degree of intensity or anticipation.

Control of the sources of such emotion clearly depends upon knowing what they are. It is one thing for priests to exorcise haunted houses and graveyards, it is another to know how to deal with fear the precise nature of which is not known.

We must, in other words, distinguish between fear which is seen or known to be controllable at the outset or shortly after its expression and which, because it can be controlled by others is a potential weapon of authority wielded by these others, and fear which is, so to speak, "raw" fear.

Controllable fear presupposes respect for authority. This is nineteenth century Fear of God. Uncontrolled or raw fear stands on its own, dissociated from any connotation of respect for authority. In present-day English we have almost abandoned these two connotations of fear. Publicly at least, we still claim to have respect for authority and reject the idea that this authority could legitimately use fear as its primary sanction.

We reserve the concept of fear for the raw emotion, though, admittedly, as often in a weak as in a strong sense, e.g. "I fear it may rain today" as against "I fear flying more than any other mode of transport." The strongest expression of the inner state seems nowadays to take the form of such associated terms (and their derived forms) as dread, terror, or horror.

Perhaps through the mass media, including horror movies, and through reports of human atrocities committed throughout the world in the name of politics, including terrorism and tyrannies, our consciousness of the fear-to-horror spectrum is semantically heightened: we use such terms frequently and in different combinations and possibly with less and less emotional loading.

I wish in this chapter first to concentrate on this basic distinction between what I will call *respectful* or authorized fear and *raw* fear, and then to follow its implications. Respectful fear assumes a predictable response to behavior. It approaches knowable fear. Raw fear assumes an unpredictable aspect sustained by the victim. It is, literally, fear of the unknown. The first is emotionally integrated. If you cross your divine or secular lord, then you may fear his wrath but at least have only yourself to blame and could have prevented it. Falsehood and guilt prompt the fear while truth and innocence suppress it. In this way these emotions or "inner states" occur in some kind of balance.

However, raw fear is, so to speak, dislocated from any underlying emotional consistency. You may suffer it even though you did no wrong. The innocent as well as the guilty are its victims. Thus, respectful fear is based on some system of reasoned consequences, while raw fear is not.

Keeping in mind this distinction between respectful and raw fear, with its associated characteristics, I turn now to the question of how cultures construct emotion. As Scruton says elsewhere, it is not the phylogenetic bases of emotions that interest us, such as so-called "natural" or primate sexual activity, violence, or fear. Rather, we are interested in the transmission, recognition, and modification of these emotions through the rules of particular cultures.

We can put this another way. Phylogenetically, it may be possible to posit certain universal features of the emotions we call fear. But, translated into its particular socio-cultural expression, no such universal features may be expected. Fear in some cultures will approximate that in others, but in yet others differs significantly. We may speculate that, even allowing for problems of linguistic translation from the languages of different cultures, fear is a polythetic concept (see Needham 1975).

In one sense, different native exegeses would probably give fear the cross-cultural status of a polythetic class, i.e., the different but overlapping definitions given of the concept of fear by the members of different cultures.

But, as my limited semantic examples suggest, the two-fold distinction between respectful and raw fear seems at least fundamental, however much it is then the basis of further, variable cultural elaboration.

I am suggesting, in other words, that there is an underlying semantic distinction of this kind which is widely distributed, possibly universally, and which may be either explicit or implicit in everyday speech and behavior depending on the society or culture.

I noted that up to the twentieth century in Europe, respectful fear clearly existed as an isolable concept alongside raw fear. Since that time respectful and authority-conferring fear has disappeared or would be regarded as contradictory: we ask, how can fear ever legitimize respect? As in the shift from the hierarchical to egalitarian use of *tu* and *vous* (and comparable forms) in pronominal addresses in many European languages, the dissolution of respectful fear has taken place against an ideological background of increasing equality.

Many politically uncentralized societies traditionally regarded ritually powerful elders, priests, and other experts as local authorities who could only be effective through the fear they could instill in others. One might fear the power of witchdoctors but it was these same people to whom one would go to purchase vengeance magic and, justifiably in one's own eyes, settle a personal wrong against an enemy.

Fear of witchcraft in Africa is not, contrary to popular opinion, raw fear. The victims of witchcraft might ascribe their misfortune similarly to the jealousy of their enemies. But, sometimes, the victims are revealed at a later stage as themselves being witches, either after seeking vengeance, or as a result of their evil intentions being discovered by a diviner as the original cause of the enmity.

The fear of witchcraft, in other words, is immediately caught in a web of well-established and sometimes novel interpretations which presuppose cause and effect. As among the Azande, this is part of a more general African metascience which never allows a phenomenon to remain unexplained for long. In Europe, too, before the Enlightenment and rational positivism, metaphysical explanations were promptly demanded.

In other words, fear, then and in much of Africa now, had some difficulty in remaining raw; in no time at all, it was gobbled up by an explanation of its cause and effect. It is thus always nearer to, and immediately transformed into, respectful fear.

To take a particular case from a people among whom I worked in Kenya, this easy assimilation of fear with respect for authority is evidenced in the Giriama use of the verb *ku-ogoha*, which means both to fear and to respect. Formal respect relations exist between members of immediately adjacent generations, as in many other areas of Africa and the world, and a Giriama says of his father *namwogoha*, I respect him. He may use the same verb to refer to a harmful spirit or a possible source of danger. Another politically uncentralised African people whom I studied, the Luo, whose Nilotic language is quite unrelated to that of the Bantu Giriama, also merge respect with fear: "I fear them" is *aluorgi*, while a "respected person" is *moluor*, the common root being *-luor-*.

There is a Giriama term borrowed from the Swahili-Arabic, which means to respect, *ku-heshima*, but it has no connotation at all of fear. Similarly, in the closely related Bantu Swahili language and in Luo, there are numerous other terms for fear and respect, the two generally being clearly distinguishable, as they are in modern English, and as they were and are in Hebrew which has two terms demarcating respect from fear.

The Giriama dominant use of the term ku-ogoha, the Luo use of -luor, the nineteenth century English usage, and examples from other languages, do however suggest that the inclusion of respect within fear and its attachment to legitimate authority occurs widely in space and time and is not confined to politically centralized, despotic societies. The politically uncentralized Giriama and Luo group respect with fear but so did the centralized Zulu under Shaka who, according to Walter (1969), instituted political consensus through terror. Perhaps the governing distinction is not that between centralized and uncentralized polities but between dominant cultural epistemologies.

Paradigmatically this may be seen in the commonly alleged, though probably biblically erroneous, change from the Old Testament with its fearful warnings of brimstone and fire, to the New Testament, which denounced fear as a religious sanction and substituted a philosophy of love.

Love has become an analytically embarrassing emotion for Westerners. Yet, requited love (which is presumably the kind most widely sought), is surely the counterpart of respectful fear. Both are reciprocal: I have reason to fear my Lord or sovereign if I fail to respect my obligations to Him, but He has obligations to me too; love, similarly, can be exchanged.

Unrequited love, by contrast, is in one sense the counterpart to raw fear, for neither involves an obligation to exchange. Their course is indeterminate. While respectful fear and requited love predictably perpetuate themselves, both preserving in different degrees relationships of authority, answerability, and dependence, raw fear and unrequited love are jarring intrusions which can lead anywhere, to violence to oneself or others, or to different kinds of withdrawal.

It is likely that children's curiously ambivalent, fearful liking of horror tales in societies throughout the world is a tacit recognition of the randomness of raw fear. For, through such tales, we capture the raw fear, place it in known social relations, and so embed it in a system of morality and hence of religious or secular authority.

Rather than arguing that any one kind of society would necessarily emphasize one of the two kinds of fear over the other, I would rather see the two as always present, though to variable degrees, depending on the situation and persons involved. It is in fact better to regard the two as in some kind of struggle with each other, even in a dialectical relationship. To put it simply, some societies stress an Old Testament view of the world, others a New Testament. But changes are always likely to occur in the dialectic.

Early positivists of the Enlightenment insisted that everything could eventually (if not immediately) be explained "scientifically" and so logically there need never be raw fear of anything. By the same token, religion and the occult should then have withered away as irrational activities and there should have been no need, either, of respectful fear of God or of God-abiding authorities.

This clearly did not happen. Alternating emphases on respectful and raw fear have continued to present day. The Nazi regime of Germany was attracted to Nietzsche's doubts that love or consensus alone could facilitate government and that only harsh, sometimes fearsome sanctions could prevent disrespect for authority. In modern Euro-American society most people have not moved in that direction, for they do not accept that good authorities rule by fear, (though representatives of their governments often support tyrannies elsewhere out of political expediency). But, if the more modern emphasis on horror movies and on sometimes sinister occult sects is any guide, we seem to have allowed raw fear to occupy a growing area of our cosmology. Why should this be so?

Perhaps one answer is that many people are tacitly questioning the positivist premise, on which our civilization has been sustained for so long, that science can explain everything. We still have cancer. New diseases occur. Third World poverty worsens as the global population rises unabated. Western democracies produce elaborate economic theories which still cannot regulate inflation. Wars and the arms race intensify. Doubts deepen.

Paradoxically, the revolution in mass communications has crammed into the head of the individual more information than might reasonably be expected, but which, presented in the form of insoluble problems, creates a colossal uncertainty. Under such conditions an increase in raw fear, isolated from recognizable cause and effect, seems inevitable.

The danger is that, if my hypothesis is correct, an increase in raw fear may at some stage be met by its conversion into respectful fear. That is to say, raw fear rushes in to fill the vacuum created by the moral expulsion of respectful fear, but raw fear creates the uncertainty that must in turn be controlled by increasing amounts of respectful fear.

The Ayatolla's regime in Iran is an obvious recent example. How many more, perhaps closer to home, are imminent? That said, is this transformation of raw into respectful fear only ever malign and destructive? In the next section I suggest otherwise.

Fear and Creativity

There is a further paradox in the foregoing, which concerns the question of creativity. Respectful fear is associated with some degree of certainty, control, and predictability. You know roughly what will happen should you fall afoul of your ruler or god. For their part rulers and gods are not disposed to let you bring in new ideas. Theirs is the expectation of unquestioning obedience. Respectful fear hardly seems good for innovation, therefore. Does that then mean that raw fear, with all its uncertainty and capriciousness, is what we actually need to be creative?

Curiously, this does in fact seem to be the case. The dread of incurable diseases spurs us to discoveries of their causes and remedies, or at least to a faith in such discovery. The nuclear arms race and the horror of holocaust may, again on the most optimistic note, force nations to compromise and secure a lasting peace. The paradox is that the raw fear of these as yet uncontrolled phenomena creates the uncertainty which then becomes the problem which we must resolve.

To return to the earlier point, raw fear can then either become converted into respectful fear by moralists, or, if left to flourish, can provide the conditions of desperation needed for experimentation and discovery. Putting this another way, raw fear is competed for: on the one hand we have a tendency to want to tame it by turning it into respectful fear; on the other hand we wish to solve the puzzles of life which it imposes on us. The latter suggests that our creative will must be fed by constant amounts of raw fear. Without it, we lack the stimulation to create. The former tendency would rather obliterate all traces of raw fear.

In fact, neither tendency reaches a conclusion. However much a regime or a philosophy attempts to eliminate notions of raw fear by presenting them as misguided and by concentrating peoples' fears on venerated agents, amounts of raw fear will remain. Similarly, the potential for creativity that comes from our reflection on the causes of fear is never fully tapped. Indeed, as in the sad case of the fear of cancer, we really have more faith in the possibility of a cure than we have concrete evidence of a cure itself. Periods of remission may have increased over the years but we know that this is no substitute for a complete and utter remedy. Yet, the apparent success of inoculation against polio, tuberculosis, and smallpox, sustains the faith. Our faith in our capacity to overcome obstacles is not simply in proportion to the quantity of raw fear around us. Rather it is, if we are to continue to believe in life, an essential part of our experience of fear.

Once again, language provides an insight into this mutual embed-dedness of faith and fear. The word "apprehension" has the three major connotations of capture, understanding, and uneasiness, the latter amounting to a weak form of raw fear. If we wish to understand things in a new way, we have to reach out and grasp hold of concepts in a creative manner which may nevertheless be dangerous. Such was Galileo's experience. But, however fearful he may have been of the consequences of snatching concepts out of their existing epistemology he had faith in this necessary route to understanding. Apprehension, therefore, summarizes the transition from fear, through faith, to understanding.

If our experience of raw fear is not also accompanied at some point by faith, then we have in effect given up life itself. For we have let ourselves become dominated by the unknown; we have allowed it to become forever the unknowable. Those in whom frightening experiences induce a heart attack are a special case, but the cases of people reduced to gibbering madness or suicide after such experiences are no more than extreme instances of allowing fear to stifle life.

More normally, colossal fear paralyses or immobilizes temporarily but also prompts thereafter a questioning response, if not by the victim himself, then at least by others. Thus, from the fiction-like reports of haunted houses, we move to a more serious concern with poltergeists, and thence to scientific investigations into paranormal phenomena, the pursuit of which is more motivated by faith in results than by their demonstration.

In these equations of raw fear with creativity and of respectful fear with unquestioning and therefore uncreative obedience, another distinction arises. Raw fear gives us the choice, so to speak, of whether to understand its origin or to ignore it. Respectful fear offers no such choice. Those who flinch from questioning the causes of raw fear are, then, like those who unquestioningly obey the dictates of respectful fear. Put another way, the responses to raw fear sort out those who can challenge from those who can or will not.

This optative feature of raw fear has two related implications. First, it offers a mode by which individuals shape their own self-perceptions, reputations, and theories of personal existence. Am I cool or a coward? Is either bravery or cowardice a necessary condition of my existence, and of existence generally? This leads to the second implication. If I and others decide that a positive and creative response to raw fear is a necessary condition of our existences, then we must face the further question of whether we are also to challenge the dictates of respectful fear. Followed out in this way, peoples' responses to raw fear must contain the seeds of revolutionary thought. This may be the usurpation of religious as well as of political dominance. Galileo upset the existing theological-philosophical paradigm; Marx disturbed that of middle capitalism.

However, it is not necessarily the case that those who confront and understand the perils of raw fear, will next tackle the church or state. After all, scientists and academics generally have been noted for their conversion of raw fear into rational understanding, yet have included only a few who rebelled against the establishment. They will call this conservatism their respect for the establishment but may it not also be their fear of dismissal or of being deprived of rewards? The creativity inspired by raw fear is, then, not enough to turn heroes who confront fear of the unknown into rebels against the familiar. Similarly, the converse applies: it would be easy to imagine a fearless revolutionary, capable of removing the most despotic regime, nevertheless having a paralytic fear of being alone in the dark or a deserted graveyard.

Those who do combat first the unknown and thereafter the known sources of fear face in turn unnamed and named phenomena. That is to say, raw fear refers to sinister forces, which, simply because they are unknown, are by the same token unidentified and therefore nameless. By contrast, respectful fear is of a specific person such as a ruler, a god, and even of a demon or occult force. These are identified by personal or descriptive names. Respectful fear tends, therefore, to be personified. This is obviously so in the case of human despots. But gods and demons take on certain human characteristics while remaining distinctly nonhuman. Gods may be churlish and angry, even jealous, as well as loving and benevolent. Demons reveal their own human-like desires and weaknesses. And even such occult forces as sorcery and witchcraft may be differentiated by names which suggest human emotions. The Giriama classify many types in this way.

Identification and classification through naming is of course a method by which scientists reveal their understanding of phenomena. We convert the unknown into the known by naming their properties and giving them distinctive characters. The sometimes physicists' concept of ether has been reclassified in terms of particle and electro-magnetic wave theory. The moon is made up of chemical elements rather than cheese. Volcanoes are not the work of gods, and so on.

Although we cannot bargain with chemicals and volcanoes (or do not normally perceive ourselves as able to do so), we can negotiate with the gods, demons, and human despots whose fearsomeness we respect. It is true, as I noted above, that such agencies expect unquestioning obedience and are loathe to entertain new ideas. Yet, simply because they can be identified and appealed to, we can sometimes redefine the relationship and negotiate with them.

Thus, just as our responses to raw fear vary from the paralytic to the creative, so we either obey or challenge respectful fear. In both cases, of course, the more positive response has its dangers. Gods, rulers, and occult forces have a nasty habit of getting back at us if we defy them. In both cases, the result is to redefine our previous relationship and understanding. Raw fear becomes known and classified, and renamed as something else: e.g. ghosts becoming aspects of the paranormal. Respectful fear is renamed as our subjection to tyranny, or as our acceptance of benevolent despotism or simply of rule by rightful and just (divine) law, depending on the extent to which the incumbents are redefined.

In the Giriama view of spirits and occult forces, we see this classificatory creativity and dynamism very clearly. A person may first be diagnosed as suffering from sinister forces which the diviner is unable at that time clearly to identify. Later, she/he, or another diviner may suggest that a particular kind of sorcery is responsible for the patient's ills. Still later, one or a number of named demons or spirits may be blamed by the diviner for possessing the patient. Once a consensus has been reached, a cure may be suggested. Since most patients recover, the cures are seen to be effective and peoples' initial fears are assuaged. Thus, raw fear of the unknown is progressively reexperienced as fear of particular spirits or forces, to be followed by their expulsion. Yet, while particular cases may be successful, new spirits and occult forces are always being "discovered," giving rise to, or perhaps merely accompanying, new human fears. Throughout all this diviners come and go as their reputations wax and wane. But some, like the famous Kajiwe (Parkin 1968) are for a time genuinely feared and respected, and command large followings.

Therefore, while neither raw nor respectful fear are eradicable, and affect us in all societies and eras, it may be helpful to see them together as the conditions we ourselves set for our own creativity. It would be dangerously complacent to excuse the tyrannies of rule and belief throughout the world which cause so much human suffering. But, if we have to live with the Devil, both out there and in us all to a greater or lesser degree, then let us at least negotiate with him.

To negotiate a phenomenon is to treat it as a "thing" to be transacted. Yet, while fear may indeed be viewed in this way as a passive commodity, it can in other respects seem actively to exert power over people. I now turn to the tension in this idea of fear as autonomous agency and as negotiable object. More generally, the tension results in part from the semantic ambiguities of terms for emotions. Such terms do not refer unambiguously to discretely experienced inner feelings but are rather to be seen as associative networks of words and ideas (Rey 1980), which may subtly be converted one into the other. But who or what effects such conversions? Is it the cultural network which directs the person along conceptual pathways, or does the person himself fit words to his experiences? Or is neither interpretation appropriate?

Fear as Commodity and Fear as Humanity

I believe that it was Wittgenstein who pointed out that while dogs may have fear, it is only humans who have remorse. Humans have fear, too, of course. Among humans, too, fear is convertible into other emotions at two levels: that of the unreflective dog, whose fear of a stranger may turn into pleasure at the sight of meat in the stranger's hands, and that of contemplative man, whose fear of being discovered of having perpetrated an evil deed becomes, as the danger of discovery recedes with time, remorse at having committed the deed itself. Dostoyevsky's Raskolnikov seems to have traversed almost the whole gamut of emotions, principal among which were fear and remorse, the one constantly becoming the other.

Fear can similarly lead to anger, as we all know, often as a cathartic release: a child narrowly misses falling from a precipice as a result of carelessness and, once safe, is castigated by the parents, now furious at the near loss which moments earlier had gripped them with fear. Anger itself leads to ideas of agitation, of being upset: the Swahili-Arabic loan term *ku-kasirika* and the Swahili Bantu word *ku-hangaika* roughly translate both and reflect a Swahili view, held in other parts of Africa and elsewhere, that anger and inner agitation are the same thing (Harris 1982; Lewis 1980; Rosaldo 1980, on the concept of *liget*). Finally, agitation is the crux of emotional expression: emotions communicate powerful messages yet, paradoxically, they are rarely at all clear either to the sender or receivers. Emotions enjoy, so to speak, a certain poetic licence, forcefully evoking a response either from a self or an other, yet uncertain, and indefinite, and with a communicative intentionality that is easily convertible.

It is this convertible, dynamic quality of our inner states that I wish to emphasize here. It is invariably captured by language, but we can only know this if we engage in cross-cultural translation. Thus, just as the Swahili terms ku-kasirika and ku-hangaika are in different ways and to different extents associated with emotional hurt, grief, and anger, i.e. with what English speakers regard as different emotions, so the word "pride" in English fails to translate the Swahili word *kiburi*, even though this is one of the dictionary renderings. Kiburi has the negative connotation of arrogance or conceit, which is the obverse of the modern positive one of "pride" in English (e.g. "pride in his achievements"), for which there is no easy equivalent in Swahili. More examples could be given.

Two points emerge so far. First, emotions engage in a communicative paradox: they elicit powerful responses, but they confuse the bearer's intentions and entail slippage from one inner state to another. Second, a cross-cultural view of different linguistic expressions for emotions reveals that words and inner states are not isomorphic: there is nowhere a neat labelling of emotions which "really" marks them off from each other. This does not mean that there may not be a universally limited range of phylogenetically defined emotions, though cultural emphasis may vary. I might surprise readers by suggesting that the Western concept of fear both occupies a more focal role in our thinking and has a larger number of associated concepts than among a number of African societies of my acquaintance, principally the Giriama of Kenya and some related Bantu peoples, and the East African southern Luo and other Nilotic peoples. I do not mean to say that, in such African societies, people feel less fear. Rather, I contend that fear, as a concept translatable into the Western equivalent as best it can be, does not figure so largely in peoples' minds and talk. I have already suggested that fear among the Giriama and some other peoples is often linked to ideas of respect, and so is both a more normal feature of, and also more embedded in, social life, and is more easily identified in association with other inner states.

In all this, I have to suspend immediate problems of cultural translation. That is to say, I have to assume on the basis of my own and others' ethnographic experiences that the emotions of fear, remorse, anger, and excitement, are everywhere present but that they may be identified differently and may not everywhere be of equal cultural significance.

To return to my suggestion, then: why do the heirs of the Judaeo-Christian-Islamic tradition (to lump together much that is in common) and, more narrowly, Western thinkers, place so much emphasis on fear as a force to be respected, obeyed, or passively accepted, or actively to be countered?

Let me return here to the distinction between respectful and raw fear, the former institutionalized as a legitimate means of authority and coercion, and the latter, raw fear, which is characterized as an elemental force which grips peoples' hearts in a random or at least uncontrollable manner. I think that this distinction is particularly marked in Western society, being often used to classify the proclivities of other peoples or of divisions and classes within Western society. The shift from one to the other type of fear changes people themselves, however temporarily, and may justify either their right to rule or their subjugation.

While raw fear is an elemental force, respectful fear is a commodity: that is to say, you can increase the amounts of fear you might inject into your authority system. To do this you capture, so to speak, elemental fear and incorporate it within your right to rule. Roosevelt's insistence that peoples have nothing to fear but fear itself implicitly recognizes this potential commoditization, transferability, and utility of fear. The admonition is to recognize raw fear but then to tame it. Roosevelt would wish thereafter to banish it. But tyrants can set it loose on the people. In short, then, treating fear as a "thing" has a number of consequences. It makes it easier to extricate fear as an isolable concept from the shifting emotions by which we are "really" constituted. Thus extricated, it can be controlled by a minority and turned against a majority. The capacity to produce and project fear can be transferred to another group or elite, or appropriated by one. Finally, and most importantly, this transferable capacity to produce and project fear, i.e. its overall commoditization, enables people to dissociate fear and its effects from the intentions of those who exploit it. For instance, it becomes possible to blame the evils of a regime or situation on fear as an independent thing rather than on those who produce it. Or, to put the point another way, when the sources of fear are unexplained, then those who initiate it are excused.

We are familiar enough with this situation in a number of totalitarian regimes. The sources of fear become displaced: in the early days of Nazism, Jews were portrayed as sinister monsters of immense power to be stamped out. Certain capitalist regimes generate fear of left-wing "agents" and vice versa. Even in war-time Britain enemies were characterized as evil, though also, paradoxically, as comic figures. Sometimes we are taught by our rulers the fear of impersonal agents such as inflation, Western economic decline, racial invasions, the threat of war, etc. Displacing the sources of fear is an aspect of scapegoating and can lead to witchhunts. It hides the identities and intentions of those who produce the fear. It separates the emotion from the person and casts it as an independent entity. For fear is both object, in that it can be manipulated, and yet also subject, in that it is assumed to generate its own effects once launched.

All this results, I believe, from the way in which Westerners semantically mark out and then commoditize fear. A recent commoditization is of course the large-scale manufacture and sale of horror-video films. I am not saying that this tendency is absent in other cultures, but only that it is more emphasized in the West and other parts of the Northern industrialized world.

Let me now turn to what I believe are examples of an opposite tendency. This is where fear is viewed not as a manipulable commodity separate from personhood, but as an intrinsic part of humanity and as an inseparable part of what people define as the normal person. Thus, the first tendency, let us call it A, is not to see fear and its manipulation as an inherent part of man's nature. In the West we try to eliminate all fears from our minds. The second tendency, let us call it B, is to regard fear and its manipulation as an inevitable and necessary part of being human.

Thus, the Giriama regard evil acts and intentions as an inevitable characteristic of authority figures, such as the members of a ruling secret society of senior elders called the Vaya. These Vaya elders have the knowledge of numerous oaths, the most feared and efficacious of which is called the hyaena oath. Anyone who lies in taking the hyaena oath is expected to die. The belief is a powerful one. Fear of the Vaya elders and their oaths upholds their judicial authority.

The Giriama actually regard the Vaya elders ambivalently. On the one hand the elders' authority is necessary for law and order. On the other hand the Vaya elders are ordinary mortals, distinguished only by their immense age, and so suffer the usual range of human emotions of greed, jealousy, anger, and fear, as well as altruistic concern. Like other persons, then, the Vaya are expected occasionally to vent their angers and fears through the malevolent use of their powers. They too, it is believed, must from time to time avenge themselves of wrongs and, possessing absolute power, are in an unassailable position. So, Giriama say, ordinary people tolerate the Vaya's occasional acts of evil as the necessary price of their role as arbiters. It follows from this that the fear of oaths which supports their authority is also regarded as an inevitable necessity. Without fear there is no authority. People must put up with it (see Parkin 1985).

All this stems from the assumption that these are general features of human nature. Certainly, people are expected to try to control excessive evil, but it is also expected that people must protect and avenge themselves. Vengeance *is* a form of protection. And revenge can only succeed as a belief system based on invisible relations of cause and effect provided that it instills fear in others. The rationale is that, just as evil is naturally in all of us, so also is our fear of others and our capacity to frighten them. Fear is inseparably part of being a normal, law-abiding person. No Giriama suggests that fear can be eliminated from the human condition. That would be an illogical denial of normality and of the capacity of persons to defend themselves—a denial, indeed, of human rights.

Further, this humanization of fear, as distinct from its commoditization, links it more easily to the other "normal" emotions. If both fear and anger are regarded as normal, then their identification and expression are that more readily merged than if only one, fear, was regarded as abnormal and therefore eradicable. The language of emotions among peoples like the Giriama reflects this overlap. In English, by contrast, fear stands out from the corresponding lexicon. "Fear" as a term shades into such others as "dread," "doom," "horror," "terror," and the weaker "apprehension," "temerity," "nervousness," etc., and there is no doubt as to the rhetorical and literary strength of their focal domain.

Hume's notion of primary and secondary emotions may indicate a Western proclivity both increasingly to differentiate our inner states through a poliferation of terms, and to heighten their relative significance as distinctive clusters. I do not think that this difference in tendencies between Westerners and a people like the Giriama reflects a difference in personal reflexivity. The Giriama reflect on themselves much as we do. But they do so from a different perspective. We call emotions "inner states," but then try to externalize our control of them through self- and psycho-analysis, aided by an immense vocabulary of terms to identify them. The Giriama do sometimes see the body as a container of emotions. But they also equate specific parts of the body with emotions, as in many other parts of Africa and as, to some extent, in pre-Renaissance Europe. In other words, they see the body as both constituting and constituted by the emotions. Body-parts, emotions, and the person are the same. The potentiality is there, but not yet the predisposition, for the separation and subsequent commoditization of these three. For the moment, at least, fear is not to be feared.

I am, then, dealing with obverse tendencies, and no more than that. The category "Western" or Judaeo-Christian-Islamic" is much too broad while that of "Giriama" too minutely represents something of other African cultures, and possibly other non-Western ones. Further comparative research is certainly needed. My aim has been to explore how the ontological status of fear can be reversed, without worrying too much where this actually happens. While some persons or peoples may strive to externalize the fear that is in us all, others leave it as an essential feature. These contrasting tendencies each lends itself to extensive cultural elaboration. The first results in the treatment of fear as a thing or commodity which nevertheless takes on the characteristics of an autonomous agent of destruction. The second retains fear within the domain of human sensibilities and intentions and sees good, as well as harm, resulting from it.

Let me conclude. The manipulation of respectful fear in the service of authority can lead to its commoditization. Yet, sustained by peoples' ideological beliefs in its innate power, respectful fear can seem sometimes to turn back and confront those who produce and control it. Raw fear emanates from a universe of unsolicited experiences which are difficult to identify and control. In the end, however, it proves to be none other than a part of humanity itself and its wayward thoughts on personal destiny.

Notes

1. A letter from Kipling to Baden-Powell (displayed in Batemans, Kipling's house in Sussex, England) makes the same kind of point in referring to the belief that by instilling in a child *fear* of his father, you ensure eventual *respect*.

Appendix A

The Wolpe-Lazarus Fear Survey Schedule invites the subject's response to seventy-five items. The intensity with which fear of each stimulus is felt is indicated as follows: "a little," "a fair amount," "much," or "very much." The "things and experiences" which elicit those replies are as follows:

1. Noise of a vacuum cleaner
2. Open wounds
3. Being alone
4. Being in a strange place
5. Loud voices
6. Dead people
7. Speaking in public
8. Crossing streets
9. People who seem insane
10. Falling
11. Motor cars
12. Being teased
13. Dentists
14. Thunder
15. Sirens
16. Failure
17. Entering a room where others are already seated
18. High places on land
19. Looking down from high buildings
20. Worms
21. Imaginary creatures
22. Receiving injections
23. Strangers
24. Bats
25. Journeys by train
26. Journeys by bus

27. Journeys by car
28. Feeling angry
29. People in authority
30. Flying insects
31. Seeing other people injected
32. Sudden noises
33. Dull weather
34. Crowds
35. Large open spaces
36. Cats
37. One person bullying another
38. Tough looking people
39. Birds
40. Sight of deep water
41. Being watched working
42. Dead animals
43. Weapons
44. Dirt
45. Crawling insects
46. Sight of fighting
47. Ugly people
48. Fire
49. Sick people
50. Dogs
51. Being criticised
52. Strange shapes
53. Being in an elevator
54. Watching surgical operations
55. Angry people
56. Mice
57. Blood (animal or human)
58. Parting from friends
59. Enclosed places
60. Having an operation
61. Feeling rejected
62. Aeroplanes
63. Medical odours
64. Feeling disapproved of
65. Harmless snakes
66. Cemeteries
67. Being ignored
68. Darkness
69. Feeling your heart is missing a beat

70. Lightning
71. Doctors
72. People with deformities
73. Making mistakes
74. Looking foolish
75. Losing control

Appendix B

A responsible group phobia remediation program might be similar to the one described below, which we have used at Behavior Service Consultants, Inc. since 1977, with modifications as found useful with practice.

Group members are either self-referred or come at the suggestion of their individual therapists, and groups are made up of people matched for presenting fears. There is a great deal of overlap among fears presented by group participants, but they can be categorized under the diagnostic umbrellas of "agoraphobia" and "social fears." The specific kinds of fears reported include: fear of dying, of losing control or going crazy, of being physically ill or fainting in public, driving, traveling from the home, entering stores, restaurants, malls and other public places, of being alone, taking public transportation, of social contacts, talking on the telephone, speaking in public, and meeting new people. Such fears have been experienced over a range of time from four months to thirty-three years. Group members all report a narrowing in their activities, lifestyles, and social interactions, a decrease in confidence in themselves, and an increase in dependency behaviors as a result of their fears.

Prior to entering the group they have generally received some type of treatment for their fears, most frequently of a psychodynamic nature, until recently the most available treatment in the Washington area. Obviously the treatment had not typically been successful since they seek other help. Some of the group members had already started individual behavioral treatment before entering a group, for fears and anxieties and related problems.

Although medication is not formally a part of the treatment, about a fifth of participants take antianxiety medication while participating in the program. Their medication is closely monitored by their personal physicians, with whom the group leaders communicate periodically.

The group sessions are led by one or two therapists, as are the educational sessions. At the latter, there are occasionally lectures presented by other mental health specialists from the clinic.

The fifteen week program consists of two individual assessment and goal-setting sessions, pretesting, ten educational sessions which include the clients' helpers, twelve small group sessions which include invivo practice, a hot line telephone service and posttesting and evaluation. A description of the program flow follows.

The screening interview assesses appropriateness through such variables as type, duration, and severity of fears, physical health, medication history, and current medication status. Clinical judgment decides whether or not individuals will then be appropriate in terms of effective group composition.

Assessment is through questionnaires administered and scored in the office on a computer terminal. Questionnaires such as Fear Survey Schedule (adapted from Wolpe and Lang 1964); Fensterheim 1977), the Social Anxiety Scale (Wellems, Tuendes, de Haan, and Defore 1973), Cues for Tension and Anxiety Survey Schedule (Cautela 1977) and Assertiveness Inventory (Gambrill and Richey 1975). The Minnesota Multiphasic Personality Inventory (Hathaway and McKinley 1947), is administered by paper and pencil. As part of the assessment there are physiologic measures taken before and after approaching the feared stimuli.

Once the client is assigned to a group, an intake interview filters additional information relevant to the client's fears and methods of coping with them. During this interview, the five to ten stimuli that provoke the most discomfort are identified and ranked in order of severity. These contribute to the development of the individual's Behavioral Approach Test and Discomfort Rating Scale, which scale is administered before and after training and also ranked at those times by the helper. Physiologic and behavioral tests are administered in the natural environment by the therapists. Baseline heart rate and blood pressure readings are taken during a pretest interview a week before the first session. Then a written description of the behavioral approach invivo tasks are given to the interviewee. Physiologic measures are taken three minutes later. The therapist and client approach the feared stimuli to the degree the client is able. Physiologic measures are again taken and based on all the preceeding information, specific goals are then put together for each person. Testing takes about three hours.

Education sessions are attended by group members and their designated helpers, usually for ten weeks during the course of the program. Concepts relevant to fears and anxiety are presented by formal and informal lectures, through group discussion, videotaped behavior rehearsal, paper and pencil exercises, and worksheets.

The purpose is to provide the participants and their helpers with an understanding of the relevant physiologic, cognitive, and behavioral aspects of fear. Additionally, techniques for dealing with the fear and panic responses as well as supervised practice in interacting constructively in situations involving approach or fearful behavior are stressed. Typical session topics are: Fear as a Learned Behavior; Physiology, Cognitive, and Behavioral Components of Fear; Relaxation Training; Coping with Panic; Cognitive Restructuring; Thought Stopping and Switching; Success Rehearsal; Helper-Helpee Interactions, and Helper-Helpee Behavioral Rehearsal.

Group sessions are two hours once each week and are used for the analysis of individual problem areas and practice of approach and anxiety reduction behavior and techniques. The agenda is semistructured, with regularly scheduled practice exercises, formal and informal discussions, and homework review and monitoring. A typical session includes Relaxation Practice (10-15 minutes), Discussion of Individual Progress and Problem Areas (30 minutes), Invivo Approach Behavior practice (45-60 minutes), Homework Review and Monitoring (30 minutes), and Evaluation and Processing (5 minutes).

The relaxation exercises provide additional training in and practice of various techniques—muscle relaxation, positive imagery, Weitzman, etc. They also allow group members to experiment with methods of lowering their SUDS level in a controlled environment. This scale is officially "subjective units of discomfort" but participants frequently call it the Sudden Urge to Depart Scale.

The invivo approach exercises are planned by the group and the therapists during the session. They include imaginal and invivo desensitization, flooding, videotaped behavior rehearsal, success rehearsal, and cognitive restructuring. Frequently several members of the group share an invivo exercise, working together and serving as helpers to one another. At other times the exercise is appropriate for only one and a therapist accompanies the individual client. Assignments include entering a grocery store, waiting in a checkout line for varying amounts of time, driving a car on different types of roads and with varying amounts of traffic, riding elevators, public transportation, staying alone in enclosed places, rehearsing social or business interaction, speaking before a group, making telephone calls. There is one three hour excursion—an extended shopping trip at a mall, a subway or bus ride to a museum, eating dinner at a crowded restaurant. These group excursions are designed so that all members have an opportunity to practice in a variety of situations relevant to their fears and problems areas and at the same time to be helpful to others in analogous situations.

During the homework review and monitoring period, members take turns reporting progress made during the week and receiving direction from therapists and other members, entries on homework recording forms are shared. Appropriate individual assignments for the coming week are agreed upon, usually built upon the approach behaviors designed during the individual interviews.

Hot line telephone service provides members with a means of receiving additional support and direction between group sessions. It insures telephone access to a therapist during a specific one hour period daily. Clients are encouraged to call in to report their successes as well as difficulties. Although emergency calls are taken or returned immediately, clients are encouraged to wait until hot line time. This gives them an opportunity to try to work with difficult situations or issues themselves— with the knowledge that help is available.

The format of the telephone conversation is structured to encourage participants to use the following format when speaking of their fears or of themselves. First, appropriate social greeting and conversation, positive statements about self and steps taken, then statements of difficulty and success, followed by exploration of alternative solutions and plans, and then an appropriate termination of the conversation.

The tests involved in the admission and intake procedures are read-ministered to group members after the sessions are completed. Results for several groups have been discussed elsewhere (Cimarusti et al 1980). They sum up as having significant impact not only on phobic avoidance behavior but on psychosocial functioning, with less obsession and more competency to face difficulties, more social behaviors and greater comfort.

About the Contributors

Enya P. Flores-Meiser is a cultural anthropologist on the faculty of Ball State University in Muncie, Indiana. She holds degrees from the University of the Philippines, University of Iowa, and the Catholic University of America. Her ethnographic fieldwork and related research topics include Samal Moslems and Tagalogs of the Philippines, Japanese-Brazilians, and Filipinos in the United States. Reflecting this diversity of interest, Flores-Meiser's publications include those on evil eye beliefs, comparative fieldwork techniques, and culture change.

Colby R. Hatfield, Jr., received his B.A. in psychology from Clark University and his M.A. and Ph.D. from the Catholic University of America. He has taught at the University of Dayton, University of Colorado at Boulder, and Denver. Currently he is director of the Liberal Arts CORE Program at Loretto Heights College.

He has spent a total of ten years in East Africa, beginning in 1965 with Ph.D. research on religious specialists among the Sukuma. In 1970 he returned to Tanzania on a F.A.O. sponsored livestock development among the Sukuma and Nyamwezi. From 1973 to 1979 he was involved in a bilateral USAID/Tanzanian government livestock development project with the Maasai. In 1979—80 he also conducted a baseline survey of communities and development along the proposed routes of two "drought" roads in North and South Maasailand.

Research interests include religious systems, witchcraft, culture change and development and the dynamics of pastoral societies. His most recent publication is a joint article, written with Jon Moris, on the role of the social sciences in developing and introducing new technologies, published through the International Rice Research Institute.

William H. Key received his M.A. and Ph.D. degrees from Washington University in St. Louis. His administrative positions include sociology department chairmanships at Washburn University and the University of Denver; Director of Social Science Research at the Menninger Foundation; Director of the Academic Research Center at the University of Denver; and Vice Chancellor for Academic Affairs at the University of Denver from 1974 to 1978. Books in which he was a major contributor include: *When People Are Forced to Move; Tornado;* and *Conquering Disaster.* His articles have appeared in the Social Science Quarterly,

Mass Emergencies, and the Journal of Applied Behavioral Science, among others. He has been a consultant on research designs and organizational development to federal agencies, cities, institutions, and business organizations. Currently, he is Professor Emeritus at the University of Denver.

DeWight R. Middleton is Associate Professor of Anthropology at the State University of New York at Oswego. He has extensive fieldwork experience in Manta, Ecuador, Tampa, Florida and St. Louis, Missouri. He has published numerous urban analyses ranging from families and ritual kinship, to ethnic group dynamics and urban regional systems.

David Parkin is Professor of African Anthropology at the School of Oriental and African Studies in the University of London. His books include *Palms, Wine and Witnesses* (1972), *The Cultural Definition of Political Response* (1978), *Semantic Anthropology* (ed) (1982), and *The Anthropology of Evil* (ed) (1985), as well as others specifically on Africa, where he has conducted many years of fieldwork, principally in Kenya and Uganda. He is interested in language use and the anthropology of practical philosophies, and ritual and the arts in Africa.

Molly G. Schuchat is a cultural and applied anthropologist who does program planning and evaluation consultation in the areas of mental health, adult education and ethnic health programs.
She has studied food habits, ethnicity, migration and travel in the USA, Eastern Europe, and East and South Asia. Recent publictions include *The Comforts of Group Tours* in Annals of Tourism Research, Vol. 10 (1983) and essays on aspects of Jewish-American life for a variety of magazines (in collabortion with Elaine Shalowitz). With James Jordan, she wrote a chapter on the Chinese village for Westview Press's *Village Viability in Contemporary Society* (Ed. Priscilla Copeland Reining and Barbara Lenkerd). She is completing a book on American mobility—*Rooted/Restless: Why we go and why we stay.* She received the Ph.D. in anthropology from the Catholic University of America in 1971 and an undergraduate degree in economics from Vassar College in 1948.

David L. Scruton is Professor of Anthropology at Ball State University and currently is chairman of the Department of Anthropology. His degrees are from the University of Oklahoma, Washington University, and the University of Washington. His interests and publications have been in the areas of futures' research and Africa.

Marcella G. Walder is a clinical social worker in private practice who works with individuals, couples, families, and groups. She has done research and practical work in behavior therapy, skill training, parent education, and the development of programs for youth. She is director of Behavior Service Consultants' Stress Management program which is offered to federal and private agencies as well as in-house. Mrs. Walder is a member of the National Association of Social Workers and the Greater Washington Society for Clinical Social Work.

She is a member of the Academy of Certified Social Workers and is licensed in the State of Maryland. She is currently Director of Group Therapy programs and the Therapeutic Companion Program at Behavior Service Consultants, a multi-profession mental health and consultation agency, of which she is also Vice President.

Bibliography

Agar, Michael H. 1980. The Professional Stranger: An Informal Introduction to Ethnography. New York: Academic Press.

Akutagawa, D. 1956. A Study in Construct Validity of the Psychoanalytic Concept of Latent Anxiety and Test of a Projection Distance Hypothesis. Unpublished doctoral dissertation, University of Pittsburgh.

Angelino, Henry, Joseph Dollins, and Edmund V. Mech. 1956. Trends in the "Fears and Worries" of School Children as Related to Socio-economic Status and Age. The Journal of Genetic Psychology 89:263-276.

Arnold, Magda. 1960. Emotion and Personality, Vol. 1: Psychological Aspects. New York: Columbia University Press.

Ausubel, David P. 1955. Relationships Between Shame and Guilt in the Socializing Process. Psychological Review 62:378-390.

Averill, James R. 1976. Emotion and Anxiety. In Emotions and Anxiety. Marvin Zuckerman and Charles D. Spielberger, eds. Hillsdale, New Jersey: Lawrence Erlbaum Associates.

Averill, James R. 1980. Emotion and Anxiety. In Exploring Emotions. A. O. Rorty, ed. Berkeley: University of California Press.

Bailey, F. G. 1983. The Tactical Uses of Passion. An Essay on Power, Reason, and Reality. Ithaca: Cornell University Press.

Bamber, James H. 1974. The Fears of Adolescents. The Journal of Genetic Psychology 125:127-140.

Bamber, James H. 1979. The Fears of Adolescents. New York: Academic Press.

Bates, H. D. 1971. Factorial Structure and MMPI Correlates of a Fear Survey Schedule in a Clinical Population. Behaviour Research and Therapy 9:355-360.

Benedict, Ruth. 1946. The Chrysanthemum and the Sword. Boston: Houghton Mifflin.

Bernstein, D. A., and G. J. Allen. 1969. Fear Survey Schedule (II): Normative Data and Factor Analyses Based Upon a Large College Sample. Behaviour Research and Therapy 7:403-407.

Bock, Philip K. 1970. Culture Shock. New York: Alfred A. Knopf.

Bock, Philip K. 1980. Continuities in Psychological Anthropology: A Historical Introduction. San Francisco: Freeman.

Bohannan, Laura. 1964. Return to Laughter. Garden City, New Jersey: Doubleday/Anchor.

Braun, P. R., and D. J. Reynolds. 1969. A Factor Analysis of a 100-item Fear Survey Inventory. Behaviour Research and Therapy 7:399-402.

Breton, Raymond. 1964. Institutional Completeness of Ethnic Communities and Personal Relations of Immigrants. American Journal of Sociology 70:195-205.

Brownell, Blaine A. 1975. The Urban Ethos in the South, 1920—1930. Baton Rouge: Louisiana State University Press.

Bulatao, Jaime C. 1964. Hiya. Philippine Studies 12:424-438.

Cancian, Frank. 1963. Informant Error and Native Prestige Ranking in Zinacantan. American Anthropologist 65:1073ff.

Cannon, Walter B. 1927. The James-Lang Theory of Emotion: A Critical Examination and an Alternative Theory. American Journal of Psychology 39:106-124.

Castaneda, A., B. R. McCandless, and D. S. Palermo. 1956. The Children's Form of the Manifest Anxiety Scale. Child Development 27:317-326.

Cautela, Joseph R. 1977. Behavior Analysis Forms for Clinical Intervention. Champaign, Illinois: Research Press.

Chambless, Dianne L., and Alan J. Goldstein. 1982. Agoraphobia: Multiple Perspectives on Theory and Treatment. New York: John Wiley and Sons.

Church, Austin T. 1982. Sojourner Adjustment. Psychological Bulletin: 91,3:540-572.

Cimarusti, Linda et al. 1980. A Fifteen Week Anxiety/Phobia Remediation Program. Paper presented at the Second Annual Phobia Conference, Arlington, Virginia, June 14-15.

Clubb, Jerome M., and Howard W. Allen. 1977. Collective Biography and the Progressive Movement: The "Status Revolution" Revisited. Social Science History 1 (Summer): 518-534.

Cohen, Abner. 1969. Custom and Politics in Urban Africa: A Study of Hausa Migrants in Yoruba Towns. Berkeley: University of California Press.

Cohen, Abner. 1974. Introduction. *In* Urban Ethnicity. Abner Cohen, ed. Pp ix-xxiii. London: Tavistock Publications.

Cohen, Abner. 1979. Political Symbolism. Annual Review of Anthropology 8:87-113.

Cole, Luella. 1959. The Psychology of Adolescence. New York: Holt, Rinehart and Winston.

Coulter, Jeff. 1979. The Social Construction of Mind. Totowa, New Jersey: Rowman and Littlefield.

Croake, James W., and Nancy Catlin. 1974. Adlerian Theory and Children's Self-reported Fears. International Journal of Sociology of the Family 4:56-74.

Darwin, Charles. 1872. The Expression of Emotions in Man and Animals. London.

De Vos, George A. 1974. Psychologically Oriented Studies in Comparative Cultural Behavior. *In* Frontiers of Anthropology. M. J. Leaf, ed. Pp. 189-230. New York: D. Van Nostrand Co.

Dixon, James J., Cecily de Monchaux, and Joseph Sandler. 1957. Patterns of Anxiety: An Analysis of Social Anxieties. The British Journal of Medical Psychology 30:107-112.

Douglas, Mary. 1966. Purity and Danger. London: Routledge and Kegan Paul.

Douglas, Mary, and Aaron Wildavsky. 1982. Risk and Culture: An Essay on the Selection of Technical and Environmental Danger. Berkeley: University of California Press.

Durkheim, Emile. 1951. Suicide. Trans. John A. Spaulding and George Simpson. New York: Free Press (original 1897).

Eames, Edwin, and Judith Goode. 1977. Anthropology of the City: An Introduction to Urban Anthropology. Englewood Cliffs, New Jersey: Prentice-Hall.

Eckman, Paul. 1974. Universal Facial Expressions of Emotion. *In* Culture and Personality: Contemporary Readings. Robert LeVine, ed. Pp. 8-15. Chicago: Aldine.

Edgerton, Robert. 1979. Alone Together: Social Order on an Urban Beach. Urban Anthropology 8:208.

Elgin, Lorna. 1974. Girl of Two Worlds. Kijabe: Kesho Publications.

Ember, Carol R. 1978. Men's Fear of Sex with Women: A Cross-cultural Study. Sex Roles 4:657-678.

Epstein, Seymour. 1976. Anxiety, Arousal and the Self-concept. *In* Stress and Anxiety, Vol. 3. Irwin Saranson and Charles D. Spielberger, eds. Pp. 185-225. New York: John Wiley and Sons.

Farley, R. H., A. Cohen, J. Goldberg, and Y. Yinon. 1978. Fears in American and Israeli Women. The Journal of Social Psychology 106:17-24.

Fensterheim, Herbert, and Jean Baer. 1977. Stop Running Scared! Fear Control Training: How to Conquer Your Fears, Phobias and Anxieties. New York: Rawson Associates Publishers, Inc.

Fischer, Steven C., and Ralph M. Turner. 1978. Standardization of the Fear Survey Schedule. Journal of Behavior Therapy and Experimental Psychiatry 9:129-133.

Fisher, Elizabeth. 1979. Woman's Creation. Garden City, New Jersey: Doubleday/Anchor.

Fosbrooke, H. A. 1948. An Administrative Survey of the Maasai. Tanganyika Notes and Records 26 (December): 1-50.

Freedman, Alfred M., Harold I. Kaplan, and Benjamin J. Sadock. 1975. Comprehensive Textbook of Psychiatry—II. Baltimore: The Williams and Wilkins Company.

Freilich, Morris, ed. 1977. Marginal Natives at Work: Anthropologists in the Field. Cambridge, Massachusetts: Schenkman Publishing Co.

Fried, Marc. 1963. Grieving for a Lost Home. *In* The Urban Condition. Leonard J. Duhl, ed. New York: Simon and Schuster.

Fry, W. F. 1962. The Marital Context of an Anxiety Syndrome. Family Process 1:245-52.

Gambrill, E. D., and C. A. Richey. 1975. An Assertion Inventory for Use in Assessment Behavior and Research. Behavior Therapy 6:550-561.

Geer, James H. 1965. The Development of a Scale to Measure Fear. Behaviour Research and Therapy 3:45-53.

Geer, James H. 1966. Effect of Fear Arousal upon Task Performance and Verbal Behavior. Journal of Abnormal Psychology 71:119-123.

Geertz, Clifford. 1973. Thick Description: Toward an Interpretive Theory of Culture. *In* The Interpretation of Cultures. Selected Essays. Clifford Geertz, ed. Pp. 3-30. New York: Basic Books.

Geertz, Hildred. 1959. The Vocabulary of Emotion. Psychiatry 22:225-237.

Gerber, Eleanor Ruth. 1975. The Cultural Patterning of Emotions in Samoa. Unpublished doctoral dissertation, University of California, San Diego.

Giddens, Anthony, ed. 1972. Emile Durkheim: Selected Writings. Cambridge: Cambridge University Press.

Gluzman, Semyon. 1982. Fear of Freedom: Psychological Decompensation or Existentialist Phenomenon? American Journal of Psychiatry 139:57-61.

Goffman, Erving. 1971. Relations in Public: Microstudies of the Public Order. New York: Harper and Row.

Gray, Jeffrey. 1971. The Psychology of Fear and Stress. New York: McGraw-Hill.

Grossberg, John M., and Helen K. Wilson. 1965. A Correlational Comparison of the Wolpe-Lang Fear Survey Schedule and Taylor Manifest Anxiety Scale. Behaviour Research and Therapy 3:125-128.

Guthrie, G. M. 1975. A Behavioral Analysis of Culture Learning. *In* Cross Cultural Perspectives in Learning. Abrislin, S. et al. New York: John Wiley and Sons.

Hafner, R. J. 1977. The Husband of Agoraphobic Women: Assortative Mating or Pathogenic Interaction? British Journal of Psychiatry 130:233-9.

Haldipur, C. V., Mantosh Dewan, and Michael Beal. 1982. On Fear in the Countertransference. American Journal of Psychotherapy 36:240-247.

Hallowell, A. Irving. 1938. Fear and Anxiety as Cultural and Individual Variables in a Primitive Society. The Journal of Social Psychology 9:25-47.

Hallowell, A. Irving. 1967a. The Self and its Behavioral Environment. *In* Culture and Experience. A. Irving Hallowell, ed. Pp. 75-110. Philadelphia: University of Pennsylvania Press.

Hallowell, A. Irving. 1967b. The Social Function of Anxiety in a Primitive Society. *In* Culture and Experience. A. Irving Hallowell, ed. Pp. 266-276. Philadelphia: University of Pennsylvania Press.

Hand, I. et al. 1974. Group Exposure (Flooding) in vivo for Agoraphobics. British Journal of Psychiatry 124:588-602.

Hannerz, Ulf. 1969. Soulside: Inquiries into Ghetto Culture and Community. New York: Columbia University Press.

Hannerz, Ulf. 1981. Exploring the City: Inquiries Toward an Urban Anthropology. New York: Columbia University Press.

Hatfield, Catherine. 1983. Education and the Schoolgirl. The Case of Tanzania. University of Denver. Mimeo.

Hatfield, Colby R. 1968. The Nfumu in Tradition and Change. A Study of the Position of Religious Practitioners Among the Sukuma of Tanzania, East Africa. Anthropological Studies #12. Washington, D.C.: The Catholic University of America.

Hatfield, Colby R. 1973. Does the Punishment Fit the Crime: Witchcraft and Social Justice Among the Sukuma. Session 5, African Studies, RMSSA/WAA Meetings. Laramie. Mimeo.

Hatfield, Colby R., and Rueben ole Kuney. 1976. Current Trends in Maasai Development: A Baseline Survey. Maasai Project Evaluation Paper No. 3. United Republic of Tanzania Regional Development Directorate. Arusha. Mimeo.

Hatfield, Colby R. 1983. Fear and Trembling: Stress, Trance, and the Maasai Warrior. Paper given at the Sociophobics Symposium. XIth International Congress of Anthropological and Ethnological Sciences. Vancouver.

Hathaway, S. R., and J. C. McKinley. 1970. Booklet for the Minnesota Multiphasic Personality Inventory. New York: The Psychological Corp.

Hersen, M. 1971. Fear Scale Norms for an In-patient Population. Journal of Clinical Psychology 27:375-378.

Hoelter, Jon W., and Leslie Street. 1978. Sex Differentials on Fears of Death. NCSA Series.

Hoffman, Lois W. 1982. Methodological Issues in Follow-up and Replication Studies. Journal of Social Issues 38:53-64.

Hughes, Michael. 1980. The Fruits of Cultivation Analysis: A Reexamination of Some Effects of Television Watching. Public Opinion Quarterly 44(Fall):287-302.

Izard, Carroll E. 1977a. The Emotions and Emotion Concepts in Personality and Culture Research. *In* Handbook of Modern Personality Theory. Raymond Cattell and Ralph M. Dreger, eds. Pp. 496-510. New York: John Wiley and Sons (Hemisphere Publishing Corp.).

Izard, Carroll E. 1977b. Human Emotions. New York: Plenum Press.

Jacobs, Alan. 1965. African Pastoralists: Some General Remarks. Anthropological Quarterly 38:144-54.

Jacobs, Alan. 1979. Maasai Inter-Tribal Relations: Belligerent Herdsmen or Peaceful Pastoralists? *In* Warfare Among East African Herders. Katsuyoshi Fukui and D. Turton, eds. Senri, Osaka: SENRI Ethnological Studies #3, National Museum of Ethnology.

James, William. 1884. What is an Emotion. Mind 9:188-205.

Jellicoe, M. R. n.d. Survey of Lake Region. Dar es Salaam Ministry of Cooperatives and Community Development. Ref N. Surveys/Lake 14. Mimeo.

Jersild, A. T., and F. B. Holmes. 1935. Children's Fears. Child Development Monograph 20.

Johnson, Frederick. 1967. A Standard Swahili-English Dictionary. London: Oxford University Press.

Johnson, Norris Brock. 1984. Sex, Color and Rites of Passage in Ethnographic Research. Human Organization 43:108-120.

Kemper, Theodore D. 1978. A Social Interactional Theory of Emotions. New York: John Wiley and Sons.

Kirk, Lorraine, and Michael Burton. 1977. Meaning and Context: A Study of Contextual Shifts in Meaning of Maasai Personality Descriptors. American Ethnologist 4:734-761.

Kirwen, Michael. 1979. African Widows. New York: Orbis Books.

Krippendorff, Klaus. 1980. Content Analysis: An Introduction to its Methodology. Beverly Hills, California: Sage Publications.

Kroeber, Alfred L. 1959. The History of the Personality of Anthropology. American Anthropologist 61:398-404.

ole Kulet, Henry. 1971. Is it possible? Nairobi: Longman Kenya Ltd.

ole Kulet, Henry. 1972. To Become A Man. Nairobi: Longman Kenya Ltd.

Kurtz, Howard. 1984. U.S. Probes Fear of Nuclear Power. The Washington Post. October 30:A1.

LaBarre, Weston. 1947. The Cultural Basis of Emotions and Gestures. Journal of Personality 16:49-68.

Landy, Frank J., and Larry A. Gaupp. 1971. A Factor Analysis of the Fear Survey Schedule—III. Behaviour Research and Therapy 9:89-93.

Lang, P. J. 1969. Factor Analysis of the 122-item Fear Survey Schedule. Behaviour Research and Therapy 7:381-386.

Lang, P. J., and A. D. Lasovik. 1963. The Experimental Desensitization of an Animal Phobia. Journal of Abnormal Social Psychology 66:519-525.

Lanyon, Richard I., and Martin Manosevitz. 1966. Validity of Self-reported Fear. Behaviour Research and Therapy 4:259-263.

Last, Cynthia G., and Edward B. Blanchard. 1982. Classification of Phobics Versus Fearful Non-phobics: Procedural and Theoretical Issues. Behavioral Assessment 4:195-210.

Lawlis, G. F. 1971. Response Styles of a Patient Population on the Fear Survey Schedule. Behaviour Research and Therapy 9:95-102.

Leach, E. R. 1971. Rethinking Anthropology. London: Athalone Press.

Lebra, Takie Sugiyama. 1971. The Social Mechanism of Guilt and Shame: The Japanese Case. Anthropological Quarterly 44:241-255.

Leighton, Dorthea, and Clyde Kluckhohn. 1947. Children of the People. Cambridge: Harvard University Press.

Levy, Robert I. 1974. Tahiti, Sin and the Question of Integration Between Personality and Sociocultural Systems. In Culture and Personality. Robert A. Levine, ed. Chicago: Aldine Publishing Company.

Lewis, Michael, and Leonard A. Rosenblum, eds. 1974. The Origins of Fear. New York: John Wiley and Sons.

Liebow, Eliot. 1967. Tally's Corner: A Study of Negro Street Corner Men. Boston: Little, Brown, and Company.

Lindenbaun, Shirley. 1979. Kuru Sorcery. Disease and Danger in the New Guinea Highlands. Palo Alto: Mayfield Publishing Company.

Llewelyn-Davies, Melissa. 1981. Women, Warriors, and Patriarchs. In Sexual Meanings. The Cultural Construction of Gender and Sexuality. S. B. Ortner and H. Whitehead, eds. Pp. 350-358. Cambridge: Cambridge University Press.

Lofland, Lyn H. 1973. A World of Strangers: Order and Action in Urban Public Space. New York: Basic Books.

Lutz, Catherine. 1982. The Domain of Emotion Words on Ifaluk. American Ethnologist 9:113-128.

Lynch, Kevin. 1960. The Image of the City. Cambridge, Massachusetts: Technology Press.

Malatesta, Carol Zander. 1982. The Expression and Regulation of Emotion. In Emotion and Early Interaction. Tiffany Field and Alan Fogel, eds. Hillsdale, New Jersey: Lawrence Erlbaum Associates.

Mandler, George. 1975. Mind and Emotion. New York: John Wiley and Sons.

Manosevitz, Martin, and Richard I. Lanyon. 1965. Fear Survey Schedule: A Normative Study. Psychological Reports 17:699-703.

Marcus, George E., and Dick Cushman. 1982. Ethnographies as Texts. Annual Review of Anthropology 11:25-69.

Marks, Isaac M. 1978. Living with Fear: Understanding and Coping with Anxiety. New York: McGraw-Hill.

Marshall, Mac. 1977. The Nature of Nurture. American Ethnologist 8:643-662.

Matthews, A. M., M. G. Gelder, and D. W. Johnston. 1981. Agoraphobia: Nature and Treatment. New York: The Guilford Press.

Mavissakalian, Matig, and David H. Barlow. 1981. Phobia: Psychological and Pharmacological Treatment. New York: The Guilford Press.

Mayer, Philip. 1961. Townsmen or Tribesmen: Conservatism and the Process of Urbanization in a South African City. 2nd ed. Capetown: Oxford University Press.

Mead, Margaret. 1949. Social Change and Cultural Surrogates. *In* Pesonality in Nature, Society and Culture. C. Kluckhohn and H. A. Murray, eds. New York: Alfred A. Knopf.

Mead, Margaret. 1950. Some Anthropological Considerations Concerning Guilt. *In* Feelings and Emotions. M. L. Reymert, ed. New York: McGraw-Hill.

Merbaum, Michael, and George Stricker. 1972. Factor Analytic Study of Male and Female Responses to the Fear Survey Schedule. Journal of Behavior Therapy and Experimental Psychiatry 3:87-90.

Merry, Sally Engle. 1981. Urban Danger: Life in a Neighborhood of Strangers. Philadelphia: Temple University Press.

Middleton, DeWight R. 1974. Neighborhood and City in Coastal Ecuador. Urban Anthropology 3:184-199.

Middleton, DeWight R. 1981a. The Organization of Ethnicity in Tampa. Ethnic Groups 3:281-306.

Middleton, DeWight. 1981b. The Production and Management of Fear in Urban Contexts. Paper presented at the Conference on Sociophobics at Ball State University, Muncie.

Milgram, Stanley. 1970. The Experience of Living in Cities: A Psychological Analysis. Science 167:1461-1468.

Miner, Horace. 1966. Culture Change Under Pressure: A Hausa Case. *In* A Casebook of Social Change. Arthur Neihof, ed. Pp. 109-117. Chicago: Aldine Publishing Company.

Mittlemann, B. 1959. Analysis of Reciprocal Neurotic Patterns in Family Relationships. *In* I'm Neurotic: Interaction in Marriage. V. Eisenstein, ed. London: Tavistock.

Mol, Rev. Frans, M.H.M. n.d. MMA. A Dictionary of the Maasai Language and Folklore: English-Maasai. Nairobi: Marketing and Publishing Ltd.

Newman, Oscar. 1973. Defensible Space: Crime Prevention through Urban Design. New York: MacMillan Collier Books.

Oberg, K. 1960. Cultural Shock: Adjustment to New Cultural Environments. Practical Anthropology 7:177-182.

Parkin, D., ed. 1985. The Anthropology of Evil. Oxford: Basil Blackwell.

Perin, Constance. 1977. Everything in its Place. Princeton, New Jersey: Princeton University Press.

Person, Ethel S. 1982. Women Working: Fears of Failure, Deviance and Success. Journal of the American Academy of Psychoanalysis 10:67-84.

Piers, Gerhart, and Milton B. Singer. 1971. Shame and Guilt—a Psychoanalytic and a Cultural Study. New York: W. W. Norton.

Plotnicov, Leonard. 1973. Anthropological Field Work in Modern and Local Urban Contexts. Urban Anthropology 2:248-264.

Plutchik, Robert. 1962. The Emotions. New York: Random House.

Plutchik, Robert. 1982. A Psychoevolutionary Theory of Emotions. Social Science Information 21,4/5:529-553.

Pratt, Karl C. 1945. A Study of the Fears of Rural Children. The Journal of Genetic Psychology 67:179-194.

Punamaki, Raija-Leena. 1982. War and Psychological Research. Psykologia 17:3-11.

Rainwater, Lee. 1969. Fear and the House-as-Haven in Lower Class. In Urbanism, Urbanization and Change: Comparative Perspectives. Paul Meadows and Ephraim Mizruchi, eds. Pp. 291-302. Reading, Massachusetts: Addison-Wesley Publishing Company. (Originally published 1966, Journal of the American Institute of Planners 32:23-31.)

Rainwater, Lee. 1970. Behind Ghetto Walls: Black Family Life in a Federal Slum. Chicago: Aldine.

Rigby, Peter. 1979. Olpul and Entaroj: The Economy of Sharing Among the Pastoral Baraguyu of Tanzania. In L'Equipe ecologie and anthropologie des societies pastorales. Pastoral Production and Society. (Production Pastorale et Societe). Proceedings of the International Meeting on Nomadic Pastoralism. (Actes de Colloque Internationale sur le Pastoralisme Nomade), 1-3 Dec. 1976. Pp. 329-347. Cambridge: Cambridge University Press.

Robarchek, Clayton A. 1977. Frustration, Aggression, and the Nonviolent Semai. American Ethnologist 4:762-779.

Robarchek, Clayton A. 1979. Learning to Fear: A Case Study of Emotional Conditioning. American Ethnologist 6:555-567.

Rosaldo, Michelle Z. 1980. Knowledge and Passion: Ilongot Notions of Self and Social Life. Cambridge: Cambridge University Press.

Rothstein, W., G. R. Holmes, and W. E. Boblitt. 1972. A Factor Analysis of the Fear Survey Schedule with a Psychiatric Population. Journal of Clinical Psychology 28:78-80.

Rubin, B., E. Katlin, B. Weiss, and J. Efran. 1968. Factor Analysis of a Fear Survey Schedule. Behaviour Research and Therapy 6:65-75.

Rubin, B., G. Lawlis, D. Tasto, and T. Namenek. 1969. Factor Analysis of the 122-item Fear Survey Schedule. Behaviour Research and Therapy 7:381-386.

Russell, G. W. 1967. Human Fears: A Factor Analytic Study of Three Age Levels. Genetic Psychology Monographs 76:141-162.

Saish, Philip A. 1982. The Lebanese Fear Inventory: A Normative Report. Journal of Clinical Psychology 38:352-355.

ole Saitoti, Tepilit, and Carol Beckwith. 1980. Maasai. New York: H. N. Abrams.

Sankan, S. S. 1973. The Maisai. Nairobi: East African Literature Bureau.

Schachter, Stanley, and Jerome E. Singer. 1962. Cognitive, Social, and Psychological Determinants of Emotional State. Psychological Review 69:379-399.

Scherer, Klaus R. 1982. Emotion as a Process. Social Science Information 21,4/5:555-570.

Scherer, M. W., and C. Y. Nakamura. 1968. A Fear Survey Schedule for Children (FSS-FC): A Factor Analytic Comparison with Manifest Anxiety (CMAS). Behaviour Research and Therapy 6:173-182.

Schroeder, H., and L. Craine. 1971. Relationships Among Measures of Fear and Anxiety for Snake Phobias. Journal Consulting and Clinical Psychology 36:443.

Schuchat, Molly, and M. G. Walder. 1983. Phobias and Culture Shock: Commonality and Responses in Psychological Treatment and Anthropological Fieldwork. Prepared for Second Symposium on Sociophobics, Vancouver.

Scruton, David L. n.d. Sociophobics. MS.

Sellitz, Claire, Lawrence S. Wrightsman, and Stuart W. Cook. 1976. Research Methods in Social Relations. 3rd edition. New York: Holt, Rinehart and Winston.

Selye, Hans. 1956. The Stress of Life. New York: McGraw-Hill.

Selye, Hans. 1975. Stress Without Distress. New York: Signet.

Shibles, Warren. 1974. Emotion. Whitewater, Wisconsin: The Language Press.

Shott, Susan. 1979. Emotion and Social Life. American Journal of Sociology 84:5:1317-1334.

Silva, John M. 1982. An Evaluation of Fear of Success in Female and Male Athletes and Nonathletes. Journal of Sport Psychology 4:92-96.

Solomon, Robert C. 1976. The Passions. Garden City: Doubleday/Anchor Press.

Spielberger, Charles Donald, and Rogelio Diaz Guerrero, eds. 1976. Cross Cultural Anxiety. New York: Hemisphere Publishing Company.

Strathern, Andrew. 1975. Why is Shame on the Skin? Ethnology 14:347-356.

Taylor, J. A. 1953. A Personality Scale of Manifest Anxiety. Journal of Abnormal Social Psychology 48:285-290.

Thomson, Robert. 1979. The Concept of Fear. In Fear in Animals and Man. W. Sluckin, ed. Pp. 1-23. New York: Van Nostrand Reinhold Co.

Tignor, Robert L. 1972. The Maasai Warriors: Pattern Maintenance and Violence in Colonial Kenya. Journal of African History XIII,2:271-290.

Tuan, Yi-Fu. 1979. Landscapes of Fear. New York: Pantheon Books.

Tucker, A. N., and J. Tompo ole Mpaayei. 1955. A Maasai Grammar with Vocabulary. London: Longmans, Green and Co.

Wallace, Anthony F. C. 1970. Culture and Personality. 2nd ed. New York: Random House.

Whiting, Beatrice et al. 1963. Child Rearing in Six Cultures. New York: John Wiley and Sons.

Williams, Thomas Rhys. 1967. Field Methods in the Study of Culture. New York: Holt, Rinehart and Winston.

Winick, Charles. 1956. Dictionary of Anthropology. New York: Philosophical Library.

Wirth, Louis. 1964. Urbanism as a Way of Life. *In* Louis Wirth On Cities and Social Life: Selected Papers. Albert J. Reiss, Jr. ed. Pp. 60-83. Chicago: University of Chicago Press. (1938, American Journal of Sociology XLIV:1-24.).

Wolpe, Joseph, and Peter Lang. 1964. A Fear Survey Schedule for use in Behvior Therapy. Behaviour Research and Therapy 2:27-30.

Wolpe, Joseph, and A. A. Lazarus. 1966. Behavior Therapy Techniques. Oxford: Pergamon Press.

Yancey, William L. 1971. Architecture, Interaction, and Social Control: The Case of a Large-Scale Public Housing Project. Environment and Behavior 3:3-21.